WORLD CITIZENS]

Also by Joseph Rotblat

ATOMS AND THE UNIVERSE (*with G. O. Jones and G. J. Whitrow*)

RADIOACTIVITY AND RADIOACTIVE SUBSTANCES (*with J. Chadwick*)

SCIENTISTS IN THE QUEST FOR PEACE

NUCLEAR RADIATION IN WARFARE

* STRATEGIC DEFENCES AND THE FUTURE OF THE ARMS RACE (*co-editor with J. Holdren*)

* COEXISTENCE, COOPERATION AND COMMON SECURITY: Annals of Pugwash 1986 (*co-editor with L. Valki*)

VERIFICATION OF ARMS REDUCTIONS (*co-editor with J. Altmann*)

GLOBAL PROBLEMS AND COMMON SECURITY: Annals of Pugwash 1988 (*co-editor with V. I. Goldanskii*)

BUILDING GLOBAL SECURITY THROUGH COOPERATION: Annals of Pugwash 1989 (*co-editor with J. Holdren*)

TOWARDS A SECURE WORLD IN THE 21st CENTURY: Annals of Pugwash 1990 (*co-editor with F. Blackaby*)

STRIVING FOR PEACE, SECURITY AND DEVELOPMENT IN THE WORLD: Annals of Pugwash 1991 (*editor*)

A NUCLEAR-WEAPON-FREE WORLD: Desirable? Feasible? (*co-editor with J. Steinberger and B. Udgaonkar*)

A WORLD AT THE CROSSROADS: NEW CONFLICTS, NEW SOLUTIONS: Annals of Pugwash 1993 (*co-editor with S. Hellman*)

TOWARDS A WAR-FREE WORLD: Annals of Pugwash 1994 (*editor*)

* *Also published by Macmillan*

World Citizenship: Allegiance to Humanity

Edited by

Joseph Rotblat, FRS
Winner of 1995 Nobel Peace Prize
Emeritus Professor of Physics, University of London
President, Pugwash Conferences on Science and World Affairs

Executive Editor: Tom Milne

St. Martin's Press
New York

WORLD CITIZENSHIP: ALLEGIANCE TO HUMANITY

St. Martin's Press, Scholarly and Reference Division,
175 Fifth Avenue, New York, N.Y. 10010

First published in the United States of America in 1997

This book is printed on paper suitable for recycling and
made from fully managed and sustained forest sources.

Printed in Great Britain

ISBN 0–312–17359–8 (cloth)
ISBN 0–312–17361–X (paper)

Library of Congress Cataloging-in-Publication Data
World citizenship : allegiance to humanity / edited by Joseph Rotblat.
p.   cm.
"Pugwash Conferences on Science and World Affairs"—T.p. verso.
Includes bibliographical references and index.
ISBN 0–312–17359–8 (cloth). — ISBN 0–312–17361–X (paper)
1. Citizenship—Congresses. 2. Internationalism—Congresses.
3. Citizenship (International law)—Congresses.   4. International
organization—Congresses.   I. Rotblat, Joseph, 1908–   .
II. Pugwash Conferences on Science & World Affairs.
JX4215.W67 1997
327.1'7—dc21   96–50106
                                                                                    CIP

Contents

v

Part II   Education for World Citizenship

Preface

Since their inception, in 1957, the Pugwash Conferences on Science and World Affairs – recipients of the Nobel Peace Prize for 1995 – have been mainly concerned with the nuclear issue: halting the nuclear arms race and avoiding a nuclear war. After the end of the Cold War, Pugwash initiated a project with a specific objective: creating a nuclear-weapon-free world. At the time of writing this objective is still far from being achieved, but a nuclear-weapon-free world is no longer considered a fanciful idea; it is the subject of serious studies, and endorsed by many political and military leaders. The elimination of nuclear weapons is the explicit task mandated to a high-powered Commission set up by the Australian Government.

The removal of nuclear arsenals would remove an immediate threat, but it will not provide permanent security. Nuclear weapons cannot be disinvented; the knowledge of how to make them cannot be erased. Should there occur, some time in the future, a serious conflict between major powers involving them in a military confrontation, they might be tempted to build up nuclear arsenals again, and mankind would once more be in mortal danger.

This mortal danger stems from the development of nuclear weapons. With their invention, Man has, for the first time in the history of civilization, acquired the technical means to destroy the whole of civilization in a single act. Indeed, the whole human species is threatened with extinction. We must also bear in mind that further advances in science and technology may result in the discovery of yet other means of wholesale destruction. The human species is now an endangered species.

This danger had already been recognized in 1955, in the Russell-Einstein Manifesto, which is considered to be the credo of the Pugwash Movement:

> We are speaking on this occasion, not as members of this or that nation, continent or creed, but as human beings, members of the species Man, whose continued existence is in doubt.

vii

viii   *Preface*

The Manifesto went on to state clearly the choice facing the world community:

> Here, then, is the problem which we present to you, stark and dreadful, and inescapable: Shall we put an end to the human race; or shall mankind renounce war?

Forty years after this question was posed, Pugwash began its quest for a world without war; this book presents the basic thinking, as well as initial practical steps towards the creation of a war-free world.

****

The end of the Cold War has greatly reduced the threat of global nuclear war, but regional conflicts fought with conventional weapons are still going on, with the ever present threat of a conventional war escalating into a nuclear war. The break up of the Soviet Union saw the emergence of three new states with substantial nuclear arsenals. In the Middle East, the perceived possession of nuclear weapons by Israel is a strong incentive for other states in the region to acquire, by some means or other, a nuclear capability. More generally, the drive to achieve independence by constituents of former empires, has resulted in the outbreak of regional wars, in the former Soviet Union, in Yugoslavia, as well as in the Middle East.

Conscious about possible escalations of military conflicts, and anxious to find ways to avoid the terrible carnage that results from the use of even conventional weapons, Pugwash has set up Study Groups to debate regional conflicts. One of these Study Groups is seeking a comprehensive regional security system in the Middle East. Another Study Group, with the title: 'Social Tensions and Armed Conflict: Ethnic and other Aspects', looked into the various ethnic disputes that resulted, or threaten to result, in military confrontations. In two Workshops, held in Canada and Ukraine, the unstable situation in a number of countries, specifically in Bosnia, Estonia, Ukraine and parts of Africa, was debated. We were unable to come up with a general solution, and the conclusion reached was that the only way to avoid regional and other types of war is to create a political climate in which disputes are settled by means other than military confrontations. War must cease to be an admissible social institution.

Thus, out of the study of ethnic conflicts, Pugwash has arrived at the same conclusion drawn in the Russell-Einstein Manifesto in relation to the threat to humanity posed by the invention of nuclear weapons. Our objective must be a war-free world.

****

To most people the concept of a war-free world is a Utopian dream, a desirable but unrealizable goal. In a society governed for two millennia by the Roman dictum '*si vis pacem para bellum*' (if you want peace prepare for war), and which, in consequence, has always been ravaged by war (because if one prepares for war one will get war), it is difficult to imagine the complete elimination of war. However, as Samuel Johnson pointed out, the knowledge that one is going to be hanged in a fortnight concentrates the mind wonderfully! We have now arrived at the stage when we all have to learn to live altogether, because otherwise we shall all die together. This compels us to think the unthinkable.

Actually, the realization that another world war is likely to bring catastrophe is gradually sinking in. It has already taken hold in relation to the use of weapons of mass destruction. The great majority of nations (80–90 per cent) have renounced the use of biological and chemical weapons. By signing the Non-Proliferation Treaty, 175 non-nuclear states have also renounced the right to possess nuclear weapons. Gradually, the same attitude is beginning to take hold in relation to wars with conventional weapons. In Europe, the continent where war has been endemic throughout history, the majority of states now belong to the European Union, and a military solution to a conflict between them has become inconceivable. In the whole world there is a growing realization of the futility of war; a genuine desire is emerging to avoid military confrontation.

All the same, for the concept of a war-free world to become generally accepted will require a new mindset, the adoption of thinking in global terms. At a time when the continuing existence of the human species is threatened we must think seriously about ways to remove that threat. Just as we have concerns about the safety of our family, and the security of our nation, we must now begin to be consciously concerned about the protection of humankind. Just as in the course of history we have acquired a loyalty to our family, and then to our nation, we must now take the next step and develop an allegiance to humanity.

The problem is that the concept of humanity seems nebulous and remote. It is difficult to develop any feeling towards an entity consisting of six billion units. Actually, size alone does not seem to matter. The United States has a population of about 265 million, comprising a huge diversity of ethnic and racial origins, yet its citizens have a stronger feeling of national belonging than many a state with a population of less then ten million. More important than size is sharing values, a common interest in economic, social and cultural matters. In this respect, the prospects for developing a loyalty to humankind are becoming brighter because of the growing interdependence between nations, an interdependence not only in the realm of economics but also in social and cultural areas; an interdependence brought about by the advances in science and technology.

It is a remarkable fact that the same human activities that have created the potential to destroy the human species have also provided the means for its salvation.

The fantastic progress in communication and transportation has transformed the world into an intimately interconnected community, in which all members depend on one another for their well-being. We are now able to observe instantly what is going on in any part of the globe and provide help where necessary. By means of the various electronic networks we are able to talk to each other, wherever we may be. Language is still a barrier, but this will no doubt be overcome by further improvements in computer technology.

Of course, interdependence is not always a blessing; indeed, some of its negative aspects are quite serious obstacles to peace and security in the world. In the economic sphere, globalization has resulted in the setting up of huge multinational enterprises, operated from the industrialized countries for their own profits; often this is detrimental to the standard of living of people in the developing countries, and thus constitutes a perpetual cause of strife. There are also adverse problems in relation to the environment; certain human activities in the industrialized countries threaten to disrupt global life-supporting processes, the developing countries being the main sufferers. The depletion of natural resources, particularly water, coupled with the continuous increase in the world population is also a perpetual threat to the security of the world.

These threats are an additional incentive to safeguard humankind, by accelerating the positive aspects of globalization, made possible by the progress of science.

We have to build on the achievements of science to get people to know each other better. Access to full information will help to remove prejudices and mistrust which stems mostly from ignorance. We must utilize the new tools for intellectual intercourse to overcome chauvinism and xenophobia, those malevolent fomenters of strife and war. We must exploit the many new channels of communication to bring us together and form a truly global community. We must become world citizens, and, as a first step, educate the people for world citizenship.

World citizenship – in the context of this book – is not meant in the sense of us becoming formally subjects of a world government, with passports and the other trappings associated with a central administrative regime. Some form of global governance is very likely to evolve from the ever-growing interdependencies. It may range from a modification of the United Nations Charter to a fully-fledged World Government. There is certainly the need to redefine the concept of the nation state, involving individual nations relinquishing some of their sovereign rights. But long before any formal political structure is established – and as a step towards it – we have to develop in ourselves the feeling of belonging to the world community, and be beholden to it as we are now to a our family and to our nation. It is in this sense that world citizenship is discussed, and education for it is advocated, in this book.

****

The ideas outlined above were the basis for the discussions at the Pugwash Workshop held in July 1994, in the village of Pugwash, Nova Scotia, the site of the First Pugwash Conference in July 1957. Twenty-five scientists and scholars, from 13 countries, came together to present and debate the chapters of the monograph *World Citizenship: Allegiance to Humanity*.

The material in the book is divided into two parts, the first dealing with the rationale for world citizenship, and the second with ways to achieve it, through education and communication.

As befits a movement of scientists, the book begins with a review, by M.G.K. Menon, of the impact of modern science and technology on all aspects of human society. Science has become an all-permeating agent for social and political change. The Earth, as viewed by an astronaut, appears as a fragile sphere, lone in the universe; but it is the only home for humanity, and it is our duty to ensure that our actions – whether it is the use of weapons of mass destruction or the daily activities that gradually poison the environment – do not harm the life-support systems.

The environmental impact of human activities is the main theme of the chapter by Anne Ehrlich. She points out that we are squeezing the planet by the exploitation and remorseless depletion of our global endowment of resources. We live on capital. The ever growing world population is partly responsible for this, but to an even greater extent it is the *per capita* growth in the use of resources and the increasing poisoning of the environment that spell doom, unless we mend our ways. The industrialized countries are the main contributors to the pollution but it is the people in the poor countries that suffer most, because they are least able to make adjustments.

The economic plight of the developing countries is taken up in the next chapter by Morris Miller. In a detailed analysis and comprehensive review of the – generally adverse – effects of globalization, he discusses the main reasons for the widening gap between the rich and the poor, including those brought by changes in technology, as well as those due to the dominance of the multinationals. All this augurs badly for peace and stability, and calls for drastic measures. He goes on to suggest specific ways to remedy the situation, the most important being a new Bretton Woods agreement.

These three chapters, illustrating different aspects of worldwide interdependence, are followed by Anatol Rapoport's seminal paper on the role of the nation state in the evolving world community. After reviewing the historical evolution of the concept and function of the nation state up to the present day, with its emphasis on sovereignty, the author concludes that sovereignty is incompatible with the global integration necessary in the interdependent world of the future. We must find a way for states to retain a sense of individuality and yet be part of the world community. The concept of sovereignty must give way to the notion of autonomy in the global system of governance. Sovereignty and autonomy must be separated, both conceptually and materially.

Rapoport's paper includes a number of ideas put forward in papers and in the discussion by Natalie Belitser, the late Andrus Park, Rita Rogers and Robert Schaeffer.

In a continuation of the discussion on the nation state, Francesco Calogero uses the scientific community, in the discipline with which he is familiar, as an example of a quasi nation containing the desirable features of a member nation in the future world community, except for a localized territory. He emphasizes the two most important characteristics of the scientific community, universality and openness, as pointers to the direction of future developments in the formation of world governance.

The changing role of the nation state is further developed in the paper 'Expanding Human Loyalties' by Douglas Roche. He analyses the ethical problems facing the world community, in particular, the need to safeguard human rights for everybody. We must aim at human liberation: we have to acquire the economic basis and the political freedom to develop fully our potential as human beings to keep up the common good. Loyalty to humankind will naturally follow from this.

Having elaborated the rationale for world citizenship, the second part of the book turns to two related aspects of the implementation of the objective: education for world citizenship, and enhancement of methods of communication between people.

Ana Maria Cetto discusses problems associated with the introduction of courses on world citizenship in the curricula of schools and universities. These must include codes of conduct, and an understanding of the role of people as human and social beings. Education must stress self-inquiry as opposed to indoctrination; tolerance rather than sectarianism. The paper describes in some detail the requirements of scientific education at high-school level and in universities.

The need to develop awareness of social responsibility among young people is the subject of the chapter by Jeffrey Porten, the youngest of the authors, and himself active in youth movements. He describes the special problems facing youth organizations, some functional, for example lack of funds, some conceptual, for example the aversion of young people to compromise. Youth movements must be supported and nurtured to fight the greatest enemies: apathy in relation to community problems and pursuit of self-interest.

The provision of objective information is one of the most important elements in the creation of a world community. The role of the media in this task is extensively discussed by Nigel Calder. There has been an enormous increase in the volume of news-providing agencies, radio broadcasts (still the cheapest and widest spread mass medium), and television, with huge numbers of channels, some providing 24 hours world-wide news service. But more often means worse; total information is totally indigestible. A process of selection is unavoidable, and this puts a heavy responsibility on those who compose news bulletins. But the judiciousness of the news media is less important than the impact and empathy evoked when viewing directly tragic events occurring in any part of the world.

The paper by Shalheveth Freier and Carin Wedar takes up the problem of objectivity of the information provided by the media, and the need to expose and eradicate misleading information. Taking the war in Bosnia as a case study, the authors give specific examples of the use of the media by both sides as means of propaganda. They put forward concrete suggestions of ways to correct distorted information. This chapter is an amalgam of two papers presented at the Workshop: Freier's paper on 'Exposing and Eradicating Biased and Misleading Information' and Wedar's 'Making Objective Information Widely Available via TV, Radio and Printed Material'. Regrettably, Shalheveth Freier died before reviewing the final text.

The use of the Internet for direct communication between people is the subject of the chapter by Mark Esdale, which incorporates ideas presented at the Workshop by Jeffrey Porten on cyberspace as a component of a new world order. Cyberspace can be described as the sum total of all computer-based communication and data storage. Internet, its largest manifestation, has an enormous, worldwide membership, and is growing rapidly; it has the greatest potential for becoming a parliament of mankind. Care will have to be taken, however, to prevent abuse of the Internet.

The role of the Internet in promoting world citizenship is further elaborated in the last chapter, by David Bell and Robert Logan. It emphasizes the profound effect of communication on the development of the modern state: 'the medium is the message' (Marshall McLuhan). The political implications of communication channels, such as the Internet, are equivalent to those of the introduction of print, in particular in furthering the concept of world citizenship and in dealing with ethnic conflicts. The authors conclude that the new communication techniques will play a significant role in the transformations that are bound to occur as we enter the 21st century.

Apart from the above-mentioned authors, valuable contributions to the discussion were made by Gabriel Baramki, Patrick Boyer, Giovanni Brenciaglia, Jorgen Jensen, Serguei Kapitza, Krishna Patel, Metta Spencer, Raymond Szabo and Mitja Zagar.

Tom Milne, the Executive Editor, wrote the Executive Summary, as well as carrying the main burden of the editorial work. David Rule has also helped with the editing. To all of them I extend grateful thanks, not only for the material help but also for their enthusiasm for the project.

London, March 1996   Joseph Rotblat

Notes on the Contributors

David V.J. Bell (Canada) is the Dean of Environmental Studies and the founding Director of the Centre for Applied Sustainability at York University, Toronto, Canada. He is the author of a number books and articles on political linguistics, Canadian political culture, political violence, negotiation, and sustainability.

Nigel Calder (UK) is a journalist, author and television scriptwriter on a wide range of scientific subjects.

Francesco Calogero (Italy) is Professor of Theoretical Physics (on leave) at the University of Rome, *La Sapienza*. He is Secretary-General of the Pugwash Conferences on Science and World Affairs.

Ana Maria Cetto (Mexico) is a Research Professor at the Institute of Physics at the Autonomous University of Mexico (UNAM), and lecturer in the departments of physics and biology of the Faculty of Sciences, UNAM. She is a member of the Council of Pugwash Conferences on Science and World Affairs.

Anne H. Ehrlich (USA) is a senior research associate in the Department of Biological Sciences and Associate Director/Policy Coordinator at the Center for Conservation Biology at Stanford University. She has written extensively on the human predicament, particularly on population and environmental issues.

Mark Esdale (UK), trained in computer science and electronics, is the Director of Technology for Wicat Systems Inc., a provider of computer-based training in commercial aviation.

Shalheveth Freier (Israel), who died on November 27, 1994, was a senior associate of the Weizmann Institute of Science, Rehovot. He served as Head of Israel's Atomic Energy Commission,

Director of Defence Research at the Ministry of Defence, and Chairman of the Presidential Panel for Science Policy.

Robert Logan (Canada) is Associate Professor of Physics at the University of Toronto. He is the author of two books on communications cum linguistics: *The Alphabet Effect* (Wm. Morrow, 1986) and *The Fifth Language* (Stoddart, 1995).

M.G.K. Menon (India) is a physicist and Fellow of the Royal Society. He is also a Member of Parliament in India. He has served in the government of India in various capacities - as Secretary, Minister and Scientific Adviser - to oversee the development of science and technology in different fields of national development.

Morris Miller (Canada) is Adjunct Professor at the University of Ottawa's Faculty of Administration and an economic consultant on international development issues. He has held senior positions at the United Nations and World Bank, and in the government of Canada. He is the author of many books and articles dealing with the current global economic situation.

Tom Milne (UK) is a staff member of Pugwash Conferences on Science and World Affairs and a postgraduate student in the Department of Government at the University of Manchester.

Jeffrey Porten (USA) is an Internet consultant and activist in Washington, DC. He has founded an Internet consulting firm, and works with non-profit organizations on technological impact and international governance issues. He has recently published a book on entrepreneurship for young people.

Anatol Rapoport (Canada) is Professor of Peace and Conflict Studies at the University of Toronto. He is author of *Origins of Violence* (1989, second edition 1995) and *Peace, An Idea Whose Time Has Come* (1992).

Douglas Roche (Canada), Canada's former Ambassador for Disarmament and a former Member of Parliament, is Visiting Professor at the University of Alberta. His latest book is *An Unacceptable Risk: Nuclear Weapons in a Volatile World* (1995).

Joseph Rotblat (UK) is President of Pugwash Conferences on Science and World Affairs and Emeritus Professor of Physics at the University of London. He is the 1995 Nobel Peace Prize Laureate.

Carin Atterling Wedar (Sweden) is a teacher of history of religion, ethics and international relations. She is Secretary-General of the Swedish Initiative for Peace, Security and International Relations and a consultant to Sweden's Ministry of Education.

Abbreviations and Acronyms

AIDS	acquired immuno-deficiency syndrome
ASCII	American Standard Code for Information Interchange
BBC	British Broadcasting Corporation
CERN	*Centre Européen de Recherches Nucléaires* (European Organization for Nuclear Research)
CFC	chlorofluorocarbon
CGIAR	Consultative Group on International Agricultural Research
CGIE^{2}R	Consultative Group on Internatinoal Energy/Environment Research
CNN	Cable News Network
FAIR	Federation for American Immigration Reform
forex	foreign exchange
FRG	Federal Republic of Germany
GATT	General Agreement on Tariffs and Trade
GDP	gross domestic product
GNP	gross national product
GDR	German Democratic Republic
G-7	Group of Seven industrialized countries
HIV	human immuno-deficiency virus
IATA	International Air Transport Association
IFC	International Finance Corporation
IGY	International Geophysical Year
IMF	International Monetary Fund
MIGA	Multilateral Investment Guarantee Agency
NAFTA	North American Free Trade Agreement
NEEDS	Non-linear Evolution Equations and Dynamical Systems
NGO	non-governmental organization
NIC	newly industrializing country
NPP	net primary production
NPT	(Nuclear) Non-Proliferation Treaty
ODA	official development assistance

OLR	off-line reader
SAL	structural adjustment lending
SDR	Special Drawing Right
UN	United Nations
UNCED	United Nations Conference on Environment and Development
UNESCO	United Nations Educational, Scientific and Cultural Organization
VCR	video control recorder

World Citizenship:
Allegiance to Humanity

Executive Overview

GLOBAL INTERDEPENDENCE –
THE RATIONALE FOR WORLD CITIZENSHIP

The most important problems facing the human race today are global problems. This is what is meant by 'global interdependence'. The rapid development of science and technology in the twentieth century has produced weapons capable of destroying civilization; and it has advanced human enterprise to a level that is straining the Earth's natural processes and equilibriums.

Threats of irreversible destruction on this scale have no precedent in human history. They demand a commensurate change in the way that human society is organized and managed.

Science and technology, at the heart of the problem, may also be at the heart of a solution. We need less polluting methods of generating energy, increased agricultural yields, foolproof ways to verify disarmament treaties. We need a sound scientific basis for international agreements to regulate damaging human activities. The international treaty banning chlorofluorocarbons (CFCs) followed from scientific evidence that the ozone layer is being destroyed, for example.

Yet, it would be illusory to think that technical advances alone can rescue humankind from its current predicament. For as long as human society is constituted by groups that are intolerant of one another, insular, selfish, and unable to think beyond their immediate material well-being, science and technology promise to create problems faster than they solve them. A parochial attitude to world affairs, insensitivity to the

1

destruction of the environment, a lack of compassion for fellow
human beings, insufficient imagination to see the dangers that lie
ahead: all will condemn the human race to a chaotic and violent
future.

Science and technology can help here too. Modern forms of
communication provide the means for us to move beyond these
destructive patterns of thinking. The mass media, electronic
communications and international travel systems have the
potential to expand our horizons to the global level: to inculcate
a feeling of belonging to a world community.

There are already myriad connections between every part of
the world. Finance, business, trade, tourism, culture and sport are
all international activities. We have an opportunity to learn far
more than ever before about the world we live in. We must hope
that as global connections continue to multiply we will begin to
see the Earth as it is: a small planet with finite resources being
undermined by short-sighted greed and backward social
organization.

ASPECTS OF GLOBAL INTERDEPENDENCE – WEAPONS OF MASS DESTRUCTION, A SHARED ENVIRONMENT, A GLOBAL ECONOMY

The existence of weapons of mass destruction is the most
egregious example of global interdependence. Nuclear weapons
exist in quantities sufficient to destroy the human species
instantly. It is assumed that nuclear weapons will never be used
on a large scale but this is no more than an article of faith.
There is no proof that nuclear deterrence operates as described in
text books. It may be that good luck has played an important
part in our avoiding nuclear war.

Even if nuclear weapons have made leaders of the nuclear
weapon states more cautious when confronting one another than
they might otherwise have been, this certainly was not and is not
a reason for developing or retaining them. Whatever the
probability of a nuclear exchange – no matter how low – the idea
of such a calculated risk is absurd when the consequence of a

failure of deterrence is the annihilation of the human species. In Robert McNamara's words, we need to eliminate nuclear weapons because 'the indefinite combination of nuclear weapons and human fallibility will lead to a nuclear exchange'.[1]

Similar arguments apply, with less force, to other weapons of mass destruction and to modern conventional weapons. The level of destruction that would be suffered by both sides in a war between powerful states is wholly out of proportion with any possible objective.

Besides the threat posed by modern weapons, the world is also made interdependent by a shared environment and a global economic system. Threats to the environment are unlikely to cause an immediate catastrophe on the scale of a nuclear war but may be equally deadly in the long run. Human activities consume vast quantities of natural resources and are producing large scale changes to the biosphere. Meteorologists, for example, believe that greenhouse gases will cause climate change, and biologists warn that loss of biodiversity is disrupting whole ecosystems. At the most basic level, it is calculated that human society is dramatically reducing the amount of energy from sunlight that is processed in photosynthesis and made available to the rest of the Earth's organisms.

Both non-renewable resources (fossil fuels, metals) and resources that are in theory renewable (agricultural soils, water) are being depleted. This threatens to cause conflict in areas of high population density relative to available resources; indeed, pressure on resources was part of the cause of the bloodshed in Rwanda. Currently, the shortage of fresh water in several regions of the world is of especial concern.

The bottom line is that a civilization that destabilizes life-supporting global processes and uses up its base of natural resources is not on a sustainable course. The industrialized nations are mostly responsible for the current predicament but all nations will suffer adverse consequences and the poorest will often be the most vulnerable to the disruptive effects.

There are no simple solutions, though many of the necessary steps are apparent. All approaches have complicated technical, political and economic dimensions which are not easily summarized. An essential part of any approach, though, will be limiting the world population. This is expected, at the minimum, to double over the next fifty years. Coping with this increase will be a daunting task. If population growth spirals out of control then it will overwhelm any and all progress in other areas. Limiting the impact that each person has on the environment in his or her daily life will be equally important. The twenty-fold rise in energy use in the industrial era (energy use can be taken as a rough indication of environmental impact) has resulted, in about equal measure, from population growth and increase in *per capita* use of energy.

At a fundamental level, a requirement for progress is for all groups to recognize consciously that the world is living beyond its means, and to plan and agree on a path to a viable future. An unprecedented level of global cooperation will be required. The United Nations Conference on Environment and Disarmament in Rio de Janeiro in 1992 might be seen as a first sign of such cooperation.

The forces shaping the world economy give cause for both hope and despair. The lifting of burdens imposed by the Cold War and the promise flowing from innovation in science and technology are sources of encouragement. In contrast, signs of impending crisis in development, environment, and trade and capital flows are ominous portents of problems ahead.

The tragic levels of poverty today bring into high relief the dramatically divided and inequitable state of the world. One-fifth of human beings live in absolute poverty. Four in ten of those living in developing countries are malnourished. Great numbers of people die from preventable diseases caused by poverty.

It is true that in recent decades there has been economic growth and social progress across the world. Even in the poorest countries, inflation-adjusted average income has gone up, average lifespan increased, and adult literacy improved. But progress has been erratic and very unevenly distributed both between and within countries. It has on the whole been growth without equity. More than this, the figures say nothing about the potential for progress that is not being realized.

The bald figures can also disguise the fact that the gap

between the rich and the poor is widening. The absolute difference in incomes between the richest fifth and poorest fifth in the world has increased eightfold between 1960 and 1990. This situation will worsen if, as expected, most of the population increase in coming decades is in poorer countries. Making the situation yet more bleak for the poor countries is a set of mutually reinforcing economic problems. Servicing international debt reduces the money available for social and industrial investment. So does the decreasing ability of these countries to compete in world markets as a consequence of subsidies ($300 billion a year agricultural subsidies alone in the industrialized countries), trade barriers, declining export markets for primary commodities, and a lack of modern high technology. Low levels of investment sow the seeds of future problems. An underfunded education system cannot, for example, produce the highly trained workforce that these countries increasingly need. A vicious cycle of decline is thus in place. Against this background, the multinational corporations – with a justified reputation for promoting low social and environmental standards – grow stronger.

There are two key requirements for global social and economic development with equity and environmental standards. First, low interest rates and stable exchange rates; second, increased financial flows to developing countries. The former will involve finding ways to control international capital flows. With respect to the latter, current amounts of official development assistance are small, usually tied to geopolitical objectives, and do little to alleviate poverty. A variety of suggestions have been made for alternative ways to finance what might be thought of as a 'global Marshall Plan'. These suggestions include taxing use of fuel, so-called 'debt-for-nature' swaps, and a minuscule tax on international transfers of money (a tax at a rate of 3/1000s of one per cent would yield enough to finance all UN operations).

The global economic system incorporates diverse and very powerful forces. To change this system in the way described here will require a new or redesigned set of institutions and rules at the level of international economic governance. A prerequisite for progress – as for tackling environmental problems – is to develop an overall vision. First, it must be agreed that the global economic system needs reforming, not tinkering with. Second, the multifaceted objectives of the reforming process must be clearly set out.

NEED FOR THE NATION STATE TO ADAPT

The common theme that emerges in discussing the various aspects of global interdependence is that the foremost social, environmental and economic problems facing the world can only be addressed through cooperation between nations. It follows that the organization of the world in sovereign units is an insuperable obstacle to progress.

To remain sovereign a nation state keeps a military force to protect what the ruling elites judge to be the 'national interest'. This provokes neighbouring states to develop a countervailing military capability. An arms race and 'balance of power' ensue, and the result is usually a tense and unstable situation.

Despite this, it has become axiomatic to political thought to equate military strength with security and prestige. This has led to enormous expenditure on arms by rich and poor countries alike. Powerful defence-industrial lobbies have become established in arms exporting countries. The vaunted 'right to self defence' is spoken of hypocritically by profit-seeking arms exporters, warmongering governments, and military establishments intent on using military force only to protect privilege and subjugate the population.

The lack of cooperation in the global economy is equally troublesome. As discussed, economic competition between nation states, the unscrupulous operation of multinationals (which are in effect sovereign actors), and global financial flows (also beyond the control of national and international bodies) all tend to produce low social and environmental standards. Even cooperation to mutual advantage is problematic because the temptation for one party to seek advantage by undermining agreement will ultimately prove too strong.

It is true that states are progressively ceding sovereignty to regional and international bodies. This happens when they sign arms control treaties, for example the Chemical Weapons Convention, environmental treaties, such as the agreement banning CFCs, or economic agreements, like the General Agreement on Tariffs and Trade. But there is strong resistance to the limitations on sovereignty that will be needed to eliminate weapons of mass destruction and tackle global environmental and economic problems effectively.

The nation state could survive and play a useful role in a process of global integration. To do so, the idea of sovereignty needs to be replaced by a concept of autonomy in which the nation state is autonomous in specific spheres and responsible to higher levels of organization in others. The range of areas controlled by the nation state would be determined on pragmatic lines. Some matters will be best organized on a global scale, some by region, some by nation, some by local area. A balance would thus be struck between allowing a state to retain a sense of its distinctive identity while at the same time becoming part of an ongoing global integration.

The most important change would be that the right and ability of the nation state to make war would end. The only legitimate military force would be a global police force in the control of a global authority. National military establishments that survive in atrophied forms would be responsible for preserving peace, responding to natural disasters, and the like.

If nation states adapt in this way they would also give up their monopoly on internal coercive power. In the past, empires and nation states have helped to control violence between groups within their borders, as was seen when the restraints on conflict were removed in the Soviet Union and Yugoslavia. The conflicts in Somalia and Rwanda also followed from a disintegration of the controlling forces in these countries. In the world order here envisaged the global police force would intervene to prevent or quell such unrest.

The root of internal conflict is usually discrimination against a minority or weak group in a state. There are various steps that could be taken to stop such conflict arising. First and foremost it is desirable that nation states grant citizenship – with its attendant rights, benefits and duties – on the basis of permanent residence only. The conditions placed on citizenship in some states today creates groups that have a different social, economic and legal status. In particular, the so-called 'natural' bases of identification (race, ethnicity, religion) should be removed from the notion of citizenship.

A nation state can be defined by clear geographical boundaries. There is, in fact, no future in defining state boundaries on other than a geographical basis. There are no ethnically homogenous nation states, and the constituent groups of multi-ethnic states are seldom in geographically contiguous regions. For this reason, the process of 'self-determination' will lead in theory to the continuing fractionation of states with no obvious limit. Existing state boundaries may not be 'natural' or 'just', but they can be clearly defined and have the great virtue of not being based on ideology. There is, of course, no reason to preclude peaceful change by agreement if this can be achieved, as for example in the merger of East and West Germany in 1990 and the division of Czechoslovakia in 1993.

In summary, if the human species is to survive then the nation state must either wither away or adapt. In the latter case, it would become an administrative unit on some appropriate level of social organization. It would play an important role by providing a continuity of established traditions but would be subordinate to global authorities dealing with global problems.

How likely is a move away from the current system of nation states? A variety of possible 'new world orders' have been predicted in recent years. These range from a cooperative global society with world citizenship and world government, at one extreme, to a world of increasing divisions and hostility between rich and poor regions, at the other. It is also predicted that parts of the world will become deeply integrated while other areas remain isolated and disengaged from the mainstream of world affairs.

There is no objective measure of the likelihood of any of these predictions coming true, because the outcome of a political process is not independent of what is predicted. If enough people believe in the need for global cooperation – and educating the general public about the need for this is the subject of the second half of this book – then this will be a factor in helping the idea to gain still wider acceptance.

A move to social organization at the global level would continue a steady progression in which social groups have increased in size from the family, in the beginning, to the nation state/continental region, today. (This progression is modelled nicely by successive factors of ten: 10^0 – individual; 10^1 – family; 10^2 – neighbourhood; 10^3 – village; 10^4 – small town; 10^5 – small city; 10^6 – medium size city; 10^7 – large city/small state; 10^8 – medium size state; 10^9 – large state/continent/civilization; 10^{10} – entire globe.) This trend is perhaps the soundest reason to be optimistic about the prospects for moving to a world organized at the global level. Moreover, the time is right for such a transition: modern communications make this final step possible.

A second, related trend which runs in the same direction is the increasing role that communities that cut across national boundaries play in the lives of ordinary people. The scientific community is a good example. Scientists have a shared set of values, a shared language, are engaged in a common enterprise, and often establish personal friendships among themselves. To this extent the scientific community can be thought of as a 'quasi nation'. It may be that as people establish friendships and loyalties in such communities, which have no territorial locality, the tendency to associate with conflict over territory will diminish. If a sufficiently large and influential group of people become deeply involved in these communities, then this could have a significant impact on a world scale. At the least, new allegiances established alongside traditional ones may dilute aggressive nationalistic feelings.

Communities that cut across national boundaries have always existed – professional sportsmen, musicians – without seeming to do much to alleviate global tensions (though who can know what would have happened without even these international connections?). But as modern communications develop, such quasi nations seem certain to become more widespread and to play a more significant role in the lives of their members. They may in this way assume a high importance as a less disruptive form of human bonding.

Whether or not the world evolves as these trends suggest that it might, it can be predicted with confidence that the present order will not persist. In an interdependent world, there will be no prosperity for any nation in the long term while there is extreme poverty on a massive scale; no stability while the human race lives beyond its means; no security for as long as nations arm themselves to the teeth. At present, therefore, the world is not in a stable state. There will be upheaval. The question is whether it will be managed change engendering increasing cooperation for the common good or panicky change, precipitated by crisis, causing nations to think only of short-term interests in an internecine fight for survival.

It cannot be emphasized strongly enough that this is a genuine choice. Sustainable development might be achieved with far-sighted public policy. Yet, there is no sign whatever of the political will necessary for the radical measures required. The difficulty is that most people think only of next week or next year and are little concerned about what will happen to the world a quarter century from now. The gap between what is required and what seems even remotely possible is a fundamental problem.

The progress of science and technology has outstripped political and social development. The affluent are aware of the extreme inequities in the world but do not care to consider that these inequalities are a consequence of public policies that their countries implement. Nor do they care that policies that leave half the world languishing in poverty and pollute the environment will sooner or later threaten their own livelihood. Nor has the civilization of the world reached such a high level of development that it demands the same rights for all human beings.

We must strive to enlighten our thinking. The child in the rich world must come to view his or her human rights as inextricably connected with those of the child in the poor world. Men and women must come to feel many overlapping loyalty systems, from the family upwards, culminating in a loyalty to humankind.

LOYALTY TO HUMANKIND – EDUCATION FOR WORLD CITIZENSHIP

We need to make a conscious effort to educate ourselves about the world. With an increasingly interdependent world the importance of understanding all of that world is growing. A stable world community cannot be built in the face of ignorance and misunderstanding – it is often simply this that leads to conflict. The greater understanding that a person has of the culture and traditions of a country in opposition to his or her own, the more tolerant they are likely to be of the differences. If we can understand the values of others we may begin to see the world as one nation, and embrace the values of people in different countries in all their diversity as our values.

The focal point of the educational process must be the threat to the human species itself. We need to resist the complacency that prevails towards this danger before it is too late. In short, we need to develop a conscious loyalty to humankind.

Loyalty to humankind can be expressed and taught in a practical way. It requires understanding issues of peace, international understanding, and husbandry of the environment; it involves recognizing the need for a social and economic order that allows each human being to develop in all dimensions of life.

Developing a loyalty to humankind will involve learning to understand and appreciate the rich diversity of culture and tradition in the world. We should not be afraid of conflicts of interest between groups – this is a normal state of affairs – rather we should worry if there are no means to bring divergent interests together to search for accommodations.

Scientists have a special responsibility to think carefully about what they are doing because the applications of science have such far-reaching global effects. When the young scientist has learnt about the laws of nature, it is important to invest his or her theoretical knowledge with meaning by teaching how and why science has evolved, its contributions to civilizations, its limitations and potential.

There is a tendency in some scientific institutions to

discourage discussion of the social role of science, or even to dismiss such inquiry as 'anti scientific'. At the same time, the importance of science as an enormously powerful agent for social change is given emphasis. These attitudes are irreconcilable. The scientist can no longer seek the sanctuary of the ivory tower. It is desirable, therefore, that science curricula contain courses covering the history of science, its philosophical implications, its relations to other disciplines and to society.

A great edifice of science has been established: each of us should be encouraged to reflect on what we want the body of science to accomplish. Such a broadening of scientific outlook would help to inculcate a feeling of world citizenship in future generations.

Capturing and nourishing the imagination and optimism of young people by involving them in youth movements – an experience that can profoundly shape their outlook on life and future career – is another part of the educational process that is needed.

Youth movements come in a great variety of shapes and sizes. There is no general prescription for enhancing their effectiveness, but none is needed: it is natural for young people to mingle, as is the case for any group with something in common. The limiting factor is the amount of money made available to support youth organizations.

From the point of view of furthering education for world citizenship, it is most important to support groups working on international issues and/or bringing together students from different countries through conferences and exchange programmes. The high cost of air travel is often the greatest restriction on what these groups can accomplish. Either providing direct financial backing or supporting travel costs by some innovative means (making use of unsold aircraft seats, for example) would be a practical approach to take.

Promoting youth movements is just one part of the broad educational process that is needed. But if by failing to provide resources to support these movements, or by being inattentive to their work, the world community turns idealistic young people into dispirited cynics then the outlook for each of us may be that bit bleaker.

THE ROLE OF THE MEDIA AND ELECTRONIC COMMUNICATIONS IN PROMOTING WORLD CITIZENSHIP

The media and electronic communications can provide the means with which to educate and inform people about the world. It is impossible, of course, for one person to be well-informed about events in every part of the world. There is just too much going on. The media themselves are inherently parochial having evolved alongside the nation state. What is more, even if balance and objectivity were sought, achieving them would be problematic. A journalist can strive to report events in objective terms but information about the world is rarely provided as an objective statement, almost all information is embedded in a context. An attempt can be made to provide a balanced picture of events, that is, all sides to a story, but information is easily biased by our cultural preconceptions. We are more apt to react to and assimilate facts that support our sincerely held beliefs than information which contradicts these beliefs.

Objectivity in the choice of stories made by the local news editor is also problematic. It is not just that editors in different parts of the world have different agendas. There are also biases created by language, location of studios, archive material, and ease of live filming. More fundamentally, the news media are not, by and large, an enterprise dedicated to enlightening the public through objective news coverage. They are in the main a business – part of the entertainment industry – providing a service, aiming to satisfy the customer. Orchestrated distortion of the news may result from government intervention, ulterior motives of powerful media moguls, pressure from the public relations industry, or lobbying from special interest groups.

Making the assumption that it is desirable for news coverage to be balanced and objective (and this is not obviously true for all societies at all times: could China, for instance, have been guided towards prosperity by congenial liberal means?), ways should be sought to expose and remove biased and misleading information of both innocent and malicious origin.

This is most difficult in war time. External pressures put on journalists are extreme and subjective influences, stemming either from group loyalties or from random emotional involvement in the conflict, are at their strongest. One possible approach would be to establish an independent and neutral body to provide information, possibly a UN news gathering service. *Vreme*, an independent newspaper set up in Belgrade in 1990, with a mandate to provide objective information on the conflict in Yugoslavia, achieved a circulation of 30,000 and became one of the most quoted sources of news on the conflict. A *Vreme* journalist argues that the Yugoslav conflict might have been avoided had it not been for inflammatory and mendacious reporting from Serb and Croat-controlled media centres.

Other ways to increase objectivity in news presentation can be imagined. The Secretary-General of the UN could give an annual State of the World address similar to the State of the Union address given by the President of the United States, and it made obligatory for nations to discuss this statement in their legislatures (where they have them). A convention might be established in the mass media obliging media owners to give a regular space to views that run counter to the editorial line. Most important, though, is for people to be educated broadly so that they can appreciate the context of information and evaluate it in a balanced manner. This, more than anything, will make us discerning consumers of media news.

Whether or not the description that the media provide of the world is wholly fair or comprehensive, the media help to foster world citizenship. The most important way in which they do this is by engendering an emotional response to the world events that they portray. Pictures of people from foreign shores or of UN peacekeepers in the field are probably more effective in changing attitudes of mind than abstract pronouncements on world interdependence. A film of a starving person evokes the compassion and unease that many people in affluent countries feel when, for example, they pass a destitute person in the street. In another respect, media coverage of violence and repression in the world – though piecemeal and, on occasion, highly selective – does some good if it puts pressure on the offending government or dictatorship to moderate its actions. The media also promote world citizenship when they increase awareness of regional and global interdependence. Highlighting the common hazards facing countries is often more persuasive in bringing them together than pointing out benefits of cooperating.

Alongside the media, electronic communications – in particular computers linked to global telephone networks – have an almost unlimited potential for increasing communication between people from different countries.

The Internet – the largest global computer network – now extends to some 170 countries. The number of people using the Internet is estimated at 40 million and is expected to exceed 100 million by the turn of the century.

This is only the tip of the iceberg: computer communication is in its infancy and will develop and expand almost beyond recognition in coming years. Apart from improvements to infrastructure and communications hardware, the technology will be made easier to use. Computer communication will become as routine as using the telephone today and as commonplace.

Computer communication can be either person to person or from one person to multiple recipients. Person-to-person communication, known as electronic mail or e-mail, is analogous to communication by letter or fax, only faster than a letter, cheaper than a fax, and sent and received in electronic form. In one-to-many communication a person sends a message to an electronic discussion forum. Other computer users have the opportunity either to post a public response to what is written in the forum (often called 'discussion group') or to respond directly to the author at his or her e-mail address. There are already thousands of such computer discussion groups in existence, involving millions of people.

Renowned theoretical work on communications and society shows that the dominant mode of communication in a society strongly influences social organization. For example, the development of the printing press gave rise to national languages and cultures, and is closely associated with the development of the nation state. It also began the modern political age by making mass participation in politics possible.

Today, electronic communications promise to transform

social organization again. These communications give an immediacy to events taking place in geographically distant parts of the world. They also diminish – and can remove altogether – indications of race, ethnicity, nationality, gender; in fact all identities other than the human one. More and more children will grow up using these communications networks. Schoolchildren from different countries may soon communicate directly with one another in lessons on, say, geography, history or religion. In the light of Marshall McLuhan's aphorism 'The medium is the message', electronic communications can be expected to foster a strong sense of belonging to a world community.

Electronic communications already help geographically dispersed groups of people to form close ties. Indeed, a sense of community exists among many of those who use the Internet. The bonding is stronger between subsets of Internet users who share a particular interest and who are sometimes already known to one another. One example is the world scientific community, discussed above, especially scientists working in the same research field. Electronic communication is making an ever greater contribution to the structure and vitality of these and similar groups.

Electronic communities have no territorial grounding: their members interact in 'cyberspace'. Might it be that social tensions stemming from the aspirations of ethnic communities for land could be lessened in a similar way? Two types of nation could exist side by side: one, the nation state, defined geographically, which is multicultural and concerned with the economic and social well-being of its citizens (though subordinate to global authorities in some areas); the other, associations of people with a common cultural heritage, bonded together by different means of communication, including electronic, but without a defined land area.

Currently, most computer communication takes place in English, but software will be developed that will allow computer users to write in any language they wish. A much more significant breakthrough will be made if machine translation of natural language is achieved. Computer scientists and linguists have struggled with the deep problems involved for forty years.

Automatic translation might even help to resolve the dilemma that now faces those who believe both in the value of removing the language barrier between groups and in preserving cultural diversity – but this is to move into murky waters.

The minimum hardware needed to connect to the Internet is a standard personal computer, a telephone line, and a modem (a device connecting the computer and telephone line). This is a large expense for the average person in many countries. Another requirement for using the Internet is a basic education and computer literacy. On top of this, building a modern communications infrastructure is an expensive undertaking at the national level. It is not surprising, therefore, that most Internet users are in the wealthier nations.

The Internet is at present quite cheap to use once one is connected to it. But it is possible (some would say likely) that those who currently provide access to the Internet at not much more than cost price, will begin to operate as commercial concerns and increase charges accordingly. They may also start to incorporate the costs of the main communications infrastructure, currently borne by national governments.

There is thus a danger that computer communications will be restricted largely to the richer countries, even to the more affluent sectors within these countries. If this happens, the enormous potential impact that this technology has for promoting world citizenship will be reduced.

CONCLUSION

Is it Utopian to believe that a loyalty to humanity could one day prevail in the world? Loyalty to humanity is clearly not relevant to those who are fighting in bloody conflicts or struggling to find food and water to live. It seems equally far from the minds of those who blithely plunder the Earth's resources.

Against this background, we should take heart from the many politicians, civil servants, NGO's, pressure groups, academics and journalists working – at the risk of sounding melodramatic – on human survival. It is enormously significant that tangible progress is being made: international agreements to eliminate categories of weapons and to protect the environment have been reached, put into practice, and achieved their objectives. In the case of nuclear weapons – a problem which humans must solve if they are to survive – attitudes are changing noticeably. Most encouraging of all, undreamed of powers of communication are bringing people together and seem likely to profoundly integrate human society (or at least parts of it).

Too little is being done too slowly: but history tells us that human beings rarely act until forced to do so by circumstances.

At the most fundamental level, optimism about the future for a deeply complex, turbulent world can be based on humankind's capacity for ingenuity and rational and moral thinking. The reflections of Robert McNamara, more than thirty years ago, embroiled in the tragedy of the Vietnam war while serving as Secretary of Defense, strike an appropriate balance between hope and despair:

> All the evidence of our history suggests that man is indeed a rational animal – but with a near infinite capacity for folly. His history seems largely a halting, but persistent, effort to raise his reason above his animality.
>
> He draws blueprints for Utopia. But he never quite gets it built. In the end, he plugs away obstinately with the only building material really ever at hand: his own part-comic, part-tragic, part-cussed, but part-glorious nature.
>
> I, for one, would not count a global free society out.[2]

REFERENCES

1. R.S. McNamara, 'A Nuclear Free World: Is it Desirable?', speech at the Royal Society, London, UK, 11 December 1992.

2. R.S. McNamara, address before the American Society of Newspaper Editors, Montreal, Canada, 18 May 1966.

Part I

Rationale for World Citizenship

1

Effect of Modern Science and Technology on Relations Between Nations

M.G.K. Menon

One of the profound features of the present millennium has undoubtedly been the birth and exponential growth of modern science.

Science (throughout this chapter, 'science' is used to mean natural science and does not include the social sciences and humanities) in its very basic sense has, of course, been an intrinsic part of human society from the earliest times. Many important scientific discoveries have been made throughout human history. The great centres of human civilization and culture, particularly those in China, India, Mesopotamia, Central Asia, Egypt, Greece and Rome, and the Indian civilizations of South America, made important discoveries that underpinned later developments. Over these earlier historical periods there were bursts of activity but no self-sustaining growth process. Then, a few hundred years ago, in Europe, the scientific and industrial revolutions occurred and took root. Ever since, the development of science has been a continuous process on an exponential growth curve.

The twentieth century has been characterized by an explosive growth of information, knowledge and understanding through scientific research, and its rapid application. As a result, we have been witnessing many 'ages' occurring in parallel. In earlier periods of human history, one had ages named after various materials, such as Stone, Copper, Iron and Bronze. These covered enormous spans in time. In contrast, in just the past half century, we have had the age of the atom, the age of space, the age of electronics and informatics, the age of new biology, the age of new materials, and the age of spectacular scientific discoveries concerning fundamental aspects of nature, such as our understanding of the sub-structure of matter, or, at the other end of the domain, of space and time and new perspectives concerning the universe.

Each of these ages has had a profound impact on the relations between nations, as we shall see later. In order to understand the nature and scale of these impacts we need to consider the question: what are the characteristics of science in the twentieth century?

The first aspect to note is that the scale of scientific advance has increased almost out of all recognition. This is true whether measured in terms of the growth rate, in the number of active research workers, in the expenditure on science, in the number of research publications, or the extent of production in the world based on scientific advances. The first four aspects relate to science itself. But the last aspect of 'production in the world based on scientific advances' is one which has affected society. There is no need to go beyond the plastic bucket, synthetic shirt or transistor radio seen in the remotest corners of the earth to appreciate that industrial production in the world is based on modern science. Economists agree that the major driving force in industrial and post-industrial societies, which defines economic levels and activity, is science.

Such a signal change in the scale of activity in science cannot but call for a profound change in the character, management and organization of science itself, as also in its relation to and impact on society. Science is no longer a stand-alone activity, at the fringes of society, but one that is closely intertwined with industrial, agricultural and other production activities, and with governmental and inter-governmental functioning; in the manner and extent to which it permeates and affects society as a whole it now constitutes a central element.

The second important characteristic of recent scientific development is the rapidity with which scientific discoveries are being applied for practical purposes. While some part of production activities, particularly in the developing countries, derive from practices that have carried down through history, the major part of current production depends on, and can be immediately traced back to, great scientific discoveries of the twentieth century, and especially of just the last few decades. Electronics and information technology, polymers, hormones and antibiotics, nuclear energy, space technology with all of its applications, and genetic engineering are all illustrations of the manner in which fundamental scientific discoveries rapidly translate to products and processes of daily life.

The third characteristic of scientific development has been the application of science to armaments. The interest of scientists and inventors in machines of war and in consulting for the military is not something new. It has a long history. However, it is only during this century, with the use of aircraft, tanks and poison gases in World War I, and the development and use of radar, sonar, missiles and of atomic weapons of frightening power during World War II, that science truly became related to the military enterprise.

Over the past half a century, the subvention to science from governments to prepare for new and ever more scientific wars has continued to be multiplied by large factors. From wars involving armies in close conflict, the scope of war has enlarged to affect entire human populations. Moreover, it is not only in the lethal weapons, but in the large support mechanisms needed for war that modern science has begun to be an essential part of the military system.

Until relatively recently, the concern was about wars involving nations and governments, with well defined weapon systems. But the fact that many of the advances arising from work in science, such as explosives, automatic weapons, biological weapons and such like, can be used extensively by relatively small groups interested in anarchy and terrorism has added a new dimension to the terror to which science has contributed.

As in many other areas, there are very close linkages between defence, aerospace and various sectors of civilian industry. Defence industries have been responsible for a significant technological push, and they have also been responsible for significant spin-off of technology to civilian industry. The true effects of the militarization of science on the character of science, as well as its image in the public mind, have yet to be evaluated. It is clear that the result will be a significant distortion in the aims and methods of science as seen by the great pioneers and sages of science.

Another important characteristic of science today is the synergistic and symbiotic relationship that it has with technology. In early stages of human history, progress was made largely through the use of skills and techniques involving coordination between hand and eye, acquired empirically. In recent decades, however, technology has been moving forward through a basic scientific understanding of the processes involved. Electrical engineering was from the beginning wholly science based. In contrast, chemical technology was in its early stages largely empirical, but now it is also science based. The developments taking place in nuclear technology, biotechnology, space technology, information technology and the like, are all based on scientific discoveries, knowledge and understanding. In reverse, technological development is enabling science to move forward much faster. Powerful capabilities arising from the availability of new materials, of electronics and instrumentation, and so on, enable scientific work to be done much more rapidly and reliably; for example, computational technology is at the very heart of scientific activity and progress today. It is this close relationship between science and technology that is enabling each to make progress so much faster.

Until World War II science was a leisurely activity carried out with relatively small funds, largely involving groups in educational institutions where there was a highly effective teacher-student relationship. After World War II science became more organized with much larger funds poured into research.

Big facilities and major research projects and programmes came into existence. The success of organized projects during World War II, such as the development and deployment of radars, and the Manhattan Project to produce the atomic bomb, demonstrated the power of mission-oriented activities for the accomplishment of very specific tasks.

Industrial research laboratories which had existed well before World War II became larger, and began playing a significant role in high level technological innovation with a major impact on products and markets. Some made significant moves into areas at the frontiers of science, even pure science. Nobel Prize-winning work has been done in many industrial research laboratories.

Today, a large part of the expenditure on science is incurred by industry and by government, in areas such as defence research, provision of infrastructural and surveying facilities, large programmes such as space, meteorological and oceanographic research, and the like.

There are many programmes today which have to be carried out through cooperation among the various nations of the world. These include programmes in meteorology and oceanography, which call for a large infrastructure of ships, aircraft, satellites, data reception, storage and analysis systems, a very large number of observing points, and so on. These demand highly coordinated efforts for task definition, research allocation, phasing of programmes, organization and management to ensure success.

Since the end of World War II we have seen major activity in science conducted in the form of mega-science projects. These projects were initially in the areas of high energy elementary particle physics, which requires large accelerators, and in space sciences; now they include other areas, such as the earth sciences and modern biology.

Whilst these changes have been taking place in relation to science and technology let us briefly consider what has been happening on the social, cultural, political and religious fronts.

From the early stages of Neanderthal Man, through the Old and New Stone Ages, human beings moved from food gathering and hunting to primitive village agriculture. This evolution was characterized by scientific and technical advances, such as the discovery of the use of fire, and major ways of handling and shaping materials, particularly tools, which could then be used for food gathering, food production and for the creation of artifacts such as cloth, pottery and the like.

Gradually, community structures emerged in the form of tribes and villages. There was the concept of a neighbourhood, whose dimensions were largely defined by human physical capabilities. With settled agriculture and the sense of food security that it engendered, there was time for leisure, leading to a more effective use of the human brain for the development of science and of the arts, of language beyond the requirements for what were then essential needs, and the creation of products which were aesthetically satisfying and decorative. Gradually, the process of urbanization set in. Cities were built and fortified from which heavily equipped armies could be sent out and supported from within. In earlier periods there were conflicts between tribes, sometimes with territorial connotations. With the emergence of cities the incentives for war with other nearby cities developed in the form of the need to acquire more land for exploitation and production of wealth. The scope for war enlarged in the transition from city states to nation states.

Historically, there have been kingdoms and empires. These were largely a product of a power wielded from above, with no feeling of citizenship or nationality among the vast mass of the inhabitants who constituted the kingdom or empire. Their loyalties continued to be to the neighbourhood and to other ethnic, religious and such groupings. It is only in more recent times, contemporary with the development of modern science but not directly related to it, that the concept of a nation with its own loyalties has emerged. But one also notices the strong loyalties to ethnic and religious groupings that continue and coexist with those to the neighbourhood or to the nation state.

These loyalties to the neighbourhood, to ethnic and religious groupings, and to the nation are usually understood and felt by individuals. Indeed, in many cases, depending on the nature of the issue, these loyalties give rise to very strong emotional feelings and relate to deep elements in the human psyche.

We shall now see how the advances that have already taken place in science and technology, and those which one can foresee as occurring on an even larger scale in the future, call for world citizenship. The difficulty is that whilst we are moving willy-nilly in that direction, the concept of being a world citizen is far removed from the understanding and psyche of an individual. Let us now look at the compulsions arising from science and technology in this direction.

It was earlier stated that we are living in a period of several ages of humankind moving ahead with revolutionary rapidity and in parallel, and that each of these has had a profound impact on the relations between nations.

The age of the atom is based on discoveries in physics made over the past hundred years. The world got to know of the dawn of this age when atom bombs were dropped on Hiroshima and Nagasaki in 1945. Since then, through the Cold War, the world has lived under a Sword of Damocles – a possible nuclear holocaust. Fortunately, that possibility has receded with the end of the Cold War. But these developments brought starkly to notice the fact that a significant part of humankind could be wiped out in a nuclear war, with untold devastation. Indeed, after such a major nuclear war, the world would never be the same place. One recalls in this context the stirring words of the Russell-Einstein Manifesto of 1955:

> We are speaking on this occasion, not as members of this or that nation, continent or creed, but as human beings, members of the species Man, whose continued existence is in doubt . . . Almost everybody who is politically conscious has strong feelings about one or more of these issues; but we want you, if you can, to set aside such feelings . . . we appeal as human beings to human beings: remember your humanity and forget the rest.[1]

This is an appeal to come together as citizens of one world to prevent nuclear disaster.

One need not go further into the impact of these developments of the atomic age on the relationships between nations, since these have been the basis for the initiation of and continuing discussions at the Pugwash Conferences. The events of 1994 in the People's Democratic Republic of Korea (when the government announced that it intended to withdraw from the Nuclear Non-Proliferation Treaty, presumably to develop nuclear weapons) only illustrate the validity of this point even in the post-Cold War World. It is absolutely clear that the only long-term solution to this problem is progress towards global nuclear disarmament leading in the long-term to general and complete disarmament. Nations will have to forgo their right to be armed to the teeth, taking note of the overall global interest.

The other major age in which we are living is the space age, which dawned in 1957 with the launch of the Sputnik, during the International Geophysical Year (IGY), which was a year of truly international cooperation in science. The space age has had a multifaceted impact on human future.

We have all seen photographs of the earth as an isolated blue marble in the blackness of space. The astronaut William Anders who had just returned from a flight around the moon said:

> The earth appeared as a small, blue-green sphere like a beautiful ornament, very delicate and limited, the only colour in the dark universe, the only friendly place we could see. The ancestral home of mankind did not appear vast, unlimited and indestructible as we often see it when groping here on its surface. It seemed much more like a delicate and fragile ornament that you must learn to preserve and protect with appropriate care. Looking back, I saw no national boundaries, no dividing up of the earth into separate states, each with a different colour as you see on a globe in a schoolroom, a globe divided on the surface by man but obviously not by nature. When viewed from this perspective, I saw instead a small but inviting oasis in the vast blankness of space. While viewing the home planet from nearly a quarter of a million miles away, the words of the American poet, Archibald MacLeish, came to mind: 'The earth, as it truly is, is small and blue and beautiful in the eternal silence where it floats.'

The space age has truly highlighted the fact that we are all children of this earth. There may be ethnic, linguistic, religious, political and geographical divisions amongst us, but ultimately, for all of us, this is home.

The second aspect that the space age is responsible for relates to the development of enormously powerful capabilities usable in military conflicts: the technology relating to missiles, reconnaissance satellites, 'Star Wars' concepts, and the many facets of militarization of outer space.

The third aspect relates to capabilities made available for peaceful uses of outer space: for telecommunications, television and radio broadcasting, and remote sensing, including large scale uses for meteorology.

While the space age has shown us so visibly the lonely fragile planet that is our home, it has also provided capabilities which have made the earth a small place. It is through satellite communications that the possibilities opened up for a global network for information transfer. Apart from tele-communications, which link people through voice, there is now a vast transfer of information taking place linking computer systems all over the world. These are used for finance, business, trade and many areas where nations interact. There is also information relayed through radio and television networks. Around 600 million people watched the first man land on the moon on 20 July 1969. Almost double that number watched the World Cup football games in Italy around two decades later. Current assessments range from 1.5 to 2 billion people for a major international event. Images and descriptions of the famines in Africa burst upon the consciousness of the public, particularly in the affluent countries in Europe, North America and Japan. One has recently seen the tragic events in the former Yugoslavia, Somalia and Rwanda, bringing us all face to face, in an almost literal sense, with suffering on such a scale that it challenges our notions of what it means to be human. It brings about an expansion of our moral universe.

Equally, with these worldwide channels of communication, life styles all over the world are becoming increasingly common knowledge. As a result, the poor aspire to the life enjoyed by the rich; the developing world hopes to attain the affluence and ways of life of the industrialized nations, which appear so tempting. There is a rising tide of expectation, and of clamouring demand, which governments are unable to fulfil. Frustrated aspirations lead to social discontent. This is seen in increasing degree all over the world.

Apart from the space age, what has contributed so significantly to the above impacts of science and technology on society, and the relations between nations, is the age of informatics and electronics that we live in. The origins of these developments go back over a hundred years, but in its present form it is based on solid state electronics born in 1947. Since then we have seen the rapid development of micro-electronics: from the transistor to the integrated circuit, and increasing levels of integration up to a million transistors on a chip. This has enabled circuits of increasing complexity to be produced at greatly reduced costs. With these developments it became possible to have electronics systems light in weight, small in volume, with low power demands, of great reliability, and capable of very complex operations. This has been the basis of a great deal of the achievements of the space age. Computers, instead of being large stand-alone systems for experts, have become a part of daily life through the pocket calculator and personal computer. Telecommunications have become digital, with switching systems moving from the original mechanical systems to wholly electronic ones. There has been a merging of the fields of computing and telecommunications with a common binary language. Increasingly, a whole range of devices are being linked together to form a complex network for real time work, involving storage, access, transmission, dissemination, analysis and display of data. Apart from communication systems based on satellites, one now has extremely high density opto-electronic pathways based on laser and optical fibre systems. In recent times previously unimaginable financial transactions and currency trading has been carried out using these communication networks. The scale of this has been bewildering, far exceeding official national financial capabilities. This has had an enormous impact on the economic and political systems of nations.

Another major development has been the fact that, apart from the movement of ideas and data, it has now become possible to move people in very large numbers and goods in huge volumes across the globe. This has come about with the development of large wide-bodied jet aircraft, and huge ships specially designed for bulk transportation and containerized cargo.

The pattern of business, industry and trade is transforming in a very significant way with this ease in the movement of ideas, information, people and goods, leading to truly transnational efforts.

To facilitate the movements of goods and services with minimal barriers and hindrances, a multilateral global agreement has been agreed, under the auspices of GATT, which will in turn define the relations between nations in the future.

But in spite of all the spectacular advances just described there are many who would say that the future belongs to the life sciences. We have in recent decades seen spectacular progress in our understanding of the living system at molecular and cellular levels. Biotechnologies born of this understanding hold great promise, and are poised for development, as was atomic energy in 1945, solid state electronics in 1947, and space technology in 1957.

There have been great advances in medical genetics, with identification of genes responsible for, or acting as predisposing factors in, specific diseases, and corresponding possibilities of gene therapy; in immunology, with the development of diagnostics and immunoprophylaxis covering a wide range of disease situations in humans and animals; in agriculture, with the possibility of transferring designated genes to produce specific desired end results; and the substitution of many chemical processes by biological techniques that are less energy intensive and involve less complex situations.

These developments in modern biology have brought before us the all-embracing concept of the common fundamental basis of all living systems. This fundamental unit of all life as seen by science has truly to permeate the human psyche. Such an understanding will make us all feel more humble, and more related to one another, and indeed to all other parts of life on earth. Yet, every individual (plant, animal or human) is different and unique – and we must therefore respect each individual.

However, these advances have brought with them many new issues for humanity to grapple with. Should there be limits to manipulation of human genetic material? Should there be genetic manipulation of human embryos or reproductive cells? Would the genetic inheritance of humanity be dangerously modified by such experimentation? Would the activity to decode the human genome diminish our humanness? Even though genes lie at the very core of our cells and link us with the past through evolution and determine the future of our health, what are the roles of education, the environment, cultural factors, and the like, in shaping the human being? Are we helpless products of genetic directives without freedom for our responsibilities and our acts? There are many biologists who are opposed to the use of genetic material by the police or in forensic science. Then there is the area of eugenic information and its use – in particular its use as a means of discrimination. Euguenics in terms of coercive social politics has not disappeared; it is alive in some countries in which there are at present even sterilization codes. These and many other ethical, philosophical, legal, social and cultural questions are coming to the fore as we probe deeper into human genetics.

In view of these issues there is already an allocation under the human genome project to look into ethical, legal and social issues, apart from the benefits that would flow from increased scientific understanding.

UNESCO has set up an International Bioethics Committee to go into these issues. Indeed bioethics will be one of the major areas for discussion in society as we move into the future.

A major concept which has brought humanity and nations closer together in the recent past is that relating to the common heritage of humankind. This is a relatively new concept, existing in its present form only over the last quarter century.

The concept is essentially that the interests of all of humanity should be safeguarded in predetermined areas by special legal regimes. Historically, international law involved relationships between states on the basis of reciprocity. There was a change in 1815 when the Congress of Vienna set principles which were general in scope, such as freedom of navigation on international rivers (later expanded to inter-oceanic canals), prohibition of the slave trade, and the like. However, the first expression concerning the common heritage of humanity was in the Antarctica Treaty signed in 1979 to preserve and conserve this area in the common interest of humankind, and exclusively for peaceful purposes. The moon has also been made a common heritage of humankind by a treaty adopted in 1979. The use of the radio spectrum (which is a limited resource) on an appropriate agreed basis, as also of dedicated satellite orbits, are examples of the developments in science and technology which necessitate internationally agreed management of common resources. The most developed formulation relating to common heritage of humanity is the Law of the Sea Convention of 1982. Again, earlier, UNESCO had adopted the Convention for the Protection of the World's Cultural and Natural Heritage in 1972. The objective in this case is to ensure conservation and preservation of areas and objects identified as of outstanding universal value. Whilst these would undoubtedly belong to the nation state where they are located, this convention seeks to convey the thought that this is a heritage of such significance that in a sense it does belong to all humanity. The (neighbourhood, ethnic, religious, national) group which has inherited this is to be a trustee of the heritage on behalf of all of humanity.

There are many who have been unhappy that the common heritage concept has been very restrictive in its application, dealing largely with cultural heritage or areas outside national boundaries, like the moon or Antarctica. Indeed, some have asked whether knowledge and technology are not a common heritage. The answer is that the concept is growing and enlarging as we shall see in the next paragraphs.

In 1992, the United Nations Conference on Environment and Development (UNCED) was held in Rio De Janeiro, Brazil. It derived its *raison d'être* from the Report of the World Commission on Environment and Development, which had called for a global agenda for change, so that the process of development would be sustainable and in harmony with the life support systems on the earth and with its carrying capacity. It placed development in a context far beyond economics alone; development had to ensure equity within the present generation as also between generations. The output from UNCED was the Rio Declaration, which consists of 27 principles to cover the transition to sustainability; the Framework Convention on Climate Change; the Convention on Biological Diversity; and the (non-binding) Declaration of Principles on Forests.

The Framework Convention on Climate Change was essentially based on the very detailed work done by the Inter-Governmental Panel on Climate Change, whose report was endorsed by the Second World Climate Conference held in late 1990 in Geneva. The thrust of the Convention is that measures should be taken so that human activities do not bring about changes in the composition of the atmosphere and climate on a scale which would adversely affect long-term sustainable development. In particular, it deals with those human activities that result in large scale additions of greenhouse gases (principally carbon dioxide) to the Earth's atmosphere. It is interesting to note that the entire basis for this convention was the very detailed and careful scientific work that was carried out over a long period of time. This is an issue which would never have come to the notice of society or of governments except through such scientific work. There is also increasing awareness that the atmosphere does not respect the various boundaries that human beings create through ethnicity, language, religion, nationality, and the like.

The Convention on Biological Diversity was essentially based on pressure from the scientific community and environmentalists. They argued that with the present pathways of development, major reductions are taking place in existing global biodiversity, and that measures to reverse this trend are called for. The Convention recognizes the importance of biodiversity for long-term sustainable development.

Since UNCED, there has been greater emphasis relating to biotechnology in regard to the Bio-Diversity Convention, because of increasing awareness that the available biodiversity has in it enormous potential for the creation of new products of great value in agriculture, medicine and industry. This has given rise to very significant interest in this area on the part of the biotechnology industry. On biodiversity and forestry there is recognition of the sovereign rights of nations with regard to the resources in their territories. At the same time, there is implicit the common interest of all humanity in ensuring that this richness can survive, and all actions are taken to ensure this.

Another area where, in recent years, nations have come together, again based entirely on scientific work and forewarning, relates to the earth's ozone layer. It is now well known that the ozone layer is subject to damage as a result of certain chemicals, the CFCs, which have been used extensively in the refrigeration, air conditioning and aerosol industries. International agreement has, therefore, been reached that these chemicals, harmful to the ozone layer, should be phased out, and substituted with ozone-friendly chemicals.

We have seen in above paragraphs an account of three areas relating to the atmosphere, biodiversity and ozone in which nations of the world have been forced to come together in their common interest. The awareness in all three areas, which has given rise to the agreements, has come about because of careful, detailed and extended scientific work. It is this work, placed before governments and society, which has forced them to come to this level of agreement.

****

I have tried to show in this paper how modern science – in symbiotic relationship with technology – has grown to become what it is: an all permeating, enormously powerful agent for social and political change, and the most important driving force, other than the human spirit, for economic activity in the world; how it has provided humankind with destructive capabilities that could wipe out a large part of humanity in a nuclear holocaust; how it has demonstrated that the Earth is a lonely fragile spaceship that is the only home for all of humanity, however riven by divisions based on nationality, religion, colour, community or ethnicity; how it has made the world a small place with the capabilities now available for movement of ideas, information, people, goods and services; how it has demonstrated the fundamental and essential oneness of all living systems; how it has brought about an awareness of changes taking place in many parts of the Earth system, because of human activities, which are not tangible directly to our senses, and call for concerted international action; how it has demonstrated increasingly the concept of common property and common heritage which we would do well to respect.   Science and technology have made human society highly interdependent. There is no going back on all of this. Indeed, the only direction that I see is towards an increasing coming together. Science and technology have profoundly altered the relationships between nations and will continue to do so.

But we must keep in mind the fact that science and scientific education cannot provide us with guidance concerning moral and spiritual values.   There is nothing in the whole range of its precepts which can point a finger at the most heinous crime.

It is, therefore, important that the progress of science and technology is tempered with wisdom.

In a 'Declaration of Human Duties' which a large number of scientists have recently signed, the adoption is urged:

> . . . of a different way of thinking and a different value system. The change must be as revolutionary as that which emerged after the Middle Ages. The new way of thinking must be centred on humans as an integral part of their planet.[2]

For centuries the great religions of the world have taught us the essential oneness of the human race. Science objectively shows that this is indeed so. It has brought about international interdependence. Wrongly used, science and technology can lead to exploitation and domination. But it can also be directed to be fully consistent with the reality of international pluralism.

Any call for strong international consensus raises fears of a tyrannical imposition of a uniform system of values on a highly pluralistic world. This need not be so; just as no reasonable nation imposes any such system on its citizens. International consensus should be a flexible, dynamic and minimalistic one, which respects the virtue of existing pluralism, and is based on a few irreducible values. The most important element is for each individual to extend his or her loyalty, beyond the now familiar groupings based on ethnicity, religion, community or nation, to the human race as a whole. That is the concept of world citizenship. Science and technology are increasingly taking us towards this.

REFERENCES

1.   The Russell-Einstein Manifesto, in J. Rotblat, *Scientists in the Quest for Peace*, MIT Press: Cambridge, MA, 1972, pp.137-40.

2.   *The Trieste Declaration of Human Duties - A Code of Ethics of Shared Responsibilities*, The International Council of Human Duties, University of Trieste.

2

Worldwide Interdependence in Ecological Matters

Anne H. Ehrlich

It is almost a truism that the world is becoming more interdependent, with economic and financial linkages dominating and leading the trend, while political arrangements appear to be lagging. To a large degree, of course, economic and political developments were stalled for four decades by the Cold War and resultant bipolar orientation of nations. Still, technological development continued mostly unhindered and was ready for global linkage when the bipolar political structure finally broke down. Satellite communications, international corporations, financial links among world markets, and rapid travel have knit disparate societies closer together even as ethnic tensions and ancient feuds have ironically erupted into conflict within and between some nations. Never have humanity's myriad societies seemed at once more interconnected and more fractured.[1]

Underlying the fits and starts and social gropings towards Wendell Wilkie's 'One World' is the truth that the world has physically always been a unit – a single planet with a varied surface and an atmosphere, hosting a thin envelope of biosphere. The oceans, although superficially separated by the continents, are nevertheless continuous and united by a vast current known as the 'conveyor belt' that moves vast quantities of water from surface to bottom and all around the planet over a thousand-year span. The atmosphere is shared to an even greater degree, with air moved and mixed through heating by the sun, cooling, and by air currents that girdle the globe. Water constantly cycles between oceans, atmosphere, and land. The organisms of the biosphere play important parts in moderating or controlling the great biogeochemical processes that keep the planet habitable.[2]

Human beings, like other animals, are products of nearly four billion years of evolution since life originated, and started slowly modifying Earth's characteristics, making it generally more hospitable to life.[3] Humanity began (much later) in small groups; but as populations grew and people spread to occupy virtually all of the world's land surface, their activities also began to have worldwide effects. With nearly six billion individuals as the twentieth century draws to a close, *Homo sapiens* is perhaps the most widespread and numerous large-sized species on the planet (the only other contender for the title being domesticated cattle, which owe their numbers and distribution to human intervention).

Human beings not only live almost everywhere, they have taken over and modified or exploited most of the world's productive lands. More than two-thirds of the land is used for habitation (2 per cent), cropland (11 per cent), pasture for livestock (25 per cent), or forest (31 per cent).[4] Most of the remaining third is too cold, rugged, inaccessible, wet or dry to be useful. Human impacts on the oceans are smaller but far from negligible.

The development of modern technology and industrial processes have enabled people to live in otherwise inhospitable places and to support a far larger population than could be sustained with pre-industrial agricultural and trade practices. At the same time, they have enormously increased human impacts on the biosphere, displacing or degrading natural ecosystems and escalating losses of the world's rich heritage of biodiversity. The magnitude of changes has reached the point where human activities are altering fundamental life-supporting global processes.[5]

A century ago, environmental problems were mainly local in effect and easily remedied with local action. Soon after the mid-twentieth century, environmental problems related to industry (such as air and water pollution) had achieved national prominence in most developed nations, and regulation at the national level became necessary. Problems arising from increasingly intensive agriculture (such as land degradation and desertification, as well as pollution of water sources) began to be felt, although soil erosion and land degradation often went unnoticed because synthetic fertilizers masked early losses of productive potential.

By the 1970s, as national environmental regulations were being emplaced in industrialized countries, international problems were appearing, such as effects of acid precipitation caused by transported air pollutants originating in other countries. By the 1980s, problems of truly global scope had emerged: the destruction of the stratospheric ozone shield caused by the release of human-made chemicals, the chlorofluorocarbons (CFCs); the potential hazards of global warming due to rising emissions of carbon dioxide and (it was finally realized) other greenhouse gases, including CFCs;[6] and the long-predicted emergence of the first global epidemic caused by a novel virus – HIV, which causes AIDS.[7]

Of course, not all societies are equally responsible for causing these problems. The affluent industrialized nations bear the bulk of responsibility for most of the global problems, many of which can be traced to use of fossil fuels. Nevertheless, all societies will suffer the consequences. Indeed, the members of poorer societies who are least responsible for causing the problems are often most vulnerable to their disruptive effects.

CFCs have mostly been used in developed nations, but developing nations are equally if not more vulnerable to the impacts of increased UV-B radiation, which include damage to agricultural productivity as well as to human health. The disruptive effects of climate change on agriculture and of sea-level rises on lowland populations that may result from global warming are threats to all; but poor people will have less ability to make adjustments, especially since the specific consequences of climate change cannot be predicted for any particular area.

As the AIDS epidemic has already shown, impoverished and underdeveloped societies are poorly equipped to control emergent diseases. Indeed, even industrial societies are not well prepared for them; yet, the expanding human population, much of it crowded, poor, ill-nourished and often highly mobile, is increasingly vulnerable to pandemics.[8]

The human enterprise has reached a scale where it rivals or even exceeds that of global biogeochemical processes, including the cycling of vital elements such as carbon and nitrogen through oceans, atmosphere and land, threatening the integrity of many of them. Yet, civilization is totally dependent on the functioning of these processes to sustain its activities, especially the production of food and other essential commodities. In attempting to support an ever-greater civilization, human beings are weakening the very underpinnings of their recent success.

What forces are driving this deepening dilemma? A major component obviously is the size of the human population itself, which, on entering the twenty-first century, will be over six billion in number and still growing rapidly. Some 80-90 million people – the equivalent of another Mexico or Germany – are added to the population every year. Recent demographic projections by the United Nations indicate that the world population could more than double again before growth stops in a century or so.[9]

The other principal driving force behind the human dilemma is the massive increase in the mobilization of resources by human beings and the environmental impacts arising from that. While the world population has increased fivefold just since 1850 (from about 1.1 billion to 5.6 billion in 1994), global energy use has increased nearly 20-fold, mostly as a result of discovering and deploying fossil fuels in that period.[10] Energy use, especially use of fossil fuels, which accounts for three-quarters of it, can serve as a reasonable index for resource mobilization. Combustion of fossil fuels is also the source of many important environmental impacts, including most air and water pollution, many toxic substance problems, acid precipitation, and the build up of excess greenhouse gases in the atmosphere. Of the 20-fold rise in energy use during the industrial era, population growth is responsible for about half of the increase, and growth in *per capita* use accounts for the rest.

A large portion of the growth in population, energy use and economic activity (customarily measured by GNP) has occurred in the last half-century, as the human population's growth has virtually exploded. Indeed, the population has nearly tripled since just 1930. The most recent United Nations medium demographic projection indicated that the population is likely to pass 8.5 billion by 2025, reach 10 billion near mid-century, and ultimately stop at 11.6 billion.[11] Of course, unexpected changes in reproductive or mortality rates could cause growth to be either considerably higher or lower. The UN's high alternative projection shows no end to growth, with the population soaring past 28 billion around 2150 – a clearly unsustainable scenario. The low projection indicates a peak population size of 8.5 billion around 2050, followed by a slow decline, and passing five billion again within a century. The key assumption here is that the average family size worldwide (currently 3.3 children a couple) would soon fall below 'replacement reproduction', where parents on average just replace themselves in the next generation: about 2.2 children a couple.

SQUEEZING THE PLANET

Whether the world's future demographic path will actually coincide with any of these projections depends to a great extent on humanity's ability to support, even for a few decades, a much larger population than today's. To biologists, the symptoms of population overshoot are already increasingly evident. We are doing what no responsible family or corporation would do – living on our capital. The capital in question is the global endowment of resources, both renewable and non-renewable. That civilization is depleting reserves of non-renewable resources, such as metals and fossil fuels (especially petroleum), is well known (although many economists are convinced that acceptable substitutes can always be found for any resource).[12] Less appreciated but more worrisome are the depletion and degradation of putatively renewable resources, such as agricultural soils, fossil groundwater,[13] and biodiversity.[14]

Some 24 billion tonnes of topsoil have been estimated to be lost each year from the world's farmland, an amount that is far from sustainable even in the medium term.[15] A recent study of the world's productive land by the United Nations Environment Programme concluded that significant land degradation has occurred since 1945 on every continent but Antarctica.[16] Affected lands include cropland, forests, and grasslands; the causes are agriculture, deforestation, and overgrazing. Some 11 per cent of the world's productive lands have been moderately to extremely damaged, and another six per cent lightly degraded. Moderate to severe damage implies some loss of productivity, and restoration would be difficult and costly. Extremely degraded lands are deemed beyond reclamation. Moreover, much good land is lost each year as cities grow and more roads, factories and airports are built over it.

Many regions are already seriously short of fresh water, not only for producing food but even, in some areas, for domestic use.[17] Water has become a major limiting factor for development in areas such as the Middle East, northern India, much of China, and parts of Africa, regions where populations are mostly still growing rapidly. Shortage of water (like other resources) can also be a major source of political conflict.[18]

Irrigation has been an important contributor to the near-tripling of global food production since 1950, and much of the water has come from groundwater sources.[19] To support high-yield agriculture, aquifers in many areas are being drained at rates far above natural recharge. Today farmland is increasingly being taken out of production as groundwater sources become so depleted that further pumping is uneconomic. In many areas, water sources have been seriously polluted with toxic substances and thus made unusable for agriculture or domestic consumption.

The increasing degradation or loss of agricultural land poses a serious problem for a population still committed to substantial growth. The green revolution, which enabled grain production nearly to triple between 1950 and 1990, has largely run its course, with no convincing encore in sight.[20] On a *per capita* basis, grain production (humanity's feeding base) has been declining since 1984. The outlook for keeping food production rising faster than population growth (which is necessary to improve the diets of the poor) is not heartening. The accelerating loss of biodiversity is probably least appreciated by the general public but of gravest concern to biologists. As the planet's land areas have been increasingly taken over for human uses, degraded by overcultivation, overgrazing or large scale deforestation, or assaulted by human-released toxins from acid precipitation to pesticides, habitats for other organisms have disappeared, causing an epidemic of extinctions.[21] As ecosystems are degraded or destroyed outright, essential services that they provide to society are impaired or lost: maintenance of the gaseous composition of the atmosphere; modulation of climate and regulation of the hydrological cycle; cycling of nutrients (vital for agriculture), replenishment of soils, and disposal of wastes; detoxification of poisonous substances; pollination (including numerous crops); control of the vast majority of pests and disease vectors; provision of forest products, fisheries, and other foods and materials; and the source or inspiration for countless potential new products, from foods, medicines and spices to industrial chemicals to be found in nature's vast genetic library.

Most ecosystem services are taken for granted and valued only after being lost.[22] Even if people knew how to replace these services (in most cases they do not), technological replacement would not be possible on the scale required. Replacements of services that are attempted (such as management of the hydrological cycle through dams and water projects) are far from perfect, and generally unsustainable in the long-term.

The profound changes being imposed on Earth's ecosystems can be seen in the impact on the planet's biological production – the most fundamental resource of all, the basis of all food for ourselves and other animals. Net primary production (NPP) is the energy from sunlight made available through the process of photosynthesis by green plants, algae, and some kinds of bacteria – minus the energy used by these organisms for their own life processes. Humanity uses directly (for food, feed, fibre and forest products) or indirectly (by creating human-directed ecosystems composed of different organisms than would otherwise be present) some 33 per cent of the total amount of energy made available as carbohydrates by photosynthesizers on land.[23] Because of the widespread degradation of natural ecosystems or conversion of them into less productive ones, such as farms, or unproductive areas, such as highways and cities, much potential NPP is foregone. Thus, the total human impact on the world's potential terrestrial productivity is about 40 per cent. The world has been rendered biologically less productive by human action, although an enormous share of it now goes into the human account; the result is a far diminished share for the other organisms of the planet.

Human diversion of NPP from the oceans, most areas of which are much less productive than an equivalent area of land, is a comparatively modest 2 per cent. The NPP in ocean systems is produced by highly dispersed, microscopic organisms, which are not likely soon to become an important part of the human diet. Rather, we will continue to depend on fishes, mostly at the top of the food chain, as marine food sources, thus harvesting only a small fraction of the oceans' NPP. Human impacts, however, are by no means negligible, since the pollution of coastal areas and the increasing depletion or even commercial extinction of many fish stocks are serious concerns.[24] Most fisheries experts agree that the global maximum sustainable yield for marine fisheries has been reached or (given current unsustainable methods) exceeded.

MEASURING IMPACT

Human beings today can be seen as a force that is mobilizing resources on a scale comparable to, or in some cases exceeding, natural cycles. We also now are threatening to destabilize major elements of the natural life-support system through such changes as large scale deforestation,[25] depletion of the stratospheric ozone shield, and the build up of greenhouse gases in the atmosphere.[26] A civilization that allows the degradation of its essential resource base, and the destabilization of global climate and biogeochemical processes, is very far from sustainable.

Twenty-five years ago, Paul Ehrlich and John Holdren devised a simple equation to describe in very simplified terms the multiplicative effects of numbers of people and their use of resources in generating environmental impacts.[27] The equation (more accurately, an identity) is

$$I = P \times A \times T$$

where I represents the total environmental impact of a society, P is the population, A is the affluence (or consumption) of each individual on average, and T is a measure of the impact of the technologies used to supply each unit of consumption.

Although reasonably accurate statistics are available for population sizes, no useful measure exists for total consumption per person or for the impacts of technologies. Indeed, the latter two are very difficult to untangle, and all three factors are by no means independent of each other. Yet, a rough appreciation of the relationship can be gained by using *per capita* energy use as a measure of a society's A x T (or AT). Considering the central role that energy use plays in generating so many environmental impacts, this is a useful approximation that, although greatly oversimplified, nonetheless offers some insight into human impacts.

By this measure, each person in an industrialized nation can be seen on average to have seven times the impact of a person in a developing nation. At the extremes, the average American (whose *per capita* energy use is 50 to 100 per cent higher than that of the average European or Japanese) has six times the impact of a person in Mexico, and about 30 times that of someone in a very poor nation like Bangladesh or Chad. Thus, even though the populations of industrialized nations are growing relatively slowly or not at all, they consume a disproportionate share of the world's resources. The industrialized nations have only about a fifth of the world's population – 1.2 billion – but they control and consume about three-quarters of most resources. Consequently, they are causing far more than their share of damage to the Earth's life-support systems. Moreover, they are still striving to increase their consumption per person.

Although the populations of most developing nations are growing much faster (at an average rate of about 2.3 per cent a year, excluding China), their collective contributions to deleterious global change are still much smaller. But their share is rising rapidly, and the potential for far greater contributions in the near future is considerable, given substantial growth in both their populations and their economies.[28]

Claims are often made by people in the industrialized world that the 'population problem' is a problem of developing countries, because their populations are growing rapidly whereas those in most rich nations are growing very slowly, if at all. Conversely, people in the developing world often assert that the problem is not overpopulation, it is overconsumption and overexploitation of poor nations by the rich.[29] As the I = PAT identity shows, both views are partly right. Yet, overpopulation drives much of the overconsumption in rich societies; clearly, if half as many people were consuming at the same rate *per capita*, they would be doing far less damage.

Meanwhile, the poor aspire and plan to consume as the rich do; in societies that are rapidly industrializing, population growth drives rising consumption rates and pressure on resources. In poorer nations, which usually have the highest birthrates, population growth often has the effect of increasing pressures on the land, accelerating land degradation, and deepening poverty.[30] One result is massive migration of rural people to cities, often overwhelming the cities' ability to accommodate them, or to other countries seeking a better life.[31] Though often called 'economic refugees', more and more such migrants are in reality environmental refugees fleeing from damaged and exhausted lands.

As biologists know, when animal populations approach or exceed their local carrying capacities, more individuals are forced to live in marginal situations, and resource-abundant areas also become more crowded.[32] For human beings, this can be seen in heavily populated nations where the poorest families are often forced to live in either less productive or high risk areas. In

Bangladesh, poor farmers in the Ganges delta are vulnerable to severe floods and cyclones which have several times killed tens of thousands of people. Continued population growth among the world's poorest can be expected to worsen this trend, regardless of other efforts to relieve poverty.

Similarly, high population density relative to available resources can lead to increased conflict among animals, and the same is well-known to be true for human populations.[33] The carnage in grossly overpopulated Rwanda is a glaring case in point, but similar factors have been at play in numerous other areas, such as the Sudan, Somalia, West Africa, the Middle East and the India-Pakistan confrontation in Kashmir, even though political factors are most often cited by political scientists and the press.

ADDRESSING THE HUMAN PREDICAMENT

The growing precariousness of the human situation and its increasingly global nature have been clear to much of the scientific community, especially environmental scientists, for some time; now it has at last reached the attention of political decision-makers (as demonstrated by the 1992 United Nations Conference on Environment and Development in Rio and the 1994 International Conference on Population and Development in Cairo). It also is increasingly apparent that no simple or superficial solutions will be sufficient to reverse the dilemma. Nor will addressing only one or two of the $I = PAT$ factors be adequate in the long run for most facets of the predicament, even though certain measures, such as increasing energy efficiency, switching to more benign energy sources, developing less damaging agricultural systems, and strengthening family planning programmes, would each be fairly essential.

But the human enterprise cannot be put on a truly sustainable basis until it is recognized that we are now living beyond our means, and that a path towards a viable future must be carved out and agreed on. The next century or two will not be easy ones. The principal challenge will be to manage the transitional 'overshoot' phase, while populations and resource use exceed carrying capacities and stresses on life-support systems continue to mount. Humanely reversing the population explosion itself will require many decades to accomplish, and more than family planning programmes will be needed to meet the basic needs of the poor. Reducing the material throughput of over-industrialized societies and kicking the fossil fuel habit will be equally difficult, requiring some fundamental changes in lifestyles. Detoxifying and restoring damaged and decimated ecosystems, and developing sustainable and productive agricultural systems, will be needed in both industrial and developing countries. Somehow, serious international warfare must be avoided in the process.

Without some clear vision of an attractive, attainable shared future, these difficult commitments are not likely to be made and carried out. Each society needs to evaluate its own territory's carrying capacity (including resources available through trade with other societies), reach a consensus on its preferred living standard and lifestyle, and decide on an appropriate size for its population. Then reasonable policies should be adopted that will ease the transition and move towards the chosen goals. Of course, these decisions cannot be made in isolation but will require an unprecedented level of cooperation, trust and coordination among societies. Industrialized nations will have to curb their consumption and share with developing nations their technologies for efficient energy use and development of alternative sources. Cooperation in curbing greenhouse gas emissions will be critical.

Providing the basic necessities of life – adequate food, clothing, shelter, sanitation services and clean water, education, health care and employment – for people in every nation must be a global priority. It has become increasingly clear that the perpetuation of poverty and powerlessness deepens the human dilemma in a variety of ways. The rural poor often contribute to land degradation because they lack the means of increasing food production and have little control over their local resources. All nations must be involved in reversing the population explosion. Empowerment and education of women is key to reducing birthrates, as is improving the well-being of everyone.

Some progress has been made in international cooperation at the political level, as global economies are increasingly woven together, but much more is needed. We can take heart that the Cold War has ended without a catastrophe. We can view its termination as presenting an opportunity to create a new cooperative world structure. We cannot afford to miss this opportunity.

REFERENCES

1.   R.D. Kaplan, 'The Coming Anarchy', *Atlantic Monthly*, February 1994.

2.   *See* P.R. Ehrlich, A.H. Ehrlich, and J.P. Holdren, *Ecoscience: Population, Resources, Environment*, W.H.Freeman & Co.: San Francisco, 1977 for a description of the biogeophysical processes that characterize Earth.

3.   A good recent summary of what is known about Earth's beginnings can be found in V.R. Oberbeck and R.L. Mancelli, 'Asteroid Impacts, Microbes, and the Cooling of the Atmosphere', *BioScience* 44:3, March 1994, pp.173-7.

4.   Figures from UN Food and Agriculture Organization (FAO), 1992, *World Food Production 1991*, FAO, Rome. See also World Resources Institute, *World Resources 1992-3*, Oxford University Press, Oxford and New York.

5.   P.R. Ehrlich and A.H. Ehrlich, *Healing the Planet*, Addison-Wesley: Reading, Massachusetts, 1991.

6.   J. Houghton, G. Jenkins, and J. Ephraums, eds, *Climate Change: The IPCC Scientific Assessment*, Intergovernmental Panel on Climate Change (IPCC), Cambridge University Press: New York, 1990; Ehrlich and Ehrlich 1991, *op.cit.*.

7.   P. Ehrlich and A. Ehrlich, *Population, Resources, Environment*, W H Freeman & Co.: San Francisco, 1970.

8. For example, a recent report of the US Center for Disease Control, cited in L.K. Altman, M.D., 'Infectious Diseases on the Rebound in the US, a report says', *New York Times*, Science section, 10 May 1994.

9. United Nations Population Fund (UNFPA), *State of the World Population, 1992*, United Nations: New York, 1992. UNFPA based its summary on United Nations Population Division, Long-Range World Population Projections, ST/SEA/SER.A/125, United Nations: New York, 1991.

10. J.P. Holdren, 'Population and the Energy Problem', *Population and Environment* 12:3, Spring 1991, pp.231-3; and J.P. Holdren, 'Energy in Transition', *Scientific American* 263:3, September 1990, pp.156-63.

11. UNFPA 1992, *op.cit.*.

12. H.E. Daly and J.B. Cobb Jr, *For the Common Good*, Beacon Press: Boston, 1989.

13. S. Postel, 'Water for Agriculture: Facing the Limits', Worldwatch Paper 93, Worldwatch Institute: Washington D.C., 1990.

14. P.R. Ehrlich and A.H. Ehrlich, *Healing the Planet*, Addison-Wesley: Reading, Mass., 1991, ch.1; E.O. Wilson, 'Threats to Biodiversity', *Scientific American*, September 1989, pp.108-16.

15. L.R. Brown and E.C. Wolf, 'Soil Erosion: Quiet Crisis in the World Economy', Worldwatch Paper 60, Worldwatch Institute: Washington D.C., 1984.

16. L. Oldeman, V. van Engelen, and J. Pulles, 'The Extent of Human-induced Soil Degradation', Annex 5 of L.Oldeman *et al.*, *World Map of the Status of Human-Induced Soil Degradation: An Explanatory Note*, rev. 2nd ed., International Soil Reference and Information Centre: Waginengen, Netherlands, 1990. The findings are

summarized in World Resources Institute, World Resources 1992-3, Oxford Univ. Press: New York, 1992.

17. P. Gleick, *Water in Crisis*, Oxford University Press: New York, 1993.

18. P. Gleick, 'Water, War, and Peace in the Middle East', *Environment* 36:3, April 1994, pp.6-15ff.

19. Postel 1990, *op.cit.*.

20. P.R. Ehrlich, A.H. Ehrlich and G.C. Daily, 'Food Security, Population, and Environment', *Population and Development Review* 19:1, March 1993, pp.1-32.

21. P.R. and A.H. Ehrlich, *Extinction: The Causes and Consequences of the Disappearance of Species*, Random House: New York, 1981; E.O. Wilson and F. Peter, *Biodiversity*, National Academy Press: Washington D.C., 1988.

22. P.R. Ehrlich and A.H. Ehrlich, 'The Value of Biodiversity', *Ambio*, 21:3, May 1992, pp.219-26.

23. P.M. Vitousek, P.R. Ehrlich, A.H. Ehrlich and P.A. Matson, 'Human Appropriation of the Products of Photosynthesis', *BioScience*, v.36, June 1987, pp.368-73.

24. P. Weber, 'Reversing the Decline of the Oceans', Worldwatch Paper 116, Worldwatch Institute: Washington D.C.; World Resources Institute 1992, ch.12.

25. N. Myers, *Deforestation Rates in Tropical Forests and their Climatic Implications*, Friends of the Earth: London, 1989; World Resources Institute 1992, ch.8.

26. J. Houghton, G. Jenkins, and J. Ephraums, eds, *Climate Change: The IPCC Scientific Assessment*, Intergovernmental Panel on Climate Change (IPCC), Cambridge University Press: New York, 1990; Ehrlich and Ehrlich 1991, *op.cit.*.

27.   P.R. Ehrlich and J. Holdren, 'The Impact of Population Growth, Science', v.171, 1971, pp.1212-17; see also Ehrlich and Ehrlich 1991, *op.cit.*.

28.   P.R. Ehrlich and A.H. Ehrlich, 'How the Rich Can Save the Poor and Themselves: Lessons from the Global Warming', in S. Gupta and R. Pachauri eds, *Proceedings of the International Conference on Global Warming and Climate Change: Perspectives from Developing Countries, Tata Energy Research Institute, New Delhi, 21-23 February, 1989*, pp.287-94.

29.   A brief book that makes the latter points well (but says little about the role of population growth) is A. Makhijani, *From Global Capitalism to Economic Justice*, Apex Press: New York, 1992.

30.   UNFPA 1992; World Bank, World Development Report 1990, Washington DC.

31.   UNFPA, *State of the World Population, 1993*, United Nations: New York.

32.   G.C. Daily and P.R. Ehrlich, 'Population, Sustainability, and Earth's Carrying Capacity', *BioScience* 42:10, November 1992, pp.761-71.

33.   For example, T. Homer-Dixon, J. Boutwell and G. Rathjens, 'Environmental Change and Violent Conflict', *Scientific American*, February 1993, pp.16-25; Kaplan 1994, *op.cit.*.

3

The Threat and Promise of Globalization: Can it be Made to Work for a Brighter Future?

Morris Miller

> The history of man is a graveyard of great cultures that came to catastrophic ends because of their incapacity for planned, rational, voluntary reaction to challenge.
>
> Erich Fromm

THE SETTING AND THE CHALLENGE: TROUBLING TRENDS

Powerful dialectical forces are at work as the world economy undergoes a structural transformation, one that promises hope and opportunity and the other that threatens a future of despair and breakdown. The lifting of the enormous psychological, social and financial burdens of the Cold War and the tantalizing promise of scientific/technological innovations, symbolized by the computer chip and fibre optics, encourage hope and opportunity; the despair and the traumatic fear of slow or cataclysmic breakdown stems from the symptoms of global crisis, or rather of three overlapping and mutually-reinforcing crises of trade and capital flows – the debt crisis; of equity – the poverty crisis; and of ecology – the environment/energy crisis.[1]

The optimists/rationalizers, as supporters of the prevailing system, have always been with us. The ranks of the doomsters ebb and swell, but of late they have tended to swell. 'What lies ahead', a reviewer wrote in commenting on Paul Kennedy's book, *Preparing for the Twenty-first Century*, 'are famine, endemic poverty and malnutrition, irreversible environmental damage, mass migrations, regional wars, disease – and no solutions'.[2] In his best-selling opus, Professor Kennedy has drawn a lavishly detailed picture of 'a troubled and fractured planet' with reams of statistical and descriptive back-up to make his point that the global state of health is parlous. In a featured cover-story article in the February 24, 1994 issue of *The Atlantic Monthly* entitled 'The Coming Anarchy', a perceptive journalist, Robert Kaplan, spelt out in graphic terms one possible 'preview of the first decades of the twenty-first century':

> nations break up under the tidal flow of refugees from environmental and social disaster; as borders crumble, another type of boundary is erected – a wall of disease; wars are fought over scarce resources . . . and war itself becomes continuous with crime as armed bands of stateless marauders clash with the private security forces of the elites.

Heeding the lesson of the shepherd boy parable, there are, admittedly, very good grounds to be cautious about crying 'crisis!' One could argue that there has been a continuing increase in aggregate global income even when the 'decade of the miserable 1980s' is included, and that even the trend in the average *real* annual *per capita* income in both the low- and middle-income developing countries has been positive – albeit very modestly – when the period considered spans the post-war decades. Furthermore, taking these countries as a group, average longevity has risen to 63 years from 46 only a generation before, adult literacy has increased over the same period from about 20 to 60 per cent, and key morbidity rates have fallen dramatically.[3]

Conventional thinking about the global economic process – that is to say establishment-supportive economic theory – attributes this growth in incomes and related benefits in large part to the beneficence of trade. They can cite the rise in the gross domestic product of almost all countries that has accompanied the rise in the value of trade. There has, indeed, been an intensification of the interdependence of nations through trade and capital flows that goes well beyond that of previous eras. It follows, therefore, that there is a causal link between global growth and both the nature, scale and scope of the trends of international trade and capital flows, and their underlying productive and exchange relationships that goes by the name of 'globalization'. By this line of reasoning, the phenomenon of globalization has been one of the main factors playing a role in determining the speed and shaping the pattern of global growth – and bears a large measure of responsibility for both the negative as well as the positive attributes of this growth.

At the outset it is important to note that the positive trends attributed to globalization have been very unevenly distributed and have been erratic from year to year. Furthermore, the circumstances of the periods when the correlation of trade and growth has been universally positive include such factors as steady-handed statesman-like leadership that has underpinned the stability of key currencies, kept real interest rates low and stable, induced a fairer sharing of the rising incomes through measures improving market access and the terms of trade for the poorer trading partners, and such like.[4] In the course of recent history, that is, dating back a few decades, such favourable periods of growth *with equity* have been the exception rather than the rule, while, at the same time, the spread and speed of globalization has accelerated steadily. Thus, relying on a simplistic cause-and-effect relationship that is supported by a limited set of upbeat numbers is a recipe for delusion about the benefits, stability and sustainability of our present global system with its distribution of incomes and powers – and with its concomitant process of globalization. In any case, these numbers tell us little or nothing about the potential for a better life that is not being realized under the present order of things, that is, about the shortfall between 'what is' and 'what might be'.

The parlous nature of the current state of health of the global economy must be recognized before it can be remedied. The trauma of the 1930s that culminated in a world war of unparalleled ferocity seems far behind us but needs to be remembered lest we be complacent about the possibility of another tragic denouement. We, therefore, have to ask: where is globalization taking us? In the answers we may find guidance as to the policy and related institutional changes that are called for. If the trends are seen to be deep-seated or systemic, there is reason for concern beyond that of compassion: the situation in its dynamic is then unsustainable and, at the same time, more difficult to reverse.

A few examples of troubling trends sketched in broad-brush fashion should suffice to make the point that there is good cause for concern about the dynamic of the deterioration with regard to several critical aspects of life on this small planet. The following is a list of several key trends that appear to be deeply sourced within the global social/economic/financial system and can, therefore, be regarded as systemic.

1/ The gap between the rich and the poor is widening with immiserization remaining persistent and widespread

The statistical picture, as set out in the World Bank's *1994 Social Indicators of Development* and *1994 World Tables*, reveals that the 'low-income developing countries' enjoyed an annual average rate of increase in gross domestic product (GDP) of 7.2 per cent in 1992, and that their *per capita* incomes have grown since 1975 at a respectable rate of 3.6 per cent. This has been heralded as a great achievement, especially when contrasted with the rate of growth of the 'high-income group of countries' that averaged GDP growth in 1992 of 1.7 per cent, and barely averaged over 2 per cent *per capita* income growth over the period since 1975. These numbers would suggest that over the last two decades the income of the average person has been rising and that the income gap between the rich and the poor has been narrowing.

When account is taken of the *absolute* numbers, the inferences to be drawn from this comparison are not encouraging.

Percentage changes are deceptive when the base numbers differ very widely, as they do in this case: the low income countries in 1992 had an average annual *per capita* income of less than $400, while the high-income countries enjoyed an average annual *per capita* income level of almost $22,000 – or more than 50 times higher![5] With contrasts as great as these numbers indicate it should hardly be surprising that the percentage rates of change of the poorer countries are higher than those of the richer ones.

However, when one gets behind the averages and looks at the dispersion, the gap between the rich and the poor on this planet is seen to be widening: between 1960 and 1990 it has been estimated that the absolute difference in incomes between the richest fifth and the poorest fifth increased eight-fold! It seems that neither in the industrialized nor in the developing countries has the increase in incomes been widely shared. Thus, the most illuminating comparisons are not those made on a country-by-country basis, but those between the absolute and relative incomes of the elites (or the top income decile) and of the urban and rural 'working people' (or the bottom income decile, including those dependent on wages and seeking work and the landless and small land-owning peasants). The income gap can then be seen to be widening to a degree and at a speed that provides the recipe for civil unrest. The revolt in Mexico's province of Chiapas is symptomatic. Even in a region that is described as 'resurgent', such as Latin America, the average *per capita* income in real terms is still 5 per cent below what it was in 1980, but the average obscures the fact that the drop has been much greater for the poorest and most vulnerable segment of their societies.

One of the key factors contributing to this polarization trend is the higher rate of population growth in the developing countries – particularly among the poorest segment of the populations of both developing and industrialized countries. In the developing countries the growth rate of population has been over 2 per cent a year as compared to a 0.7 per cent rate of increase in the highly industrialized countries. On the basis of present trends, world population will almost double by the middle of the next century *with over 90 per cent of that increase occurring in the developing countries* – and particularly in their cities. This will make it increasingly difficult to improve *per capita* income levels in these countries, and will undoubtedly exacerbate the already acute social and environmental problems in the poorer ones.

Whatever the relative rates of change, the hard fact remains that one in five living on this planet – or over 1 billion persons – are existing in conditions of 'absolute poverty' (roughly identified by an income level of less than $1 per day), and are thus unable to feed, clothe and house themselves in a manner that can sustain health and human dignity. Four out of ten of those living in the developing countries are considered to be malnourished and functionally illiterate. To put this in graphic terms, leaving aside special tragedies due to droughts and war, about 20 million persons a year, or 50,000 a day, or 2000 an hour, are dying from preventable diseases related to poverty. Of those children who survive, about 100 million are being denied any educational opportunities, and hundreds of millions more are being denied adequate school facilities and well-trained teachers. This has profound implications for their nations' hopes of ever escaping from a state of technological and scientific backwardness that, in turn, leads to perpetual economic, cultural and political dependency.

Lest it be thought that this is a contrast between the industrialized countries and the developing ones, it should be noted that the North too has its own figurative South. The industrialized countries have not been spared the impact of this distributional trend: in the USA, for example, over the two decades from 1969 to 1989 the *real* income of the poorest fifth of the wage-earners declined by about 25 per cent, while the richest 1 per cent managed to increase their after tax incomes by well over 50 per cent.[6] How is one to characterize a societal condition in which about one-fifth of the US population live in dire poverty and the broader wage-earning population suffers from declining wages and living standards and dimming prospects of finding steady work?

This situation has had broad societal implications related to the increase in crime and violence. The numbers engaged in criminal activities and drug-related activities are now large enough to justify the characterization of the present situation in almost all industrialized and developing countries as a 'social and cultural crisis'. As an example of the nature of the deteriorating societal scene that is close to home it might suffice to note the rise of violence in the world's largest economy: in the 15 May 1994 issue of *The New York Times*, a columnist, Anthony Lewis, cited Senator Bradley's call to Americans 'to join in a national rebellion against violence', noting in this connection that 'violence in America is so pervasive we most often take it for granted, like background noise' – and the statistics bear this out. Is it any wonder, then – to cite but two related and telling statistics – that in the USA the number of gun dealers now exceeds that of gas stations and grocery stores, and that the number of private security guards is now greater than the publicly-financed police forces?

2/ The nature of technology is changing rapidly, widening the educational/informational gap and increasing the unemployment rate

Almost all the industrialized countries and a few of the developing ones are well embarked on what has been aptly labelled 'the Third Industrial Revolution' or 'the information age', and some are already in the midst of what Professor Robert Heilbroner has called a 'transformational boom'.[7] Rapid changes are stressful enough, but when the spearheading technologies are 'high-tech', labour-saving, and involve extremely mobile intangible assets, the social impact is magnified. Unable to keep up with the rapidly and profoundly changing nature of technology, most of the developing countries are falling further and further behind the industrialized nations in the acquisition and deployment of these technologies that are opening the way to new modes of production and distribution and, in effect, to new modes of economic and social life.

One of the most significant implications is the structural shift towards production and distribution operations that require a well-trained skilled labour force and, *pari passu*, the reduced need for the unskilled and the low-skilled members of the labour force who make up the far larger proportion of the working population. This is reflected in the widening of the wages gap between the well-educated/skilled and the unskilled, and in the much higher levels of unemployment with a rate of youth unemployment that is much higher yet. In the case of Europe, for example, the forecast for 1994 is that it will be as high as 12 per cent with over half of those unemployed having been out of work for more than a year. This situation has prompted the observation that 'the surplus of gifted, skilled, undervalued and unwanted human beings is the Achilles' heel of this emerging system'.[8]

Given the rate of population increase and the consequent annual flow of new entrants into the labour force, and given the phenomenon of what has been labelled 'jobless growth' with its implication of a continuing high overall rate of unemployment and of underemployment, there is a spreading recognition that the rise in unemployment is structural rather than simply cyclical. This has tempted establishment-supporting commentators to regard a high rate of unemployment as 'the natural rate' – or, euphemistically, 'the equilibrium rate', a view that has provoked Professor William Vickrey, a former President of the American Economic Association, to assert that the natural rate of unemployment (justifying a historically high rate) is one of the most vicious euphemisms ever coined.[9] In this sentiment he joins another famous economist, John Maynard Keynes, who observed in the mid-1930s in his *General Theory of Employment Interest and Money* that 'the outstanding faults of the economic society in which we live are its failure to provide for full employment and its arbitrary and inequitable distribution of wealth and incomes'. Not only have these failings not been corrected but the current rates of unemployment and underemployment have not been seen since the Great Depression of the 1930s. The concern is compounded both by the gradual acceptance of a new 'conventional wisdom' that this has to be accepted as 'normal', as an unavoidable cost of 'progress', and by the gradual sense of despair that no effective policies have even been proposed, let alone tried, to bring down the exceptionally high percentage of unemployment other than weakening/smashing unions or aborting their formation, reducing real wages, worsening working conditions and such that goes under the euphemism of 'making labour markets more flexible'.

The concern goes beyond the employment issue to focus as well on the decline in the real levels of wages and salaries, and on the 'social wage', that is, the benefits every citizen enjoys as entitlements through the spending undertaken by their respective governments for education, health and programmes related to 'social welfare'. In the name of 'fiscal responsibility', and in the cause of 'debt reduction', the amount of funding and the nature of social programme spending – that now comprises about 25 per cent of the budgetary expenditures of the industrialized countries – is under great pressure. Much of that pressure, vigorously supported by politically powerful multinational corporations, is rationalized as part of the price to be paid for the benefits derived from the process of 'globalization' and its close cousin, 'regionalization', with its so-called 'free trade' agreements or treaties. With the zealot's faith in the beneficence of so-called 'market forces' – and, thus, of the globalization process – a political/cultural assault has been launched on welfare systems that have been in place for decades, many components of which emerged out of the social/economic trauma of the Great Depression.

One commentator, a trade unionist, expressed in graphic terms the fears that this phenomenon has engendered:

> The emergence of the global corporation has provided management with the means to weaken or even to destroy unions. The traditional ultimate weapon of a union is the strike, but how does one picket a plant that has been closed by a corporation now getting the work done in another part of the globe? . . . Viewed globally, the ultimate effect of the strategies pursued by global corporations in their immediate best interests is to convert the globe into a Dickensian England – a world of underpaid and unemployed people unable to buy what they produce.[10]

The worsening situation faced by the greater part of the world's population is troubling enough for those directly and adversely affected, but the anxiety is exacerbated by the rising chorus of scepticism voiced by the affluent – and generally the most politically powerful – about the concept and practice of supporting programmes of 'welfare', or 'the social safety net', both within their own countries and abroad. That there is waning support for the global poor and needy is reflected in the stagnating size of the flow of development assistance, especially that provided on concessional terms.

The spurious rationalization for this waning support for foreign aid goes under the name of 'aid fatigue', that is, it is justified by the simplistic cause-and-effect argument that such aid has been plentiful but largely wasted if one looks at the meagre results. The moral is that the aid is virtually useless. It hardly seems to matter to the critics of foreign aid that the cited results are often measured by nebulous or misleading criteria and that there are myriad factors at play. Of the most important of these factors, one is the current set of policies associated with the globalization process. Another factor is simply that the amounts transferred under ODA programmes have, in real terms, not been that large and may, indeed, be judged to be minuscule. A large amount of this has been 'tied', and an even larger amount has been geopolitically and militarily motivated. It thus turns out that less than 10 per cent of ODA is focused on poverty eradication programmes. Furthermore, the degree of deprivation has been accentuated by the shift of a large percentage of the aid and lending from projects to what is called, 'policy lending' or 'structural adjustment lending' (SAL) that calls for the recipients to reduce subsidies and realign exchange rates, raise prices for basics, and undertake a host of 'belt-tightening' measures.

With the diminution of genuine aid and concessional lending, and with the nature of the policy and institutional changes that have been made in the grants and lending programmes, it should come as no surprise that the global underclass has been growing in number and facing greater stresses.

3/ The pressure on the environment is increasing, exacerbated by the spreading poverty and by the debt overhang

If more employment opportunities are to be provided for a growing labour-age population that will be increasingly urbanized and seeking non-farm jobs, the growth of industrialization is an imperative; with this comes both greater energy use and – to a greater or lesser extent depending on the sources and the uses to which energy is put – greater pressure on the ambient environment. In cities the environmental problems of urban waste disposal and of rising carbon emission levels from vehicles, power plants and the like have already begun to reach worrisome stress levels. Given the greater intensity of energy use in the earlier phases of industrialization, and given the plentiful availability and, therefore, lower financial cost of coal, a rapidly increasing reliance on high carbon fuels is virtually certain, unless alternative environmentally-benign fuels can be developed and made available, or the pattern of energy use can radically improve the energy/output relationship. There is no prospect of either without bold, innovative approaches that can address this challenge on an international scale. (An encouraging precedent is provided by the experience of the Consultative Group on International Agricultural Research (CGIAR) that contributed to the development of new wheat, rice and other varieties of food by using the available research funds more effectively. To focus research funds on the energy/environment connection in an analogous organizational manner, that is, on the feasibility of establishing a $CGIE^2R$ might seem an appropriate initiative. After all, funds are already available for research in a dispersed manner in dozens of underfunded organizations.[11])

The developing country debt issue is off the front pages, but is still alive. The total debt owed by these countries to their official and private banking creditors has more than doubled in the past decade, amounting to more than $1700 billion by the end of 1992. It is still going up – by over 5 per cent in 1992. Meanwhile, according to the latest tabulations, the outflow from the developing countries to the banks and governments of the industrialized ones is running as high as $40 billion and, at the same time, the arrears of all indebted developing countries have been mounting, doubling over the course of the last five years to total more than $100 billion.[12] The arrears reflect a desperate situation for those countries involved as they face a situation characterized by falling incomes and rising poverty, with suffering exacerbated by an awareness that their debts have been mounting rather than decreasing.

The debt numbers, by themselves, provide no clue as to their significance. The level of foreign debt is a relative concept. The implications of devoting an average of 25 to 30 per cent of foreign exchange earnings to servicing foreign debts becomes clear when examining the reduction that the debt servicing implies in terms of the amount of capital that is available for consumption and, as importantly, for investment in infrastructure, education and health. Because the debtor countries are in a phase of development that is – or should be – capital-intensive, the damage inflicted by this drain of capital is thus especially profound and long-lasting, dampening the hope that within the foreseeable future these countries as a group – allowing for a few exceptions – can rise out of the poverty trap in which they find themselves. Weighted by the debt burden, their economies are less able to compete and, as a consequence, the great mass of the citizens of these countries are doomed to sink further and further into the pit of excruciating poverty, if present trends continue. The bold initiative that is called for is, however, unlikely under the prevailing institutional arrangements.

4/ The capacity of developing countries to compete is decreasing and that of the large multinational companies is increasing with particularly distressing socio-economic-political consequences for developing countries

With the exceptions of the newly industrializing countries (NICs) and China, almost all the developing countries are finding themselves less and less able to compete in world markets for both primary and manufactured higher value-added products. Leaving to one side the conventional trade obstacles of tariff and non-tariff barriers, the primary commodity exports of the developing country have been losing markets to substitutes (fibre optics for copper, nylon for jute, aspartame for sugar, and so on). But perhaps the more formidable competition comes from the products that are subsidized by the governments of the industrialized countries. When the estimated annual total of agricultural subsidies in the industrialized countries is about $300 billion, the impact on the exports of the developing countries is devastating. They find themselves unable to compete in the subsidies contest, and lack the flexibility to shift production to take advantage of market opportunities beyond their limited domestic ones.

Under these circumstances, as the tax base shrinks or fails to expand rapidly enough, the financial burden that has to be imposed on the formal sectors of the economy becomes heavier. This results in strong incentives for producers and distributors to operate in the tax-evading 'informal sector', which is now estimated by the International Labour Organization to account for as much as 35 per cent of the GDP of many developing countries. Then a vicious circle begins: with this reduced ability to finance their education, health and infrastructure programmes and projects, these governments become less and less able to find the financial and other resources that are necessary to change the economic and socio-political structure so as to raise the productivity of the economy; this, in turn, puts more pressure on the formal sector . . .

The victims most severely affected by this vicious cycle are those at the bottom of the income and power scales, largely women and, in particular, peasant women. But with these changes in the economic and socio-political structure, the power of labour *vis-à-vis* indigenous and foreign capital is also weakened. This exacerbates the vicious downward spiral, further widening the gap between the rich and the poor.[13] It also has the effect of weakening the bargaining power of the host country *vis-à-vis* the foreign investors, especially if, as is likely, the bargaining is with any of the larger of the 35,000 multinational companies that might seek to invest.

The comparative financial strength of the multinationals can be gleaned from the 'fact' (an estimate by *The Economist*) that 300 of the largest companies control about one-quarter of the world's $20 trillion stock of productive assets, and 600 of the biggest, with annual sales above $1 billion, account for more than a fifth of the world's total value-added in manufacturing and agriculture.[14] The largest 20 have a total of sales volumes exceeding the total of the gross domestic output of 80 of the poorest developing countries.[15] These organizations are not simply atomistic economic agents searching out profitable opportunities. Their size in terms of capital and sales networks confers enormous power. They can shape markets and production relationships. Since 1983 the amount of annual flows of private international investment has grown four times as fast as global output and this resurgence of private international capital flows has been largely due to multinational companies that annually account for over $150 billion of the flow.

Their role in the global economic system has, indeed, fostered growth in the few developing country economies that have been favoured with their investments, but their impact on the *distribution* of the putative benefits is quite another matter. In a cover story of the May 14, 1990 issue of *Business Week* entitled 'The Stateless Corporation: today's giants that are really leaping boundaries', the authors note one of the implications of the estimated annual flow of $150 billion that multinational corporations invest abroad:

> What is clear is that sorting our national economic interests will be harder than ever. Washington can hardly monitor the international trade and investment activities of US businesses and is blind when it comes to determining what foreign corporations are doing in the US . . . There has been a reversal of roles between government and corporation [with] governments acting as if they are fully sovereign within their own borders on economic policy, [while] stateless corporations have increasingly learned to shape national climates by offering technology, jobs and capital.

How much more difficult must it be for economically weaker

countries to both know about and control such investments so as to capture the putative benefits of such investments? This distributional aspect sheds a different light on the benefits that the globalization process is supposed to confer. One has to ask: who benefits and who pays? In this regard it is relevant to note that almost all of the multinationals have a well-earned reputation as fierce opponents of organized labour and, as a corollary, they display a strong preference for countries where they can engage in non-unionized low-wage production with accompanying low safety, environmental and social standards. In non-democratic developing countries they need only make common cause – 'splitting the spoils', so to speak – with the elites of the countries in which they invest to ensure that these conditions are maintained. The lop-sided nature of the outcome is reflected in the character of the notorious *maquiladoras* located along the Mexican-US border, with its sharp contrast between gleaming (but polluting) factories and nearby slums, and in the dramatic contrast between the $20 million remuneration of Michael Jordan, the American basketball star, by the Nike Company and the lesser amount paid to 'all the [thousands of] Nike workers in the Indonesian factories that make them [Nike products]'.[16]

5/ 'Off-shore' international financial flows are large and growing rapidly – and the rate of increase, composition and volatility of these flows has been increasingly beyond governmental control

The global integration of financial markets on a large scale can be dated back to 1963 with the launching of the first Eurobond bond issues totalling $164 million. Financial innovations that were made possible by new technologies gave a tremendous boost to the volumes of capital handled by the fledging markets, bringing the annual compound rate over the intervening three decades to more than 36 per cent. As the volume increased, the pressure mounted for the removal of restrictions applied to cross-border financial flows.[17] This typifies the rate of increase in the volume of financial transactions through all of the world's financial markets: by 1994 the daily flow through the foreign exchange (forex) centres around the world exceeded $1 trillion, or the rough equivalent of the foreign exchange holdings of all the central banks of the major industrialized nations. Given the relative size and nature of these flows with their impact on exchange rates and interest rates, the issue of control of these off-shore financial activities has emerged recurrently as a priority item on the agenda of meetings of the Group of Seven (G-7). The lack of ability to dampen the fluctuations had long ago become worrisome. A minor concern related to the injury inflicted by the speculative and volatile attributes of much of these capital flows on the developing countries, which generally lack adequate financial resources to take hedging measures against the turbulent financial waves, and to 'roll with the punches', so to speak, by being policy-flexible. By early 1994 there was a perceptible rise in the level of concern with the focus placed on the business of derivatives that are estimated to be outstanding in the amount of about $16 trillion.[18] Their size and volatility have provoked a Congressional committee hearing and prompted *The Economist* to devote the cover and lead editorial of the 14-20 May 1994 issue to the theme 'Your financial future' and to ask what the fuss is all about. The reasons given is that:

> the industry is new, global and already very big: the telephone number figures for the supposed value of outstanding derivatives (. . . $16 billion +) make the eyes spin . . . Lastly, there are fears that derivatives fuel financial-market uncertainty by multiplying the leverage, or debt-based buying power, of hedge funds and other speculators – an uncertainty that could, if things went wrong, threaten the whole of the world financial system. [The journal's editorial judges this fear to be 'overdone' with the underlying reason being that 'in general, financial systems are self-correcting and the conclusion being that 'derivative misfortune-tellers are wrong.'[19]]

The risk-engendered fear of playing with such large financial stakes has spread beyond the derivatives business that many regard as being only a part and a symptom of the broader phenomena of high and gyrating interest rates and sharp and wide fluctuations in exchange rates. This anxiety is combined with concern about the low proportion of the capital flows that is being channelled towards productive purposes, and the high concentration of this flow that is intra-multinational companies and directed to a very limited number of countries. The questionable nature and composition of the capital flowing through financial markets arises from the 'fact' (a best guess estimate by *The Economist*) that only about 5 per cent is for the financing of trade and less than 15 per cent for investment. *The Wall Street Journal* (in its September 18, 1992 issue) has ventured to state that 'less than 10 per cent of this staggering sum has anything to do with trade in goods and services'. It would seem that the remaining 80+ per cent of the ebb and flow is attributable to speculative and/or 'money-laundering' motives that are in large measure beyond the bounds of serving any beneficent social purpose, and re-validates John Maynard Keynes references to the 'casino society'. Capital movements, it seems, have only a weak, tenuous connection to societal objectives; major financial decisions are made without reference as to whether the projects being financed are, or are not, 'productive' in the broadest social sense of that term.

Though the range and frequency of the volatility of capital movements, and especially of foreign exchange relationships, began to rise appreciably in the period when the Bretton Woods agreement was no longer operative, that is, in the early 1970s and thereafter, it was only in the mid-1980s that the concern was acute enough to precipitate the first of the *ad hoc* 'summitry' meetings, when the US Treasury Secretary, James Baker, invited the leaders and finance ministers of the seven largest industrialized nations (the G-7) to the Plaza Hotel in New York. These meetings became ritualized, though on an *ad hoc* basis, and some members of the group came to regard themselves as 'the board of directors of the international economy'. But the meetings became little more than symbolic events, with not much to show for all the posturing beyond the publicized communiqué as real world events went their own way seldom, if ever, affected by the pronouncements.[20]

This failure to achieve coordinated policies has given rise to the issue of leadership and raised the related critical question: have the G-7 collectively both the *will* and the *capability* to control – or even to significantly and consistently influence – global capital movements so as to:

i) dampen the extreme volatility of exchange rates and realign them to conform to underlying and sustainable realities, and, as well, in the process to dampen the volatility of real interest rates and lower them from their historically high and unsustainable levels?;

ii) ensure that the rapid rise in the rate of global foreign investment gets directed in a manner that promotes the kind of growth in poorer countries that is shared widely, is environmentally acceptable, and is responsive to democratic control; in a phrase, subject to policies that raise social, labour and environmental standards?

The evidence points to a negative response to both these questions with regard to both objectives. Thus, the pressures are mounting, heightening the awareness of the downside of the globalization process and, therefore, of the need for significant policy and institutional changes at the level of international governance so as to arrest and reverse the deplorable and dangerous trends. This calls for going beyond the objective of restoration of the debtor nations to that nebulous concept called 'creditworthiness'. After all, recovery can hardly suffice as a goal of policy, when it implies a return to a global economic system that contained within itself the seeds that germinated these unwelcome social, financial, environmental and other trends. This broader objective implies the use of resources in a different way and for different purposes; in a phrase, changes that are *systemic* in their nature and scope that would, in effect, harness the dynamic of the globalization process to achieve a more productive global economy in which there is both much greater fairness and sensitivity to the maintenance and then enhancement of social/cultural/environmental quality.

THE NECESSARY CONDITIONS FOR ATTAINING THE OBJECTIVES

The world community has long tolerated desperate poverty and extremes of income distribution, conditions that should not be acceptable on grounds of justice or fairness. Thus, hard-headed realists would expect and accept a significant degree of change only if such changes were indicated on non-compassionate grounds, that is, if they could be expected to work to the advantage of the stronger parties in trade and other relationships. On this non-compassionate basis it is possible to identify the minimal changes that are necessary – but not necessarily sufficient – for achieving the desired objectives.

The international economic scene is far from a level playing field. Globalization does not, therefore, mean a 'hands-off leave-it-to-the-market' approach especially considering that power being what it is, it is hardly surprising that the rules of the game have been tilted against the developing countries as a group. Because a few developing countries have done rather well during the last few decades, there is a tendency to ascribe the current plight of the other developing countries – and that includes most of them – to inappropriate institutional arrangements and misguided policies, that is, to conclude that their wounds have been largely self-inflicted. The popular refrain runs as follows: 'all would be well if the poverty-stricken developing countries were to rely more on the operations of "market forces" by removing the severe constraints placed on private initiatives of an entrepreneurial nature and by reducing government involvement'.

However, a convincing case could also be made that even if each developing nation 'corrected' these institutional, policy and cultural faults by 'structural adjustment', only a few of them could hope to reverse these deplorable trends so long as the international milieu remains essentially the same. This school of thought thus puts the spotlight on the weak points and unwelcome trends of the present global economy *as a system*. These unfavourable factors include:

i) secularly deteriorating terms of trade for those developing country economies greatly dependent on earnings from the export of primary commodities: the prices of these commodities have been severely depressed since the mid-70s and – in real terms – have long been at the level that prevailed during the Great Depression;

ii) the sluggish growth of the economies of the industrialized countries that traditionally have provided the main markets for the exports of the developing countries;

iii) the persistently high protectionist barriers of these industrialized economies (that, interestingly enough, have remained higher for imports from the developing countries than from other industrialized countries);

iv) historically and unsustainably high and volatile real interest rates on capital borrowed from abroad and pressure on the host country to offer highly concessional terms in order to attract capital investment from abroad;

v) exchange rates that have fluctuated widely and wildly ever since 1970 when President Nixon closed the 'gold-window' – that had until then enabled bankers and individuals to exchange gold for their US paper dollars – and, thereby, effectively terminated the 1944 Bretton Woods agreement.

If the economies of developing countries are to get back onto a growth path that is desirable in terms of both pace and pattern, 'correcting' all of these five unfavourable factors is a necessary condition – but, as noted, this is by no means sufficient since the developing countries have a role to play in terms of establishing effective, honest administrations and adopting 'appropriate policies'. But with the focus on the aspect of international governance and limited time, it may suffice to focus the discussion on the last two factors, that is, the two key economic/financial preconditions for attaining and maintaining the desired systemic objective of global growth with equity and the improvement or maintenance of social and environmental standards.

1/   Lowering real interest rates to the historic range of 1 per cent or less and dampening the volatility of exchange rates

Either or both of these financial objectives will likely prove very difficult to achieve on a sustained basis. In the early 1980s nominal interest rates reached historically unprecedented heights of over 20 per cent, and in the range of 10 per cent in real terms. This rise, known as 'the Volcker shock' (after the then chairman of the US Federal Reserve System), was a primary factor in precipitating the actions of Mexico and Brazil that brought on the debt crisis panic of 1982. The rate was unsustainably high and bears comparison with the global average real long-term rate of interest that ranged for decades in the neighbourhood of 0.3 per cent. The basis for taking the historic level of 1 per cent or less as the desired and sustainable level for Third World borrowing is simply that at an early stage of development the funds borrowed for development purposes cannot be expected to earn a higher rate of return in financial terms but may, nonetheless, yield a high socio-economic rate.

Lowering real interest rates calls for an international cooperative effort, with the USA in the linchpin role by virtue of the size of its economy and its importance in world trade and capital flows and, therefore, of its impact on the supply and demand for capital that, in the final analysis, determines the price of capital or the real rate of interest. Japan, the European Union and, to a lesser extent, others have a role to play in this process, since any actions by one to set interest rates could be offset or nullified by the actions of others. It is this interdependence that has necessitated the periodic meetings of finance ministers and their presidents and prime ministers that has now become ritualized as summitry and, as noted, shown meagre results.

This low success rate should occasion no surprise. There is, after all, little hope of lowering interest rates without action taken to arrest the decline in world savings. These fell, in aggregative terms, from 26 per cent (as a ratio to GNP) in the early 1970s to about 20 per cent by the end of the 1980s, and have continued to decline as all the major industrialized countries, with the exception of Japan and Germany, have been sliding on the downward course.[21] The chief culprit has been the US economy that has had a low rate of savings and remains heavily dependent on foreign-generated savings. Necessity will undoubtedly force changes to bring real interest rates back to their historically low levels. The big question is whether the 'necessity' is forced by cataclysmic events or by deliberate steps taken with forethought so as to anticipate the inevitable and make the adjustment a soft one.

2/ Increasing financial flows to developing countries

With few exceptions the developing countries must contend with serious financial gaps. The critical question is whether those gaps are bridgeable under any reasonable scenario that could be envisaged. On that score, the prospects are grim for most of them, since reliable forecasters see the overwhelming proportion of concessional external financing flowing to 'countries with strong creditworthiness', and any significant volume of private capital flowing to only a handful of developing countries.

The 1993 resurgence of private capital flows has confirmed this expectation. Neither the volume nor the pattern of these flows assures sufficiently high rates of *per capita* growth for *all* the developing countries, defining 'sufficiently high' as 2 per cent a year, and stressing 'all' to place the emphasis on growth *with geographic equity*. The basis for this pessimistic judgment is evident when one looks at the gap between estimates of the minimum amount of capital required and – if one judges by the past record – the likelihood of such sums being forthcoming on commercial and on concessional terms.

The questions to ask and to answer are:

- how much foreign capital is 'needed' for growth and for environmental programmes assuming – as seems likely – that 'internal savings . . . will account for the lion's share of investment?'[22]

‐ where is the capital to come from?

How much capital inflow do developing countries need?

There are many factors to consider in modelling exercises that are designed to generate estimates of capital requirement. From country to country these factors differ in their qualitative attributes and in their relationships one to the other. It is even difficult to group them by some key common characteristics. There is, in addition, the 'soft' aspect pertaining to the choice of the growth rate targets and, from the environmental perspective, the choice of the patterns of growth that must also be a component of the targeted objective. Given all this complexity and ambiguity, there is bound to be a great deal of scepticism about models churning out rather precise numbers. However, even after allowing for these conceptual, methodological and statistical difficulties, and those pertaining to the reliability and availability of the data themselves, the modelling exercises could be instructive, if used with caution.

One modelling exercise, as set out in the *1994 Human Development Report,* yields the estimated capital required to wipe out the worst forms of poverty in the world to be an *additional* $30 to $40 billion a year, an amount that would be attainable with a shifting of budgetary allocations by developing countries and donor countries. The amount is relatively modest in relation to the ambitious objective. This is an approach sharply focused on tackling the most onerous features of poverty that could be complemented by programmes to finance the research on ‐ and the eventual wide distribution of ‐ stand-alone energy technologies (solar, wind, biomass, and so on). The amount of capital required would be very modest but the pay-off would be high in eventually enabling those living beyond the reach of electrical grid networks ‐ that is where the poorest of the poor are to be found ‐ to live better in terms of housing with cheap and easy access to lighting, cooking, water and sanitation facilities, and also to be more productive. At the same time, there would be the substantial social and environmental bonus of reducing their dependence on fuelwood.

Beyond the poverty-focused programme, modellers have made estimates of capital requirements based on various assumptions. Assuming the objective is to achieve an annual 2 per cent increase in *per capita* incomes in the low- and middle-income developing countries, and that about one-fifth of the required investment would need to be supplied from foreign sources, the estimates of modellers of the *additional* annual net capital inflows have ranged from about $60 to $125 billion. When the capital requirements of the former Soviet republics and the Eastern European countries are also included, another $60 to $90 billion would need to be added. If the additional capital required annually to implement the minimal targets of UNCED's Agenda 21 is factored into the calculation, the estimates rise yet again by between $100 and $300 billion annually over the next 20 years.[23] Thus, the annual tally runs from $250 to $500 billion or about 3 to 6 times the current flow of official development assistance (ODA). Private capital flows could not be expected to increase sufficiently to meet this total volume, let alone remedy its sectoral and geographic distribution that has, up until now, been very narrowly focused on few developing countries.

What are the likely and possible sources of capital?

The main financial burden must rest on the countries themselves but the gap between what they can be expected to generate from their own internal savings would need to be filled by the governments and private investors of the richer industrialized and oil exporting countries that can carry that burden, or, as the case may be, seize that opportunity for profitable investment. It is clear that the largest part of the capital transfer must take the form of interest-free or low-interest grants and loans through substantially augmented ODA programmes.

Capital flows to the developing countries declined until 1987 and thereafter increased. By 1990 they were 30 per cent above the low point but still far short of the level of 1982, at the onset of the debt crisis. The ODA component channelled through both multilateral and bilateral aid programmes remained relatively constant in real terms. Its importance can be gauged by the fact that these ODA funds accounted in 1990 for about half of the total capital inflows to developing countries. Syndicated credits and bond issues amounted to about $16 billion in 1991, but over three-quarters of this flow went to just four Asian countries. A similar shortcoming of a narrow concentration applies as well to private direct investment flows that had declined in the early 1980s and had jumped three-fold since 1986, from less than $10 billion to over $30 billion. A recent report of the International Finance Corporation (IFC), notes that private investment to the developing countries 'has climbed back to the high point reached in the late 1970s, while public investment remains at a 10-year low'.[24] The catch is that only six of the developing countries – those with the largest markets – accounted for more than half of this total, and much of this flow has been intra-multinational firms and a reflow of 'flight capital' that has been returning home on attractive terms through transactions labelled 'debt-equity swaps'.

In relation to the magnitude of the need, the amounts involved in these private investment flows are not impressive, especially considering their limited geographic scope. They are not likely to come much greater and spread more broadly despite initiatives to encourage private capital to countries that are considered riskier, such as the Multilateral Investment Guarantee Agency (MIGA). Nor can much be expected from the private bankers who have been burnt and hold views probably well reflected in the statement of a former chairman of Chase Manhattan Bank to the effect that 'debt forgiveness and new money are incompatible'.[25] They are, however, neither forgiving nor lending to any significant degree.

Then there is the issue of the diversion of the available aid funds from developing countries to the European and central Asian 'economies in transition', which threatens to reduce the amounts going to the developing countries unless additional funding is forthcoming. The shortfall between minimal net capital import requirements and the actual flow has been enormous and, for most developing countries, growing. Now there is an additional need of even greater dimensions to meet the requirements of the economies in transition and the global environmental programmes if the developing countries are to be enabled to carry out their part. Accordingly, there has been an outpouring of suggestions regarding sources of additional funds, the most popular of which is some variant of a 'Global Marshall Plan'.[26] In addition, funding proposals have included ideas such as taxing, fining and extracting royalties on commercial operations utilizing and polluting the 'global commons' (principally the upper atmosphere, the high seas, Antarctica and areas not under any one nation's jurisdiction), taxing the trillion-a-day volume foreign exchange transaction handled by forex centres (at a minuscule rate that, nonetheless, would yield large sums), and issuing Special Drawing Rights through the IMF.[27] Then, of course, there are the 'peace dividend' proposals that would divert a stipulated percentage of disarmament 'savings' to development and environmental programmes.

In more detail, the search for further funding has given rise to the following proposals.

* A global carbon tax on the users of fossil fuels, which at $50 a tonne of carbon emission would yield annually in the USA alone about $28 billion, if 10 per cent of the revenues were allocated to environmental programmes.

* An issuance by the IMF of a substantial amount (say, $50 billion over three years) of Special Drawing Rights (SDRs), with a bias in its distribution towards needy developing countries rather than in accordance with quota entitlements which favour the industrialized nations.

* Debt-for-nature swaps which can, in some cases, provide a measure of financial relief that can be directed towards the funding for establishing and maintaining nature preserves, parks and related environmental programmes such as the environmentally beneficial forestry policies and practices that help maintain the tropical rain forests which play an important role in absorbing CO_2.

* Payment of 'rent' by the developed industrialized countries

for their past and current disproportionately heavy use of the 'global commons' as garbage disposal bins, that is, payment to compensate for their unfair share of use of the oceans and upper atmosphere. To this could be added taxes or royalties from the commercial use of the upper atmosphere.

* For international financial flows, which now amount to more than $1 trillion a day, levying taxes at a miniscule rate of 3/1000s of 1 per cent on the international transfers of money between money centres dealing in foreign exchange. This is popularly known as 'The Tobin Tax', after the Nobel Laureate Professor James Tobin. For example, it is estimated that this would yield enough to finance all UN operations, including peace-keeping.

These measures can only be achieved through both *ad hoc* agreements between nations on a regional or global basis, and through permanent institutional arrangements to ensure their implementation and enforcement. This is tantamount to saying that the appropriate action would be to launch negotiations to establish a 'global structural adjustment programme' akin to the process that established the Bretton Woods agreement of 1944, which put in place a global system of rewards and penalties designed to secure adherence to agreed-upon rules governing trade and capital movements. Today, the rules of any such agreement would be extended to ensure guidelines/adherence to norms of environmental 'good behaviour'.

THE 'NEW BRETTON WOODS' AS CONCEPT AND REALITY

The policy-makers of the major industrialized nations have only recently begun to show serious signs of worry about the implications of the growing size, and the uncontrolled and non-productive speculative nature of, financial movements. Voices had been raised before, notably Raoul Presbisch, Henry Kissinger, François Mitterrand, Robert Muldoon and others.[28] At the outset of the 1990s, the tinge of anxiety was reflected in the call by the former US Secretary of the Treasury, Nicholas Brady, for the establishment of a special commission to focus on this issue. Gerald Corrigan, former head of the Federal Reserve Bank of New York, and others, such as New York financier, Felix Rohatyn, also echoed the same refrain.

More recently, a knowledgeable observer, Fred Bergsten, the Director of the Washington-based *Institute for International Economics*, has noted that under the pressure of global stress there has emerged 'a more collective tripolar management [that has tried but not succeeded in] putting together a stable system, [but has succeeded in] avoiding crisis and total breakdown'. This has prompted him to suggest that:

> We need to get back to the global negotiations on a new world monetary system, as well as on trade, international investment, and policy coordination . . . [recognizing that] *systemic reform* takes a long time.[29] (emphasis added)

In another recent publication (co-authored with Robert Reich, now the US Labour Secretary), he went on to advocate a:

> GATT for Investment [under] new tripolar management [that] would round out a three-pronged agenda for the '90s that must address the issue of how to maintain a stable economy in the 21st century.[30]

More recently yet, the concern about the prevailing state of affairs has given rise to a report prepared by a group of prestigious international bankers, led by Paul Volcker under the auspices of the Bretton Woods Commission, in which governmental action is advocated 'to overhaul the world monetary system'.[31]

The recognition by members of the Establishment of the need to overhaul the system is perhaps more significant than the specifics of their proposals. In effect, the calls are for change in the prevailing global 'rules of the game' for trade and capital movements, but the nature and degree of change that is implied is very dependent on the objectives sought:

- is the intent limited to the avoidance of a possible catastrophic breakdown of the economic/financial system and the attainment of the nebulous phrase, 'return of debtors' creditworthiness' or 'recovery?' Or,

- does it go beyond this to envisage the creation of conditions that are conducive not only to faster global growth in real *per capita* incomes or well-being as measured in terms of national averages, but also to a more equitable sharing of this growth and to a pattern of growth compatible with standards of environmental quality, locally and globally, that would enable such growth to be sustained over the long-term?

Attaining the former objective implies acceptance of the very system that incubated the present debt, poverty and environmental crises. If, however, the objective is to attain the state of affairs congenial with high growth, equity and environmental standards, the call is for the establishment of a global set of institutions and rules analogous to what was achieved at the conference held in Bretton Woods, New Hampshire, in 1944, but going beyond the scope of that agreement to include more than rules with respect to trade and capital flows and beyond its limited number of participants. If the calls for a 'new Bretton Woods' are to have any resonance, that is, sufficient popular appeal to make progress in the face of vested interests and inertial forces, it must be broad enough in its participation, its objectives and its institutional modalities to inspire support. In a phrase, it must be sufficiently imaginative and bold to be commensurate with the challenge of the 1990s and the twenty-first century. The challenge is profoundly different from that of the 1930s and the early 1940s that led to the first Bretton Woods agreement.

There are, however, valuable lessons to be learnt from the experience of drafting and operating the original Bretton Woods agreement that emerged out of the collapse of the international system as epitomized in the agonies of the Great Depression and World War II. What emerged in the post-war world were rules governing the international movement of goods and services, and of investment based on 'an understanding' or 'a bargain' whereby the USA was to take on the obligation to act as stabilizer by exercising an overwhelming degree of control over the international financial system, such as money supply and exchange rates.[32] To carry through this agreement two new institutions – often referred to as the 'Bretton Woods twins' – were established: the International Monetary Fund (IMF) designed to act (as one commentator put it) as 'the champion of virtuous finance', and the World Bank designed to provide long-term capital for war reconstruction and for development purposes. Despite their international board of directors, neither their shareholders nor their managements had much power since – to take the case of the IMF – it was the US policy-making establishment that was vested with the responsibility of 'virtuousness' in keeping the US dollar, as the saying goes, 'as good as gold'.

In terms of trade and income growth and stability – but much less so in terms of equity and environmental concerns – the global economic/financial system operated reasonably well for the quarter century when its 'rules' held sway: the global flows of trade increased over this period by 250 per cent and incomes by 150 per cent, with developing countries growing on average at a much faster rate than the industrialized ones. In the late 1960s and early 1970s, under the pressure of financing the expensive Vietnam War, US policy-makers had to choose between adhering to the obligations their country had assumed under the Bretton Woods agreement – by reining in the inflationary forces through the imposition of tough fiscal and monetary policy measures – or breaking the agreement. They effectively chose the latter course of action by 'closing the gold window' in 1969 to private individuals and in 1970 to central banks.

After the collapse of the Bretton Woods agreement there was no longer an adequate control mechanism in place to prevent the chain of events that led to the subsequent volatility of exchange rates and interest rates, and to the enormous pile-up of an unsustainable mountain of debt, since the countries that went on a borrowing and lending binge in the 1970s would likely have been brought up short by the Bretton Woods reins. Those who call for 'rules' such as those that held sway for a quarter century from 1945 until 1970 are, however, proposing changes in scope and modalities and, possibly, institutional arrangements. These changes must be designed for an era of structural change with its massive geographic and technological shift in the international division of labour, and its implications in terms of growing inequalities in income distribution within and between countries; of rising levels of unemployment or 'jobless growth'; of demographic pressures; and of a host of social pressures contributing to unprecedented levels of ethnic and criminal violence and such.

The world has long lived with indecision, inefficiency and inequity. Few of the advocates of a new Bretton Woods would be moved to urge changes on that account, but they make common cause in feeling that, as a matter of pragmatism, the present arrangements are unsustainable environmentally, socially and politically. A Canadian academic, Professor Gerald Helleiner, has posed the pertinent question:

> who among us is confident that the existing international economic machinery will get us safely through to the end of the century . . . [so as] to ensure adequate international liquidity, a smooth adjustment to irreversible economic change, confidence in our financial systems, reasonable overall stability and growth, and equitable sharing in the fruits of such progress?[33]

If new institutional arrangements are deemed necessary or desirable to achieve the required global management on trade, capital, social and environment issues, the newness could be understood as: i) the strengthening/expanding/ rationalizing of the operations of the existing international agencies; and/or ii) the establishment of additional institutions on their own or as adjuncts to those already in operation.

The first approach is clearly preferable since starting new institutions is a difficult and lengthy process and, in any case, the existing ones may well be amenable to change in their structure, in their policies, and in their mode of operations. Thus, for example, there are advocates of assigning the job of global fiscal and monetary policy coordination to the IMF and 'development' to the World Bank and its sister regional agencies with whatever policy changes are necessary being made within their prevailing constitutional frameworks.[34]

This school of thought was supportive of the initiatives to transform the secretariat of the General Agreement on Tariffs and Trade (GATT) into the World Trade Organization which became operational in January of 1995. (Republican opposition could not derail this initiative as it did in the case of the International Trade Organization that was proposed in 1944 to complement the roles of the newly-born Bretton Woods twins.) But the necessary changes must go much further, that is, be tantamount to radical institutional surgery, if they are to succeed in rationalizing a system of international agencies that was established over time with conflicting or overlapping mandates. These changes will be made by volitional decisions in a controlled and orderly way, or they will be made by *force majeure*, that is, in an uncontrolled and precipitous manner. Should the changes come about in the second manner, the solution or outcome is likely to be a retreat from the 40-year-old trend towards interdependence to autocratic policies, as each of the industrialized countries endeavours to minimize the damage to itself by adopting 'beggar-thy-neighbour' policies. The possibility of the last outcome gives the problem and the approach to finding a solution an element of urgency.

The process of institutional change at the level of global governance has already begun but needs to be accelerated and to be led with an overarching conceptual vision that sets out the multi-faceted objectives. This needs to be combined with a down-to-earth sense of how to drive and steer the process through the political reefs, in the face of powerful cross-currents of conflicting ideas and headwinds of vested interests in the status quo. This is a situation that calls for leadership at every level of governance to provide what economists refer to as 'the collective public good', namely, the establishment and maintenance of a global milieu that is characterized by the rule of law, acceptable modes of behaviour in commerce and every-day activities, and other attributes of a desirable world in terms of stability, fairness and openness.[35] The most economically powerful nations have been judged to be failing the test of global leadership which assumes that the basic responsibility of leadership is not only to avoid cataclysmic breakdown but to go beyond that to promote the 'public good', that is, to create and/or maintain a global milieu or system congenial for achieving the desired objective of a world that is growing with equity and with high social, political and environmental standards.

This is a formidable challenge at the best of times, but especially so in this time of transformation or *mega* change. The appreciation of the dire consequences of not rising to the challenge can, perhaps, be a forcing mechanism. The fear of mutual peril might have more persuasive power than the appeals to team work and the appeal of a humane and prosperous world for all its current and future inhabitants which, for the first time in history, human ingenuity has made a realizable dream.

REFERENCES

1. For a fuller discussion of the environment/energy crisis, see M. Miller, *Debt & the Environment: Converging Crises*, UN Publications: N.Y., 1992.

2. R. Dowling, *Business Week*, March 15, 1993 in his review of Paul Kennedy's book, *Preparing for the Twenty-first Century*, Random House: N.Y., 1993 paraphrases the prognosis set forth in the book if we remain on the present trajectory.

3. The picture is spelt out statistically in various publications of which the most complete and authoritative are the annual editions of the UN's *Human Development Report* and the World Bank's *Social Indicators of Development* and *Trends in Developing Countries*.

4. For a fuller treatment of this relationship, see A. MacEwan, 'Globalization and Stagnation', *Monthly Review*, N.Y., April 1994.

5.   *Global Economic Prospects and the Developing Countries-1994*, World Bank, Washington, D.C., 1994, pp.88-9.

6.   B. Bosworth, 'Unemployed in Europe versus Poor in America', *International Economic Insights*, Washington, D.C., March/April 1994, p.3.

7.   'Anti-Depression Economics', *The Atlantic Monthly*, April 1993, p.103.

8.   R. Barnet and J. Cavanagh, *Global Dreams: Imperial Corporations and the New World Order*, Random House: N.Y., 1994, p.425.

9.   'Today's Task for Economists', *Challenge*, March/April 1993, p.10.

10.   G. Tyler, 'The Nation-State vs. the Global Economy', *Challenge*, March-April 1993, pp.30 & 32.

11.   For a fuller discussion of the proposal for the CGIE^{2}R project see, M. Miller, *The Energy/Environment Connection: Overcoming Institutional Obstacles to 'Doing the Right Thing'*, World Bank/EDI Energy Series Working Paper, Washington, D.C., 1989.

12.   *World Debt Tables*, 1992-93, World Bank, Washington, D.C., 1993, especially p.15.

13.   The trends in the key indicators of 'the human condition' is graphically documented in the annual editions of the UN's *Human Development Report*, the World Bank's annual *Atlas*, and the World Bank's *Social Indicators of Development*, The John Hopkins University Press Baltimore, Md. (Annual).

14.   'A Survey of Multinationals', *The Economist*, 27 March 1993, pp5-6; and 'Come back multinationals . . . [that] seemed fated to succeed colonial powers as the bogeyman . . . ', 26 November 1988.

15.   *The Global Corporation and Nation-states: Do Companies or Countries Compete?*, National Planning Association, Washington, D.C., 1993, p5; see also Barnet and Cavanagh 1994, *op.cit.*, *passim*.

16.   Cited by Barnet and Cavanagh 1994, *op.cit.*, p.328.

17.   See Bank for International Settlements, *Recent Innovations in International Banking*, Basle, Switzerland, 1986, p.149 and *passim*; R.C. Smith, *The Global Bankers*, E.P. Dutton, N.Y., 1989, especially the chapter entitled 'The Globalization of Capital Markets.'

18.   *The Economist*, May 14-20, 1994, p.15.

19.   *Ibid.*, pp.14-15.

20.   See P. Krugman, 'International Adjustments 1985-90: What Have We Learned?', *International Economic Insights*, November/December 1990, p.21.

21.   See B.B. Aghevil and J.M. Boughton, 'National Saving and the World Economy: Why have savings rates declined since the early 1970s?', *Finance & Development*, June 1990, pp.2-5; A.L. Bovenberg, 'Why has U.S. Personal Saving Declined?', *Finance & Development*, June 1990, pp.10-11; and J.J. Polak, 'The Decline of World Savings', *Economic Insights*, Institute for International Economics, Washington, D.C., September/October 1990, pp.18-19.

22.   S. Collins, 'Capital Flows to Developing Countries: Implications from the Economies in Transition', *Proceedings of the Annual Conference on Development Economies 1992*, World Bank: Washington D.C.

23.   For a breakdown of the estimates see M. Miller, *The Energy/Environment Connection: Overcoming the Institutional Obstacles to Doing the Right Thing,'* World Bank/EDI Working Paper, Washington, D.C., 1990, and 'Getting Grounded at Rio', *Ecodecision*, April 1992.

24. G. Pfefferman and A. Madrassy, *Trends in Private Investment in Developing Countries 1993: Statistics for 1970-91.*

25. Quoted in J. Evans, 'What If They Declared a Debt Crisis and Nobody Came?', *International Development Review*, Winter, 1989/90, p.46.

26. See, for example, P. Shabecoff, 'A "Marshall Plan" for the Environment', *The New York Times*, May 3, 1990.

27. R. Dobell and T. Parson, 'A World Development Fund', *Policy Options Politiques*, December 1988; *Our Common Future*, report of the Brundtland Commission, Oxford University Press, 1987.

28. For a long list of such voices, see M. Miller, 'Coping is not Enough! The International Debt Crisis and the Roles of the World Bank and the IMF', Dow Jones-Irwin Inc., Homewood, Illinois, 1988, pp.151-5.

29. F. Bergsten, 'A New Big Three to Manage the World Economy', *Challenge*, Nov-Dec, 1990.

30. *Ibid.,* p24; R.Reich, 'Commentary on: Globalization and the Nation-state', *Review '90, Outlook '91*, North-South Institute, Ottawa, 1991, p.21.

31. *The Wall Street Journal,* May 9, 1994

32. R. Cooper, 'A Monetary System for the Future', *Foreign Affairs*, Fall 1984.

33. G. Helleiner, 'An Agenda for a New Bretton Woods', *Foreign Policy Journal*, Winter 1987-8.

34. E. Bernstein, 'Do we need a new Bretton Woods?', *Finance and Development,* September 1984; for a critique of Bernstein's postion see, M. Miller 1988, *op.cit.*.

35.   See C.P. Kindleberger, presidential address to the American Economic Association annual meeting on December 29, 1985 reprinted in 'International Public Goods without international Government', *The American Economic Review*, March 1986.

4

The Dual Role of the Nation State in the Evolution of World Citizenship

Anatol Rapoport

THE CHANGING MEANING OF CITIZENSHIP

Five hundred years ago, the inhabitants of some European cities possessed certain rights, privileges and duties not available to people living outside the protection of city walls. Since then, the rights first associated with medieval 'city' dwellers, from which the terms 'citizens' and 'citizenship' are derived, have been extended to others and their meaning has been elaborated. But now, as then, not everyone enjoys the benefits of citizenship. Many states restrict its application and derogate its meaning. This can give rise to conflict within and between states, particularly where ethnicity and religion are used to define it.

The extension of meaningful citizenship to groups now denied it would greatly reduce the source of many, though not all, contemporary conflicts. But any effort to extend or deepen the meaning of citizenship around the world would need to be based on understanding that its meaning has changed in consequence of historical developments.

A Brief Survey of the Evolution of Citizenship

Although people in some European states and city states enjoyed citizenship in the early modern period, few others did. It was not until the eighteenth century revolutions in America and France that citizenship was dramatically extended to some residents of whole nation-state republics. The meaning of citizenship in these republics deepened during the next century and a half, citizenship becoming available to resident groups that were long denied it (for example, African Americans, women). However, citizenship did not become widely available outside the Americas. Most of the people of the world remained 'subjects' of monarchy or empire, though inhabitants of some European states enjoyed greater rights than residents of imperial colonies.

Two world wars destroyed European and Asian empires, giving the great republics – the USA and the former USSR – the opportunity to use decolonization to create a world of nation-state republics, a development that rapidly extended citizenship, or at least the formal package of rights associated with it (the right to vote, the right to equal treatment under civil law), to people around most of the world.

Even then, however, citizenship was not universally given. In addition, its meaning differed substantially from one country to the next, particularly where dictatorships and one-party regimes took power. The recent democratization of both capitalist and communist states around the world (southern Europe in the 1970s, Latin America, East Asia and Eastern Europe in the 1980s, the Soviet Union and South Africa in the 1990s) helped change that, giving new and wider meaning to citizenship in many more countries.

Still the rise of separatism and religious fundamentalism, the return of dictators to states that have briefly democratized, and the survival of dictatorships and one-party regimes in a number of other states, means that citizenship continues to be confined, restricted and derogated in important ways.

In the USA, for example, citizenship has been denied to many people on the basis of property, place of birth, gender (women could not vote until 1920 or fight in the army until

1949), race (black slaves were deprived of citizenship and African-Americans long denied many rights; American Indians placed under military and civil authority), age (minors under the age of 21 and then 18 were denied the right to vote or represent themselves in court), mental or physical health (victims of some diseases – TB and more recently AIDS – were denied entry), criminal record (felons forfeit their citizenship), reading ability (literacy tests excluded many potential voters), political affiliation (anarchists and communists were deported or denied entry), and refugee status (émigrés from communist countries could apply for political asylum, but other political or economic refugees could not).

The conditions placed on citizenship in different countries (most countries place even more restrictions than the USA) create resident groups that have a very different social, legal, economic and political status. In the modern world, there are generally three groups: citizens, denizens and subjects. In the USA, for example, European immigrants and their descendants possessed citizenship, a large and growing set of rights and responsibilities. Resident and illegal aliens, minors and, for a long time, women, possessed some but not all of these rights as 'denizens', while convicts, the mentally ill and, for a long time, slaves and Indians were treated as 'subjects' of military and civil authority. In the nineteenth century, only a minority of the population could claim citizenship, while a majority of residents were treated either as denizens or subjects. But during the nineteenth and twentieth centuries, a majority of residents acquired citizenship, reducing the population of 'denizens' and 'subjects' to a temporary or residual minority.

During the last 200 years, social movements have long sought to extend and deepen the meaning of citizenship in their own countries, sometimes in other states as well. US sailors captured by the British during the American and French revolutionary wars refused to be impressed and serve in the British navy. Their decision to remain citizen-prisoners rather than serve as subject–sailors asserted a uniquely American and republican conception of citizenship and rejected British efforts to treat them as subjects. During the nineteenth century, suffrage and anti-slavery movements sought to extend citizenship and the franchise to property-less males, African-Americans and women. In the twentieth century, the civil rights movement struggled to reclaim rights lost during the Jim Crow period. This movement was accompanied and then followed by movements of students to lower the voting age, women to equalize the application of citizenship, and gays and lesbians to end the invidious treatment of some citizens.

In other countries, dissident movements in communist countries and 'intifadas' or uprisings by Arab-Palestinians in Israel's Occupied Territories and by blacks in South Africa were more recent efforts to give new and wider meaning to citizenship.

Many of the social movements seeking to broaden the meaning of citizenship often have a global dimension. The Red Cross, food aid groups like Oxfam, International Physicians for Social Responsibility, women's movements, environmental groups like Greenpeace, and human rights organizations like Amnesty International, all try to expand global citizenship in important ways. These contemporary movements have historical precedents in American and French republicans like Tom Paine, who promoted the idea of universal human rights and the concept of 'citizens of the world', and socialist internationals, which demanded greater economic and political rights for 'comrades' in colonial and metropolitan countries around the world.

Arrayed against many of these movements were social movements that actively tried to restrict and derogate the meaning of citizenship in their own and other countries.

In the nineteenth century, slave holders and their political allies sought to extend restrictions on citizenship to non-slave-holding states. After the Civil War, Ku Klux Klan and Jim Crow legislators moved to restrict the rights of freed slaves. Numerous groups tried periodically to restrict immigrants or curb the immigration of particular groups – and this tendency has recently resurfaced in English-only movements and anti-immigration groups, like the Federation for American Immigration Reform (FAIR).

In other countries, anti-immigration and anti-semitic movements have also emerged periodically to restrict citizenship or, in the case of fascist movements, to extinguish it – a problem that has re-emerged among neo-Nazi movements in Europe today. Religious fundamentalist, communist and some separatist movements also promote restrictive conceptions of citizenship, though here it is important to note that some separatists would restrict it to members of particular ethnic groups while extending it to members of their own ethnic groups living outside the state; people who, strictly speaking, are foreigners, émigrés or even citizens of other states. So, for example, Baltic movements extended citizenship to ethnic Lithuanians living in Lithuania and in other countries, but denied it to resident Russians, Germans and Poles.

Social movements, which may be for or against an inclusive conception of citizenship, are not the only ones to shape the meaning of citizenship. Government officials also adopt policies that shape and alter its meaning, sometimes expanding it and sometimes retracting it.

In the USA, for example, government officials went to war in 1812 to prevent the impressment of its citizen-sailors, and intervened periodically to 'rescue' citizens from subjugation in foreign countries (from the shores of Tripoli to the Boxer Rebellion to the Mayaquez in Cambodia to Grenada). We may find these forcible military interventions/invasions objectionable. But we may find that the state's regular interventions on behalf of passport-carrying citizens through the extra-territorial embassy system and the diplomatic objections raised on their behalf (President Clinton's objection to the caning of an American teenager in Singapore), or on behalf of citizens from other countries (the condemnation of the *fatwa* issued on Salman Rushdie by the Iranian government), or whole groups (the Jackson-Vanik amendment insisting on greater Jewish immigration from the Soviet Union) are useful and necessary.

US officials extend the meaning of citizenship for prosaic and pragmatic reasons. They periodically open US doors to immigration to relieve labour shortages, and revise immigration laws to reunite families or to advance foreign policy goals. In 1965, for example, US officials ended anti-Asian exclusions in immigration law so that it could not be used in anti-American communist propaganda during the war in Vietnam, which was then expanding.

But while officials often extended the meaning of citizenship in the USA and around the world, they periodically restricted it, by tightening immigration laws, deporting or expelling political 'undesirables', imprisoning Japanese citizens during World War II, and supporting invidious laws adopted by state legislators (Jim Crow, English-only laws). Sometimes they do both simultaneously: NAFTA extends greater rights to professional workers moving to or residing in the USA, Canada and Mexico, but reiterates restrictions on the transnational rights of unskilled immigrant workers.

If one looks at the historical record, three general lessons can be drawn. First, the meaning of citizenship has been broadened and deepened when social movements demand it, either through peaceful methods (women's suffrage, civil rights, dissident, environmental and human rights movements), or violent means (intifadas in the Occupied Territories and South Africa).

Second, movements that seek to expand citizenship are usually more effective during periods of economic expansion and labour shortages than during times of economic crisis and high unemployment. It is during the latter periods when social movements that would restrict citizenship are more popular and effective.

Third, citizenship is generally extended overseas when nation-state republics promote decolonization, democracy and an end to dictatorship. The USA, for example, has not frequently promoted an altruistic, republican foreign policy, but it has done so periodically: after World War II during the period of decolonization and again in the 1970s and 1980s during the democratization of capitalist and communist dictatorships in many parts of the world. Why they have done so is a complex issue, which is beyond the scope of this paper, but it is largely a product of attempts to solve US economic problems (to open markets to US goods in the 1950s, to ensure repayment of US loans to Latin America during the 1980s).

THE IDEA OF THE 'CIVIL SOCIETY'

In the light of circumstances that accompanied the broadening and deepening of the concept of citizenship and those that reflected attempts to restrict it, another, apparently closely related concept emerges, namely the concept of a 'civil society'. Indeed, both the concept of a broadening and deepening citizenship and the ideal of a civil society are based on the principle of *inclusion*, whereas attempts to restrict citizenship and conceptions of society, as characterized by preoccupation with conflicts fuelled by competition or struggle for power (the antithesis of the civil society), are associated with preoccupation with *exclusion*. An especially enlightening definition of a civil society was given by Vaclav Havel:

> The perspective of a better future depends on something like an international community of citizens which, ignoring the state boundaries, political systems and blocs, standing outside the high game of traditional politics, aspiring to no titles and appointments, will seek to make a real political force out of a phenomenon so ridiculed by the technicians of power – the phenomenon of human conscience.[1]

Forms and Actors of Civil Society

The commonly accepted approach to strengthening and structuring civil society usually relates these processes to the establishment of various forms of NGO's and associations. This approach seems justified. However, it is fraught with some danger of being subverted by the circumstance that some of the so-called NGO's were created at the initiative from above rather than from below and so represent the same old structures disguised under new names. To identify the genuine NGO's and to distinguish them from the artificial ones is not easy, especially from the outside of a given society. Much preliminary work must be done collecting objective information. Obviously, such activities would differ from the techniques of seeking scientific and other professional contacts, these being facilitated by the possibility of merely evaluating CVs or lists of publication, on the basis of which choices can be made. In the more delicate sphere of seeking NGO partners, utmost discretion is necessary and personal communication at times seems indispensable in establishing fruitful partnership.   Otherwise, as has not infrequently turned out, support could be not only sterile but actually counterproductive.

Although NGO's are of utmost importance for joining people and strengthening their capacities to participate actively in social and political life, they are not the only way of getting people engaged in something broader than their personal lives. Voices of individuals not belonging to any organization or movement should also be taken into account. For this, even large scale sociological polls, though, of course, not sufficient for developing a sense of overall political responsibility, might bring some positive results. Time and again, through participation in these and other forms of studying public opinion, people become aware that their views and longings are appreciated, or at least interesting to someone. On many occasions the respondent encounters such interest for the first time in his or her life. As to the intellectual elite, especially those with high professional rating, more sophisticated ways of getting them engaged in public affairs need to be invented. Such people often take the part of informal leaders of certain groups, and their arrogant detachment from and proclaimed non-involvement in 'dirty political games' appears like a luxury which society can no longer afford, especially during critical periods.

Independent Expertise for State and Other Officials

Reports, releases, reviews and other forms of presentation by independent experts should be submitted to the wide public independently from their institutions or governments, whose established positions are usually determined by pressures exerted by narrow, egoistic interests. Subsequent governmental and interstate negotiations may benefit from such information exchanges.   Contributions from researchers, scholars and independent experts should be encouraged and appreciated, especially in the preparatory stage.

An impressive example of such a contribution is the excellent report, *The Crimean Tartars* by Andrew Wilson, Senior Research Fellow at Cambridge. This case study was requested by International Alert. Background information was collected from numerous and diverse sources with active assistance of NGO's and informal groups from both Ukraine and Crimea. Ukrainian authorities, influential politicians of many countries, international NGO's concerned with human and minority rights protection, have received copies of this report, and many seemed impressed. It seems that this report, supplemented by many other appeals, eventually moved the UN office in Ukraine to work out a project entitled *Repatriation, Resettlement and Reintegration into Crimean Society of the Deported Tartar Nation.* The project is to be completed by 1999. In case of successful realization, it will be a conspicuous example of *peaceful* international cooperation (in contrast to military interventions), in which civil society activists are taking not the least part. It is just this kind of international cooperation that might be able to address some critical issues viewed as 'domestic' problems of particular states. It provides leverage for confronting such views by a broader notion of what is a matter of general concern based on shared perception of justice, compassion and solidarity.

THE EVOLUTION OF THE NATION STATE

It appears that a major obstacle in the way of continually deepening the meaning of citizenship and extending it to ever broader categories of human beings is the notion of sovereignty as the foundation of a political body commonly called the nation state. On the other hand, it was the institution roughly identified as the 'nation state' that provided the main impetus to broadening and deepening the concept of citizenship. In assessing this dual role, we will briefly review the evolution of the concept of the nation state.

The Nation State as an Actor

It is customary to associate the emergence of the nation state with the Treaty of Westphalia at the close of the Thirty Years' War, specifically with the provision of the treaty that left the establishment of state religions to the princes of the respective domains.

From the evolutionary perspective the nation state appears as a stage in progressive growth of units representing social-political integration of human populations – from kinship groups, to clans, to tribes, to chiefdoms, to states or conglomerates of states (empires or allied blocs).

Of course, states and empires existed long before 1648, but what makes the Treaty of Westphalia seem a significant watershed is that it conferred a *juridical* status on the system of political organization that we now call the nation state. It was the first explicit recognition of that system as an acting unit characterized by 'interests', and endowed with power enabling it to pursue them.   Subsequent treaties were based on that conception.   They spelled out the 'rights' and 'obligations' of states, laid the basis of 'international law', and thus reflected conceptions of what we now call the 'world order'.   The Congress of Vienna, the Treaty of Versailles, and the Charter of the United Nations appear as formulations of these conceptions.

These conceptions of a 'world order' are distinctly eurocentric, reflecting doubtless the dominant position of European states from the time of the Voyages of Discovery (that is, conquests on the global scale) to the end of World War I. They also underlie the standard paradigm of the branch of political science that deals with 'international relations'. H. Morgenthau, the author of the authoritative work on the subject, saw political science following in the footsteps of economics, that is, dealing with the sources, accumulation and distribution of power in the same way that economics deals with the sources, accumulation and distribution of wealth. As a result, the 'nation state' became the focus of mainstream conceptions of a 'world order'.

The Evolutionary Paradigm

This paradigm has a long history, being manifested already in

Heraclitus' notion of perpetual flux, coming to fruition in Lamarck's teleological formulation in the biological context and in Hegel's self-contemplating disembodied Idea. The decisive impetus to the scientific development of evolutionary theory was given by Darwin, who revealed natural selection based on adaptation to the environment as the driving force of evolution.

The impetus carried the idea of evolution beyond the biological context. Evidence of many evolutionary processes can be seen in any museum in the form of fossil records of tools, machines, weapons, clothing, and so on. Languages certainly evolve. Their evolution is represented as a 'tree' strikingly resembling the ancestral tree of life forms with its bifurcations into phyla, classes, genera, and so on.

The same branchings are revealed by historical linguistics. Evolution of languages suggests that clearly distinguishable evolutionary processes are not confined to material entities, for example, organisms or objects. Ways of thinking and patterns of behaviour also evolve and stages of this evolution can often be discerned. In particular, organizations, institutions and systems of belief evolve. In its most general context evolution manifests itself in the historical record of systems. A system can be defined as a portion of the world that remains recognizable as 'itself' in spite of far-reaching changes going on within it. In this sense an organism is a system. Every one of us is convinced of a continuous 'identity' in spite of the fact that our material constituents are constantly being replaced. The same can be said of organizations, institutions, and the like. These may 'live' for centuries continuing to be recognized as 'themselves', in spite of the fact that their constituents (for example, personnels) are continually replaced. In fact it is not only the personnels of institutions or organizations that are replaced. Their modes of 'behaviour', the functions they serve, their relations to other systems may all change in ways that would make them unrecognizable to people who knew them in bygone eras if they saw them today. Still, their continuity and the slowness of change make it appear that they are still the same 'systems', that is, entities that preserve their identity. The present role of the nation state and its possible fate in the foreseeable future can be examined from this perspective.

Throughout the period following the Thirty Years' War the boundaries of many European states by no means coincided with the boundaries of national entities, if by such entities we mean populations sharing a common language, traditions, historical memories, and the like. This was not true of the UK, of Austria-Hungary, of the Turkish Empire, of the Russian Empire. To this day two nationalities constitute Belgium and four Switzerland. On the other hand, populations sharing the German language, many cultural traditions, and historical memories were not united in a single state until the establishment of the German Empire in 1871. About the same time also the Italian nation state was established.

It is not easy to trace the origins of the idea of nationhood. Schiller and Shaw, in their plays about Joan of Arc, would have us believe that she was a genuine patriot in the modern nationalistic sense. If so, nationalism may have already crystallized in the fifteenth century. There is some evidence for this, since Shakespeare, who was centuries closer to Joan, portrayed fully-fledged English nationalism in his *Henry V*. Possibly the idea was dormant and came to fruition only in the wake of the French Revolution and the Napoleonic wars. From then on it became a major force in European history.

The Centripetal and Centrifugal Potentials of Nationalism

In assessing the role of the nation state in the increasingly interdependent world the two contradictory aspects of nationalism must be kept in mind, namely its centripetal and centrifugal potentials. As well, in European politics of the nineteenth century nationalism fed both the right and the left ends of the political spectrum. At first it expressed itself in the aborted revolution of 1848 in Germany when the liberals pressed for a union under a constitutional monarchy. Later it was the ideological prop of staunch conservatism nurtured as an antidote to Marxism. Today nationalism exhibits similar opposite tendencies. Comparatively recently 'nation building' was a principal item on the liberal agenda, conceived as a process facilitating 'development' of former colonial dependencies.

Today flare-ups of tribal violence appear at times as an insuperable barrier to this programme. After the break-up of the Soviet empire nationalism in the constituent republics has itself exhibited aspects of militant tribalism. During World War I 'self-determination' was the rallying watchword of democrats and anti-imperialists. Today the slogan portends to induce fractionation of states without perceivable limits. Each 'successful' break-up provides a stimulus for further break-ups. The fact that constituent nationalities of several European states are seldom confined to geographically contiguous regions precludes any satisfactory solution to the 'self-determination' problem.

It follows that the term 'nation state', as it is used in discussions of prospects of a viable world order (in which some people still believe), should not be understood as an ethnically homogenous state. States nearly (but not quite) homogenous in this sense do exist today, for example Japan or the Scandinavian countries. Their stability can be regarded as assured if only because neither the Ainu nor the Lapps are likely to demand self-determination. Most multi-ethnic states, however, are vulnerable to militant ethnic ambitions.

When the questions about the 'role of the nation state' in today's world are raised, what is usually meant is the state as it is presently juridically defined, for example, as a member of the United Nations. The term 'nation' is attached simply because the terms 'nation' and 'state' are frequently used interchangeably and this usage is traceable to the mode of formation of some major states. We have mentioned the militant unification of Germany and Italy under the banner of nationalism. In the USA and in the Russian empire, on the contrary, 'nationalism' was manifested in suppression of cultural identities, as in the melting pot policy in the former or forced russification in the latter.

Serious questions about the present and future roles of the nation state are suggested by perceived incompatibilities between the roles played by states, as they are presently constituted, and the formidable problems with which all of humanity is presently faced. It became necessary to examine contexts in which states as we know them came into being in order to assess their viability under conditions now coming into being.

The Evolution of Warfare in Eighteenth and Nineteenth Century Europe

The evolutionary perspective reveals viability as dependent on adaptation to environment. Conventional wisdom has it that the viability of a state depends on its power to resist encroachments from the outside and monopolization of power over its own population. Both availability of power and its monopolization define *sovereignty*. Originally 'sovereignty' referred to the authority of the monarch supposedly stemming from stewardship bestowed by God (the so-called 'divine right of kings'). Hence it was closely associated with 'legitimacy', usually based on descent. Apparently, the institution of absolute hereditary monarchy was well adapted to its social environment. It was the basis of the order that emerged in Europe after the authority of the established church was undermined following the decay of the feudal system.

If the notion of 'world order' were current in the second half of the seventeenth century, the political theorists of the day might have hailed the establishment of a 'New World Order' by the treaty that ended the Thirty Years' War. This 'new order' was reflected in the changed origins and character of European warfare. Indeed, wars between feudal barons of the Middle Ages and religious wars associated with the Reformation were supplanted by warfare instigated by issues of 'legitimacy' reflected in the names given to the so-called 'cabinet wars' of the eighteenth century: the War of the Spanish Succession, the War of the Austrian Succession, the War of the Bavarian Succession, the War of the Polish Succession.

Also the nature of warfare in eighteenth century Europe changed, as it adapted to the predominant structure of the military establishments. Wars were fought predominantly by standing armies at the disposal of the monarchs. Long periods of service made possible large investments in elaborate training. Military expertise was a matter of mastering principles of battle tactics formalized as foundations of 'military science'. This was the business of the commanders. The business of the rank and file was the acquisition of rigidly fixed reflexes to standardized commands. The large investments in training made the armies expensive instruments, unlike the 'citizen' armies prevalent in the nineteenth century. After Napoleon lost his army in the Russian campaign, he could raise another within a few months. His armies consisted of recruits. A highly trained professional standing army could not be so easily replaced. For this reason European wars in the eighteenth century were less ferocious than either the Thirty Years' War that preceded them or the Napoleonic wars that followed.

Another reason why eighteenth century warfare was comparatively restrained was that it was not fuelled by 'patriotism', a prominent component of war characterizing the 'New World Order' ushered in by the French Revolution. In eighteenth century Europe it was as common for a general to leave the service of one sovereign to enter another's, as it is today for a professional baseball player to leave one team to join another, or for a chief executive of a corporation to change jobs. 'Patriotism' not only restricted this practice but also changed the nature of warfare. The eighteenth century soldier, frequently a mercenary, did not need to know what he was fighting for. Often he did not even know whom he was fighting. His training made him an automaton responding with standardized movements to barked commands. For this reason battles were fought in closed formations and resembled parade ground exercises. There was neither time nor necessity to train the 'citizen' soldier in this way. He was expendable and his effectiveness depended on motivation. The motivation was fuelled by the newly emerging fervour of patriotism originally linked to the defence of the Revolution against the intervention of the monarchies, later to the defence of one's country against French imperialism. It was Clausewitz, the outstanding 'philosopher of war', who recognized the profound change in the nature of warfare and spelled out the decisive role of 'morale'. In other words, the institution of war 're-adapted' itself to the world order ushered in by blows dealt to absolute monarchy following the French Revolution. In this way the institution of war fused the integrative aspects of patriotism (affection towards compatriots, loyalty, appreciation of cultural treasures) with their obverse (xenophobia, chauvinism, racism). Whatever may have been the true driving forces in World War I, the fervour of the fighting men, without which that war could not be fought, stemmed from this 'malignant' variant of patriotism that is now widely associated with nationalism.

Survival of Fixation on the Nation State

It seemed to some at the close of World War I that the trauma of the blood-letting portended eventual crumbling of we-they dichotomies based on pugnacious patriotism. Both in social criticism and in literature its rhetoric was attacked as hypocritical demagogy. In particular, among Western liberals the idea was expressed here and there that eventually Ethnic Man would become Economic Man. In the state that emerged from the Russian Revolution official ideology proclaimed that the problem of nationalities in the defunct Russian Empire was solved: Ethnic Man would become Soviet Man and presumably, following the victory of the proletarian revolution, Global Man. Nevertheless, the idea that the sovereign nation state is the most viable and reality-oriented form of social organization survived.

In the light of the evolutionary perspective this conception appears distinctly eurocentric. In view of the dominance of European states in world affairs for the past five centuries this is not surprising. The influence stems in the first instance from superior military power based on rapid advances of technology, which was in turn generated by the rapid and organized advances in science. During the nineteenth century the power of European states, conferred by military might and wielded through both political and economic institutions, was extended over most of the planet. Another source of influence is ideological and appears to stem from a critical attitude towards power embodied in liberalism and conceptions of democracy, ideas spawned by eighteenth century Enlightenment. It was these ideas that were formulated in the explicit descriptions of a 'world order' embodied in the Charter of the League of Nations, where the 'world' was still identified with the industrialized states, and their role as 'custodians' of the rest of the world was taken for granted. The ideas survived in the Charter of the United Nations, which envisaged the same 'world order' this time based on 'equality of states large and small'.

The format of the United Nations Charter is that of a world constitution. Like any national constitution it defines the rights and obligations of its constituencies. These are explicitly identified as 'nation states' (referred to as members) in the juridical sense of the term. To be sure human individuals are also mentioned as the constituency but only in the preamble:

> We, the peoples of the United Nations, determined to save succeeding generations from the scourge of war . . . and to affirm our faith in fundamental human rights, in the dignity and worth of the human person, in the equal rights of men and women and of nations large and small . . . have resolved to combine our efforts to accomplish these ends.

Note the commitment both to equality of persons and equality of states. The implication is that human rights and rights of states 'large and small' are compatible. But are they? Clearly, the doctrine of so-called 'natural rights' notwithstanding, rights exist only to the extent that they are perceived and claimed as such. In the case of persons they are embodied in perceptions of 'security', which is identified by the overwhelming majority of human beings with the absence of threats, in particular the threats of destitution, of disease, and of violence. On the level of the state, 'security' is also identified with the absence of threats or with the ability to deal with them. But those are threats of a different kind, namely threats of being attacked by other states or threats of subversion from within. More generally, threats perceived by states, especially the powerful ones, are encroachments on their sovereignty or their so-called 'national interests' (as defined by their power elites). The traditional way of dealing with these threats is by maintaining a military potential. But the military potential of one state is frequently regarded as a threat by another. So-called 'balance of power', or credible 'deterrence', has been frequently advanced as a solution to this dilemma, but the supporting arguments are based on formalistic assumptions rather than on concrete historical

experience.   In actual fact, both 'balance of power' and
'deterrence' often serve as buzz words to rationalize arms races
or the burgeoning world arms trade, which aggravate rather than
remove threats to security, as it is understood by the
overwhelming majority of people. Moreover, powerful military
establishments of small states are often no more than self-serving
enclaves of privilege or instruments of subjugation and
terrorization of populations or both.

Evolution of War as an Institution

Institutions, as well as biological species, artifacts, religions, and
so on, evolve.   Those that fail to adapt to their changing
environment – physical, biological or social – become extinct.
Chattel slavery, the Holy Inquisition, duelling, come to mind.
One would think that war had also become an institution of this
sort.   However, war has demonstrated remarkable facility of
adaptation to a great variety of social and ideational
environments. At the time when nomadic tribes were aspiring to
settled life and were looking for land, warfare was genocidal as
is evidenced by accounts in the *Old Testament*. When the scale
of agriculture increased in the Middle East, where scanty
precipitation made artificial irrigation necessary, demand for
massive supply of labour arose and with it the institution of
slavery.   Conquered populations were enslaved instead of
massacred. In the age of the great ancient empires new methods
of exploitation of conquered populations developed, for example,
taxation rather than enslavement. Both methods of warfare and
war aims were adapted to the new political needs. We have seen
how in eighteenth century Europe methods of warfare and war
aims were adapted to the 'new order' dominated by absolute
hereditary monarchy.   In 1795 Kant argued that war would
become obsolete together with monarchy. However, European
warfare became rapidly adapted to a new factor in mass
psychology, namely patriotism, identification of self with
nationality.   Militarism and nationalism marked the prevalent
European ideology throughout the nineteenth century reaching the
height of intensity in World War I.
    The latest adaptation of the institution of war to a rapidly

changing social environment was manifested in the USA, which had no militaristic tradition. That country emerged from World War II unscathed. Moreover, the rapid development of a war economy put an end to depression and remained the main stimulant to economic growth. In this case the war system became adapted not to a new basis of a we-they dichotomy (that emerged in the wake of European nationalism) but to a more pervasive feature of the American character, namely technolatry (worship of technology). While in Germany and France patriotic fervour was regarded as the ingredient of victory in World War I, in America it was technical know-how, manifested in unprecedented production volumes in both world wars and in 'high tech' virtuosity throughout the Cold War.

The nation state and war illustrate the principle of reciprocal adaptation. The state as an institution has adapted itself to war as an institution, and vice versa. It is regarded as axiomatic that the autonomy of a state is secured by its sovereignty, and sovereignty by its war potential. Thus, a war establishment is universally held to be an indispensable institution in practically every state. Conversely, the viability of a war establishment (which in many states is itself an autonomous body with its own self-centred agenda of robustness and growth) depends on the sovereignty of the state which frees it from responsibility to any higher level of organization. Witness the rapid militarization of the newly hatched states of the Third World, infected with the superstition that identifies both security and prestige with destructive potential; and note the exploitation of this superstition by the militarized states of the affluent world.

It seems, therefore, that the survival prospects of the institution of war, on the one hand, and of the nation state as we know it, on the other, are closely related.

The Nation State as Janus

In sum, as a phase in the evolution of social-political organization the nation state exhibits two faces – one towards its internal environment, one towards the external. In relation to its internal environment the nation state has been a pacifying influence mainly by monopolizing coercive power. Frequently, however, the formation of nation states was stimulated by perception of common enemies. As tribal warfare subsided, international warfare became institutionalized. The bipolar world, a product of the Cold War, while 'integrating' each bloc, brought humanity to the brink of destruction.

THE 'NEW WORLD ORDER' STILL-BORN

In the West the break-up of the Soviet Empire was hailed both by the political Right and the political Left. The former advertised it as a triumph of Free Enterprise, the Market, and so on; the latter as a giant step towards integration of humanity portending the 'peace dividend', turning attention to the common problems of humankind, flourishing of 'civil society', and so on. While the Right still basks in the glow of 'victory', the Left has suffered brutal disillusionment. We believe we are witnessing the pernicious effects of state power even when it disintegrates, as the restraints it had imposed on internal violence vanish but the identification of autonomy with power and dominance persists.

With the demise of Communism, nationalism in its most aggressive form emerged in the republics of the former Soviet Union and exploded into bitter wars. These were fuelled by: (1) migration, which has caused some nationalities to become minorities in their own lands; (2) the use of vitriolic nationalism as a tool in the power question of ethno-politicians; (3) understandable but deplorable effervescence of separatist movements.

The same factors comprised the conflagration in former Yugoslavia. Here, too, vitriolic nationalism arose on the ruins of the Communist state. It is noteworthy that it is precisely the welding of the nationalist idea with the notion of sovereignty as an undisputed right to make war that nurtures the effects obstructing the development of world citizenship.

The explosion of lethal tribalism throughout the Third World also fits into this picture.

The Epidemic of Violence

The destructive components of nationalism or tribalism, its primitive form, in their most aggressive manifestation provide rationalization of seeing others through the prism of an unbridgeable we-they dichotomy. This is what we observe today as consequences of the break-up of multi-national states and the disintegration of colonial authorities. In the last decade of our century nationalism must be acknowledged as a state of mind that denies common humanity. The collective group is prone to embrace hatred as its moulding link when the group has been exposed to humiliating experiences that have been perceived as injuries to the identity of the group. For example, during Soviet occupation Moldavians had to write their Romanian language in the cyrillic alphabet. Now that Moldavia has become a 'sovereign state', its Russian inhabitants are afraid that they will have to write Russian in the Latin alphabet.

Wars, victories, defeats, catastrophes, pogroms and hunger, in contrast to quiescent events, are embraced in our memory boxes as 'peak affective states'. These become seminal in moulding a group's perception of its role, its self-perception and its position in the world. Memories during 'peak affective states' skew reality and force assessment into primitive dichotomies – all good or all bad. The 'bad' object is both needed and desired.[2] This need and desire becomes a sure stepping stone towards dehumanization.

Dehumanization has been defined as 'a defence against painful or overwhelming emotions which decrease a person's sense of one's own individuality and perception of the humaneness of other people'.[3] The collective self under the impact of hatred perceives the 'bad' others as though they were vermin or inanimate dispensable objects.

Collective group hatred leads to violence in its need to destroy the needed object. The enemy is usually the one who is both wanted and needed, and seems to be needed for affirmation of one's identity. For example, Ukrainians seem to need Russians for their affirmation of identity, and Russians need Ukrainians for the same purpose. Cossacks are a source of negative identity to Jews and a positive identity to Ukrainians. In this way collective group hatred becomes a most successful and handy tool in the hands of political arsonists.

Bloodletting in Somalia and Rwanda can be ascribed to the same sudden disintegration of power which had constrained intergroup violence by its own monopoly of violence – the essence of the nation state.

Global Military Machine Still in Place

The evil legacy of the nation state is the pervasive identification of security with military potential. This legacy is not confined to the pervasive idea that the security of a state, culture, or way of life means the ability to repel armed attack with armed force. Even as the concrete military threat from a designated enemy disappears, the military establishment remains. The very semantics of the word 'defence' makes the dismantling of the military machine unthinkable, since it would make the country 'defenceless'. All ministries of war have become ministries of 'defence', and all war spending is invariably called 'defence' spending.

It is instructive to compare the global armament levels and 'defence' spending before and after the end of the Cold War which fuelled the arms race. The number of nuclear warheads, a good indicator, was about 70,000. At the end of START II in 2003, the number of strategic weapons is to be reduced to about 6000, or to about 15,000 if tactical weapons are to be included.[4] Aside from the fact, however, that the reduced number still represents a threat of total destruction of civilization, the agreed upon timescale (ten years) is ten to twenty times longer than necessary. The reduction could be accomplished in a few months by deactivating delivery systems and separating the warheads which could then be stored under multilateral control. Arguments against this procedure are based on the inviolate identification of destructive power with 'security'.

Global 'defence' expenditure, which peaked at $1.2 trillion in 1988, has been reduced by about one-third. The saving of $400 million is substantial and could be put to excellent use.

However, the damage of 'security=defence spending' mentality was not confined to the waste of funds. It entailed also diversion of human resources into 'defence'-related employments. Consequently, reduction of 'defence' spending entails decline of employment and of economic activity generally, and is for this reason vigorously resisted not only by the military-industrial-scientific complex establishment but by large sections of the general population. Thus, addiction to violence spiked by burgeoning killing technology is not the only evil legacy of the militarized nation state. It involves also an addiction to a war economy, identification of preparations for war with economic robustness, full employment, and so on.

WHAT SORT OF 'WORLD ORDER' IS LIKELY TO EMERGE?

Prospects for further broadening and deepening of citizenship clearly depend on the sort of 'world order' likely to emerge in the wake of radical transformations resulting from the end of the Cold War.

Political predictions are usually formulated in vague temporal language, like 'in the foreseeable future', 'over the coming decades', and so on. Paul Kennedy stresses in his book a range of 'about thirty years . . . in discussing either transnational trends or a particular region's prospects'.[5] On the basis of the events related to the emergence of a 'new world order' the following scenarios have been more or less explicitly projected: (1) a cooperative global society with a true world citizenship, universally transparent borders, respect for human rights, shared responsibilities and even with something that can be called a world government; (2) a somewhat less ambitious ideal of a closely united political bloc from Vancouver to Vladivostock, assuming a diminishing impact of the demise of Communism on the countries of the Soviet Union; (3) a disintegrationist scenario assuming that after the loss of a common enemy the West will plunge into trade wars as the interests of states like Germany, France, or the USA increasingly diverge; (4) the Western Fortress.

The last named, probably the most unfavourable to the development of the above-mentioned civil society and its universalistic goal, seems, unfortunately, at least to some, the most realistic in view of the developing course of events.

The Western Fortress

The term refers to a closely united political bloc, the core of which is formed by the advanced democratic capitalist nations of Europe and North America. The member states of this bloc will gradually dismantle interstate borders between themselves and hand more and more of their sovereign rights over to supranational bodies. The citizens of those member states will probably have common passports, will easily get permanent residency and welfare or voting rights on each other's territory. At the same time the bloc will appear as a fortress to the populations of the poorer countries in the East and South: its legislation will be toughened to keep the immigrants from the poor countries out. As during the Cold War, this bloc of Western nations will pursue a common defence policy and will move closer together along the lines of economic integration, possibly introducing a common currency. They will share basically the same understanding of human rights, representative democracy, and so on.

To sum up, the distinctive feature of the Western Fortress will be a certain opposition towards the rest of the world. There will be a basic contradiction in its construction, in that capital flows, communications and so on will move towards rapid integration with the rest of the world, while in immigration policy it will disengage itself from the other parts of the globe.

Russia's Reversion to Authoritarianism

A likely concomitant of the Western Fortress would be a return to an authoritarian regime in Russia. As the social difficulties of post-Communist capitalist transition started to mount (victimizing especially pensioners, peasants, intellectuals, and so on), the new post-Communist governments plunged into unprecedented degrees of corruption, and the societies became dominated by organized crime. The support for reform began to erode, leading to spectacular victories of blocs led by the Communist-era Communist officials, economic managers and political officials. Perhaps Poland, Lithuania and Hungary are the clearest examples of such electoral fluctuations. They are not especially threatening to young democracies, since all (even former Communist) parties and movements in those countries are generally playing within the democratic rules.[6] But the imminent threat to democracy arises when the cycle of disappointment with Western-style democracy and market economy coincides with some specific conditions that seem to be most vividly present in Russia. If democracy will not survive in Russia it will be threatened also in other post-Communist states regardless of their domestic dynamics.[7]

The likelihood of return to authoritarianism in Russia is favoured by several factors. First, Russia is too big to be helped or decisively influenced from outside – the transition will be shaped by domestic circumstances.[8] Second, Russia has a long historic tradition of non-democratic rule, which makes return to authoritarianism easier. Third, since Russia was the dominant nation in the Soviet bloc, Russian radical nationalism is strongly anti-Western, anti-capitalist and nostalgic about the imperial past.[9] It is next to impossible to mobilize Russians for painful pro-market sacrifices under nationalist banners, which means that the pro-Western function of the strongest ideological myth of the post-Communist society is somehow lost. The Russian nationalists seem increasingly dedicated to restoring at least part of the lost empire, which will further jeopardize the prospects for democracy, since Russia can be either an empire or a democracy – it cannot be both.[10]

It seems likely that most of the CIS countries may be willing (or forced) to move towards greater integration with Moscow, either because of economic dependency on Russia, or because it seems to them the only way out of civil wars. A more assertive Russia may also use its 'peace-keeping' forces to curb the post-Communist ethnic or interstate violence against the will of the local concerned governments or the major Western powers, which will unleash cycles of a new Cold War and push the Western countries towards more speedy integration among themselves. The episodes of the new Cold War will probably confirm the point that when history repeats itself, it is a tragedy the first time and a farce the second.

The Impact of American Relative Decline

The relative decline of the USA will probably contribute to the formation of the Western Fortress, especially in the sense of toughening the immigration policies of the rich countries. It is by now a part of common knowledge everywhere that there is a debate between American 'declinists' and 'revivalists'. Revivalists like Joseph Nye have stressed that 'to describe the problem as American decline is misleading . . . The United States remains the largest and richest power with the greatest capacity to shape the future. And in a democracy, the choices are the people's'.[11]   According to Paul Kennedy, however, the 'only answer' to the question whether the USA can preserve its existing position is 'no'.[12]

Even a marginal American decline, however, may have an interesting effect on the formation of the Western Fortress. The USA has been long perceived by the outside world as a noble experiment in racial and ethnic tolerance and integration. Furthermore, the perception has been that while the USA welcomes immigrants, its own rational, universalistic democratic culture somehow dominates over particular cultures that immigrants bring with them.   Consequently, the image of American decline – even if exaggerated – will convey a message of declining vigour of an immigrant-friendly, open, multi-ethnic society, which has tried honestly to accommodate increasing waves of immigrants from the poorer countries. This negative message may be a signal to other rich countries that US-type tolerance in accepting immigrants from the poorer countries may not be any longer a necessary condition for a successful economic development.

IS THERE STILL HOPE FOR INTEGRATION
OF HUMANITY?

How realistic is the most optimistic prognosis – that of global integration? No answer can be given on objective grounds. A prognosis of this sort is not like a prognosis of weather, where realization or non-realization is wholly independent of what is predicted. Predictions of events shaped by human behaviour have a strong self-realizing or self-negating component. It is not foolhardy to say that if enough people believe in the inevitability of global integration, it will become inevitable. However, the spread of this belief, itself a self-perpetuating process, strongly depends on the level of consciousness of the present and future generations. This, in turn, depends on the recognition of concrete obstacles as well as facilitating factors. We have emphasized the impeding role of the nation state stemming from its tight connection to the institution of war and consequent generation of hatred and violence in times of crisis, both when it commands the loyalty of its citizens, as in inter-state wars, and when it loses it, as in civil wars and revolutions. Let us now look at the positive role that the nation state could play in the process of global integration, which may still proceed in spite of obstacles and set-backs.

Limitation of State Sovereignty

The nation state could become a link in the chain of integrated humanity if its consolidating function were retained and its divisive effect eliminated. This could happen only if the most important aspect of state sovereignty were eliminated, namely, the right and the ability to make war. The problem is to separate both conceptually and concretely sovereignty from autonomy. Sovereignty of an actor (whether an individual or an institution) implies the absence of an authority to which the actor is responsible or else removing such an authority from the realm of the observable, for example, vesting it in a deity (recall the divine right of kings). Autonomy entails *delineating* the range of contexts in which the actor (again either an individual or an institution) is not controlled by an external authority. Ideally, the boundaries of autonomy are defined by the range of actions which have no discernible adverse effects on other actors or on systems in which the actor in question is embedded. This principle governing the limits of autonomy can be formulated in terms of determining optimal levels of decision-making.

J. Tinbergen defined the optimal level of decision making as '(a) . . . the lowest possible level in order that a maximum level of participation and maximum level of information be used, and (b) the level high enough to entail negligible external effects'.[13]

The same principle safeguards the autonomy of individuals in matters that do not jeopardize the autonomy of other individuals as well as the autonomy of larger units. The principle essentially spells out the criteria of democracy, a conception of a social-political organization in which aspirations to freedom and imperatives of responsibility are reconciled.

The role of the nation state as a *pragmatically* determined level of decision-making in a globally integrated humanity suggests a resolution of the dilemma posed by the contradiction between its integrating and its divisive functions. Sovereignty would be replaced by autonomy, that is, independence in specific spheres circumscribed by responsibility to higher levels of organization. If the institution of war atrophies (assuming that only then can a viable highly interdependent humanity be envisaged), 'defence' dependent on possessing state-of-the-art destructive power would no longer be a prerogative of the nation state. As a matter of fact, the only justifiable coercive power on the world scale would be vested in a sort of a police force responsible to a global authority. One of the functions of this coercive power would be to enforce human rights. Immunity from such enforcement is presently routinely rationalized as an adjunct of state sovereignty. This was amply demonstrated by the dogged resistance of the Soviet Union and now of China to broaden and deepen the concept of citizenship within their borders.

Positive Features of Patriotism

The positive features of patriotism are worth preserving, if ways can be found to neutralize its pernicious 'side effects'. On the one hand, patriotism (loyalty to the nation state) rallied populations to prodigious collective efforts, submerging personal and parochial interests in serving what appeared as collective good. On the other hand, the same sentiments induced murderous frenzy that dominated at least European international politics for at least a century and a half. Moreover, patriotism, as it was inculcated through educational institutions, the media, and so on, was intended to induce loyalty to the state rather than a 'nation' defined by commonality of language, traditions, and so on. As we have seen, the term 'nation state' is a misnomer when applied to the large multinational states of Europe. The term was retained in this chapter in its purely juridical sense.

In the juridical definition of the nation state the limits of its autonomy can be concretely specified. By emphasizing the cooperative aspects of this autonomy and restricting the divisive aspects, the nation state could become a link in a system of concentric loyalties based on an expanding sense of identity. Optimistic views of human nature, such as those of A. Maslow or L. Kohlberg, imply, especially in Kohlberg's treatment, such a concentric sequence. At the centre is the Self, the sense of identity protected by instinctual survival mechanisms. Surrounding that is the circle of persons on whom the individual directly depended for survival in infancy and towards whom he or she normally develops strong attachments, usually a family; beyond that the peer group, the community, the society or culture, finally humanity. Kohlberg pictures identification of the individual with humanity, that is, internalizing general human values, which take precedence over narrower ones, as the final stage of maturation.

An optimistic view of the human condition could be based on the assumption that 'maturation' of humanity is manifested in a similar process (a sort of converse analogue of ontogeny recapitulating phylogeny). This loyalty to the nation state (patriotism) would appear as an intermediate stage in the evolution of a globally integrated culture driven by increasing interdependence.

The nation state could play this role if its purely juridical aspect were emphasized in education and in conflicts arising in global politics. The reason for this is that juridical definitions of autonomy, liberties, responsibilities, and so on, can be regarded as matters of agreement rather than reflections of divine purpose, or the 'nature of things', or 'self-evident truths'. The former interpretations of legitimacy emphasize a cooperative orientation, the latter inevitably generate conflict. Examples of providential or 'natural' interpretations of bases of identification are pernicious racist and fundamentalist doctrines. For this reason it is highly desirable to remove all references to ethnicity, race or religion from the notion of citizenship, that is, the status of 'belonging' to a nation state. Juridically a nation state can be defined as a territory established by well marked boundaries, where citizenship is co-extensive with more or less permanent residence.

Much has been said and written about the artificiality of the present boundaries of states, especially in Africa, where they were established by colonial powers and bear no relation to essentially tribal identifications of the inhabitants. Such discrepancies (with ethnicity playing the part of tribalism) characterized also the formation of European states and empires. They were one of the instigating factors of World War I. Today artificial state boundaries fuel the horrendous outbursts of violence not only in Africa but also in Europe since the break-up of the Soviet Union and Yugoslavia.

It is increasingly evident that attempts to stem this violence by applying some principle of 'self determination' must fail. In Europe, especially, ethnic and religious groups are virtually 'dissolved' throughout the continent. Attempts to legitimize states on the basis of ethnic or religious homogeneity now manifest themselves as barbaric orgies of ethnic cleansing, as in former Yugoslavia, or in fundamentalist tyranny, as in Iran or Saudi Arabia. Defining states geographically seems to be a promising way out of this impasse. Of course, getting people to identify with each other and to cooperate simply because they live in relative proximity may require a great deal of effort. But so does every other attempt to link increasing interdependence of human beings with progressive integration of humanity. Here and there policies attenuating the divisive aspects of religion and ethnicity have been relatively successful, for example, in North America. This is not to say that religious prejudices or ethnic enmities do not exist in the USA or in Canada. But the fact that they are publicly disapproved and juridically proscribed has vastly improved the quality of life in those countries. Violent religious and ethnic strife has flared up in Europe, but the very anguish it induced in world public opinion speaks for at least a partial success in attenuating these bases of 'we-they' dichotomies on that continent.

In sum, the idea of basing a nation state on ethnic or religious homogeneity is not realizable. Attempts to do so only aggravate violence and sow seeds of future violence. There is much to be said for the principle of inviolability of established state boundaries. This is not to say that these boundaries are either 'natural' or 'just' but only that unlike other criteria they are clear and do not invoke a specific ideology to justify themselves, except an ideology that fosters habits of tolerance and civility to one's neighbours. Therefore, boundaries defined juridically by broad applications of a status quo principle would probably minimize the potential for violent strife or enhance the potential of adjudication in case of disputes.

Of course, this inviolability refers only to attempts to change boundaries by force. It does not preclude negotiations and changes by agreement. We have examples of both peaceful divisions of states (Sweden-Norway in 1905; Czechoslovakia in 1993) and peaceful mergers (FRG-GDR in 1990). In fact, if mechanisms of peaceful division are developed, we may see more instances of successful mergers (North and South Korea). Both division and mergers can serve to enhance a tendency of adjusting the level of decision-making to the level of participation and to the level of autonomy that does not encroach on the autonomy of others.

Then the entity that has come to be called (perhaps inappropriately) the 'nation state' will have become adapted to its (global) social environment marked by vastly increased interdependence and will, perhaps, survive as an institution. This conclusion stems from a tacit assumption that the global social environment that emerges from the present turmoil will itself be viable, which is by no means guaranteed, since increasing interdependence, as every other evolving feature of the human condition, is double-faced. It was increasing interdependence that turned initially local conflicts into world wars and threatened to do the same during the decades of the Cold War. It is interdependence that promotes new forms of imperialism (economic and cultural) and aggravates lopsided distributions of resources and power. But it is also vastly increased interdependence that brings home the imperatives of formulating and cooperatively solving global problems, and suggests pragmatically determined levels of decision-making, allotting to the nation state its proper place in a cooperatively organized humanity. The question concerning the role of the nation state in an increasingly interdependent world makes sense only if the latter potential is realized.

CONCLUDING REMARKS

To assess the role that the nation state can or should play in an increasingly interdependent world, we must first form a clear idea of what interdependence means. It means that all important problems with which humans are faced are now global problems. This is explicitly recognized in the realization that the security of a state *vis-à-vis* other states is a chimera. There is no such thing. The only security from violence on the level of states, that is, war, is the security of all. Neither 'balance of power' nor 'deterrence' can provide this security. Pursuit of 'balance of power' has consistently instigated arms races. Deterrence is predicated on the 'rationality' of the opponent and is regarded the more credible the more reckless is the deterring power. The idea of 'calculated risk' is an absurdity in this context, since no matter how small the probability of catastrophe is, its occurrence in the age of wars of total destruction makes all formal calculations of its 'probability' irrelevant.

Threats not yet imagined by the designers of a 'world order' at the close of World War II are now starkly apparent. They are generated by the rapidly accelerating degradation of the environment, which transcends all national boundaries. The consequences of this degradation may instigate struggles for arable land, or water or living space of the sort that fuelled the genocidal wars of antiquity. The ferocity of these struggles fought with weapons now developed can be readily imagined. It stands to reason that anticipating these threats and preparing to deal with them effectively requires globally integrated actions, which can be undertaken only if sovereignty of nation states as they are presently organized is drastically curtailed.

It follows that national sovereignty is an insuperable obstacle to the removal of threats to humanity that have had no precedents, namely, threats of irreversible destruction magnified beyond imagination by technology specifically developed for that purpose and threats to the very substrate of human life on this planet. A satisfactory solution to this dilemma is by no means guaranteed. It is predicated on the abrogation of sovereignty on any level below the global, which, in turn means either the demise of the nation state as an institution, or its adaptation to a new role in a hierarchy of authorities culminating in a global institution entrusted with seeking and implementing solutions of global problems.

The latter alternative seems more promising. There are indeed institutions that can no longer fit into the fabrics of more or less enlightened societies. Other institutions, however, have successfully adapted to a changed social environment and survived. An interesting example is the fate of a charitable foundation that helped unsuccessful American pioneers, people who trekked west in covered wagons and met with misfortune on the way. Survivors came back to St Louis broke. The foundation helped them to make a fresh start. The question naturally arises, what happened to this foundation? It is now Travellers Aid – a fitting successor. Other examples are the monarchies of northwestern Europe, which evolved into democracies more successfully than many republics by stripping the monarch of all political power, leaving him or her as only a symbol of the common history of a people.   In the same way military establishments may survive if they strip themselves of their mission of perpetrating violence, adopting instead a mission of promoting and preserving peace, helping victims of natural disasters, and the like.   In the same way the nation state may survive (may well *deserve* to survive) if it is divested of its sovereignty and turned into a pragmatically defined level of social organization deriving its efficacy from continuity of functions and established traditions.

Incorporated in this paper are reflections of other contributors to the discussion on the role of the nation state in an increasingly interdependent world during the Pugwash Workshop on **Social Tensions and Armed Conflict** *held in Pugwash, Nova Scotia in July 1994.   Specifically, the evolution of the concept of citizenship was discussed by Robert K Schaeffer of the USA, the role of NGO's in the building of a 'civil society' by Natalie Belitser of Ukraine, nationalism as a 'denial of common humanity' by Rita R Rogers of the USA, the possible emergence of a 'Western Fortress' by Andreas Park of Estonia.   Schaeffer, Belitser and Rogers saw the consolidated paper.   Park's deeply regretted death left me uncertain about whether I presented his ideas fairly, all the more so because I discussed them with him only cursorily at the conference.*

REFERENCES

1.   V. Havel, *Antipoliticka Politica*, 1984.

2.   O.F. Kernberg, 'The Psychopathology of Hatred', paper presented at *Symposium of Rage, Power and Aggression* sponsored by the Columbia University Center for Psychoanalytic Training and Research and the Association for Psychoanalytic Medicine, New York, 1989.

3.   V. Bernard, P. Ottenberg and F. Redel, 'Dehumanization: A Composite Psychosocial, Psychological Defense in Relation to Modern War', *Behavioural Science and Human Survival*, Science and Behavior Books, Inc, 1965, p.64.

4. J.B. Wiesner, P. Morrison and K. Tsipis, 'Ending Overkill', *Bulletin of the Atomic Scientists*, 49:2, March 1993, pp.12–23.

5. P. Kennedy, *Preparing for the Twenty First Century*, Random House: New York, 1993, p.19.

6. *Cf* A. Park, 'Turning Points in Post-Communist Transition: Lessons from the Case of Estonia', *Government and Opposition*, June 1994.

7. *Cf* A. Park, 'Ethnicity and Independence: The Case of Estonia in Comparative Perspective', *Europe-Asia Studies*, 46, 1, 1994, pp.69–87.

8. *Cf* Z. Brzezinski, *Out of Control: Global Turmoil on the Eve of the Twenty-First Century*, A Robert Stewart Book: New York, 1993, p.168.

9. *Cf* A. Park, 'Ideological Dimension of the Post-Communist Domestic Conflicts', *Communist and Post-Communist Studies*, 36:3, September 1993, p.268.

10. Z. Brzezinski, 'The Premature Partnership', *Foreign Affairs*, 72:2, March/April, 1994, p.72.

11. J.S. Nye, *Bound to Lead: The Changing Nature of American Power*, Basic Books: New York, 1990, pp.259–61.

12. P. Kennedy, *The Rise and Fall of the Great Powers*, Random House: New York, 1987, p.533.

13. *Cf* J. Tinbergen (coordinator), *Reshaping the World Order. A Report to the Club of Rome*, Hutchinson: London, 1977, ch.5.

5

'Quasi-Nations': The Scientific Community as a Component of a New World Order

Francesco Calogero

In the title of this chapter reference is made to the scientific community, but I have primarily in mind the segment of it that I know best and to which I belong, namely the community of theoretical physicists and mathematicians, and, more specifically, those of them who work on Non-linear Evolution Equations and Dynamical Systems (NEEDS). This community is reasonably well-defined; it includes persons who by and large know each other personally and/or through the scientific literature, and who, most importantly, share a common set of scientific interests and knowledge. It is a highly international community, with a substantial participation from the former Soviet Union, North America, Europe (East and West, North and South), Japan, China, India, Australia, South Africa, Latin America and indeed the entire world.

The fact that this community shares a common set of scientific interests and knowledge implies that they care for each other: they feel (more or less subliminally) that they are engaged in a common enterprise, namely the promotion of this research field and the enlargement of this body of knowledge; they know that the value of their findings – hence of the very work that is their main activity, in which they find both their professional self-esteem and the main source of life support for themselves and their families – depends essentially on the evaluation of their peers; and when, through their scientific interactions, they have gained an opportunity to actually meet (at international conferences and workshops, or through visiting appointments), they often become bonded by personal friendships which may also extend to their families.

Recently, an additional element of bonding has been provided by electronic mail, a fast and inexpensive means of communication widely used by this community, often across geopolitical boundaries which sometimes remain difficult to breach otherwise, both because of political difficulties (visa requirements, permissions to travel abroad, and so on) and – nowadays more significantly – because of the high cost of travel on a world scale compared to the present meagre resources available to support scientific interchanges (hopefully only a temporary slump, caused by the generally recessionary state of the economy, especially in the affluent societies of the 'West' where the main resources to support science now originate).

It is, moreover, clear that this community shares a common set of values, namely those associated with the correct, fair, 'honest' conduct of scientific research, and the respect and admiration for important scientific breakthroughs – which incidentally they, as a community, are the only ones capable of recognizing/defining. Of course, there also exists, within this same community, less positive behaviour: opportunism, various kinds of theft and cheating, and especially the formation of academic cliques established by individuals who support each other and bypass those fair standards of merit that should determine all decisions about individuals (appointments, invitations to lecture, and so on).

It should finally be noted that this community shares a common language, namely their scientific jargon (that they are uniquely capable of using and understanding), and also an English – often broken and generally elementary – which does however provide an effective vehicle of understandable written and oral communication.

It appears, therefore, that this community possesses many – perhaps all – of the features that are generally considered essential to characterize a *nation*. To be sure, they lack any territorial localization; but we know of course of other nations that lack such territorial identification. An important difference is, however, that while many of these other nations strive for such territorial grounding – and indeed such striving is one of the main causes of bloody conflicts in the present world – for the particular community we are talking about no such striving makes any sense. This observation – trivial as it certainly is – has an implication which perhaps merits pondering, for it suggests that – to the extent that such communities become relevant, indeed uppermost, in commanding a feeling of bonding, trust, loyalty, friendship among their members – they will make bloody conflicts associated with territorial claims less prevalent, provided that the number of individuals who partake in them becomes sufficiently large/influential to significantly affect policy on a world scale.

It is also of interest to emphasize that the community we have described is by no means conflict-free, either within itself, or with respect to other analogous communities. This is so obvious that there is no need to elaborate this point. Some – although certainly not all – of these conflicts cause alignments which reproduce division along traditional 'national' allegiances. However, it is important to note that even though these conflicts often touch deeply felt 'values' and sometimes affect truly vital interests of individuals (such as those associated with one's own scientific career, including the availability of a life supporting job and salary), they never lead to physical violence (except in rare cases of individual lunacy), not to mention war – which is instead, as we well know, a characteristic outcome of conflicts among nations.

The community whose existence we have outlined above is of course minuscule if compared with the entire world community, or even if measured against any one of the traditional nations. It does, however, exist as a fact of life – and it is by no means unique. Very many communities exist nowadays, which are analogous in some or all respects to the particular one described above. Examples of such groups are provided by segments of the scientific community in many disparate research areas; indeed the entire world scientific community constitutes itself, to some extent, such a 'quasi-nation'; and many other such 'quasi-nations' exist which cut across – more or less effectively, but certainly to a considerable extent – the standard national and geopolitical boundaries: from stamp or motorcycle collectors to professional athletes (be they skiers, tennis or football players), from employees of multinational corporations to radio hams and computer hacks, and so on (including, of course, Pugwashites!) – as well as the enormous, and still fast-growing, quasi-nation of Internet users, about which more is written in Chapter 11.

But such communities always existed, without having much, if any, relevance to the emergence of bloody conflicts and wars, nor fostering in any significant way the emergence of any kind of world governance. So why now emphasize their relevance? Because the world is changing fast in ways that clearly and inevitably imply a growing – indeed, fast growing – relevance of such 'quasi-nations', for more than one reason.

The enormously increased and increasing ease of all kinds of communication – a dominant aspect of contemporary society – plays here a most important role: direct dial, and now portable, telephones; e-mail; global radio and television coverage; and also the wide and growing availability of travel on a world scale. As illustrated by the specific case described above, the very emergence of 'quasi-nations' characterized by significantly strong interpersonal bonds is to a very large extent a result of these developments.

Since it is in the nature of things that these developments will become more significant and widespread worldwide in the next years and decades through novel technological advances and their diffusion to less affluent societies, their effects in fostering the emergence of a multiplicity of 'quasi-nations' is likely to snowball.

This motivates a close look at those cases – such as the NEEDS community above – in which such 'quasi-nations' do already exist as viable and robust entities.

The identification of a specific example rooted in science, as a typical case suitable to illustrate a general trend, is, moreover, quite significant, well beyond the contingent fact that it pertains to the personal experience of the author of this chapter. Indeed, the emergence of 'quasi-nations' along the lines indicated above is particularly natural in connection with science, due to its intrinsically universal character: Newton's law holds equally in Africa and in Asia, indeed also on the moon; no Turk will deny the validity of Pythagoras' Theorem, much as (s)he might be blinded by nationalistic antagonism against Greece (although some Nazis did deny the theory of relativity on the grounds it had been invented by a Jew; and Lysenko did succeed in destroying many of his colleagues by arguing that their acceptance of the theory of evolution contradicted the brand of Marxism-Leninism that appealed to Stalin; fortunately, those who partook in such behaviours were eventually phased out by history – unfortunately, at great cost to humankind).

There can be little doubt that science and technology (which is rooted in science, and which is also universal) are likely to influence more and more the future way of life and, therefore, eventually, the set of values of humankind. I say this in spite of the temporary explosions of irrational beliefs in some parts of the world, which find fertile ground in the ignorance still widespread worldwide.

Openness is another essential feature of the practice and ethos of modern science, and it is therefore likely to pervade more and more society worldwide, to the extent that science becomes more and more relevant to human affairs. Its emergence as a prevalent aspect of modern society is of course also facilitated by the increased ease of worldwide communication in all its various aspects, as already mentioned.

Openness is obviously a very positive component of a less conflictual world order, inasmuch as it fosters and facilitates mutual understanding, commonality, trust. Moreover, its widespread acceptance is an essential precondition for certain important and desirable developments, such as the eventual complete elimination of weapons of mass destruction.

There exist a few areas of science – and especially of technology – where complete openness entails dangers: for instance, it is obviously undesirable that the information on the design details of nuclear weapons become public. But such instances are the exception rather than the rule, and their intrinsic contradiction with the proper ethos and practice of science is well understood by the good experts who work in the few scientific fields where secrecy is required, who tend to suffer from restrictions on publicizing their own results, restrictions which may prevent them from getting the wide recognition they feel they deserve for their achievements. Secrecy is instead a great boon for the mediocre and dishonest experts, who use it to shelter themselves from justified criticism, or to win arguments and get financial support by lying – a behaviour which has been systematically practised, as is well known, by some unscrupulous weaponeers. Moreover, secrecy tends to breed catastrophic abuses, as is for instance demonstrated by the ecological disasters now discovered caused by the nuclear weapon complex in the former Soviet Union; likewise in the United States (and probably also in the other nuclear weapon countries, where the 'protection' of secrecy is still quite effective in hiding the true state of affairs).

Some will find the main line of argumentation of this paper unconvincing; others will perhaps tend to agree, but will then ask: 'so what?' Let me try and provide two answers to such a question. In the first place, if the analysis sketched in this paper is correct, it points to a direction of future development at the end of which we perceive a world order very different from the present one; a society in which the traditional allegiances of patriotism and nationalism will have lost much of their potency (hence virulence), being replaced by much less divisive values and by the formation and growing relevance of much less disruptive forms of human bonding. This will eventually also be reflected in forms of world governance, congruent with the prevalence of such universalistic values.

There is much that can be done to accelerate the moment when such a dream will come true by providing more vitality and effectiveness for 'quasi-nations' such as the NEEDS community. For instance, a case in point are the various initiatives, within this community and analogous ones, which have been advocated and undertaken by us in the affluent 'West' to help our colleagues and friends in the former Soviet Union to survive their present, hopefully temporary, predicament – to survive both in the most elementary concrete sense, but also as a viable scientific community whose existence is an asset in which we all have a share.

Secondly, there is the concrete possibility to exploit the existence of the 'quasi-nation' constituted by the world scientific and scholarly community (including all its articulations into various subgroupings) in order to help our present world, full of risks and conflicts, to cope with them, avoid major catastrophes, find a way out of dangerous impasses. The activity of the Pugwash Conferences on Science and World Affairs is itself a clear example of this approach – from its origin (the Russell-Einstein Manifesto of 1955) through its entire history to the present – especially inasmuch as it takes advantage, to pursue these goals, of the greater ease of communication natural among scientists and other scholars, even when they are associated with quite divergent ideological and political backgrounds. This is a task which remains before us, the more so since our present world continues unfortunately to be riven by conflicts and dangers, including some which still seem to provide special scope for the mitigating influence and dedicated intervention of scientists and other scholars committed to the quest for peace, conflict resolution, and problem solving.

After the above chapter had been drafted I had the sobering experience of reading the extraordinarily perceptive and informative paperback by Robert D. Kaplan, *Balkan Ghosts* [Vintage Books, Random House: New York, 1994]. In this travelogue the author – a journalist who has travelled extensively and lived in the Balkans – gives a powerful and chilling picture of the ethnic conflicts in the area, with their roots in past history and present misery, and in the extraordinary vitality and virulence of 'national' identifications. In the light of such an encompassing and discouraging picture, whose cogency is of course reinforced by the continued stream of horrible news from war-torn former Yugoslavia, what should one make of the 'Utopian' considerations about the emergence of 'quasi-nations' as an avenue to foster the obsolescence of ethnic hatreds and bloody conflicts rooted in patriotic identification and nationalistic fervour? How relevant is this to the real world of today? Is this merely 'enlightened naiveté'?

Perhaps so. But the final point I would like to reiterate is that the notion of 'quasi-nation', as sketched above, is by no means presented here as a 'Utopian' goal, as the outline of a perfect or quasi-perfect society towards which we should strive to move. I greatly doubt whether a society based *solely* on the kind of intellectual interests and pursuits emphasized above would provide a desirable future. My point is not one of advocacy; it is one of description.

The kind of 'quasi-nation' sketched above does indeed now exist as an operational entity, which affects very significantly (although perhaps largely at a subliminal level) the lives of its (few) members. Many other such 'quasi-nations' also exist and are emerging nowadays – with the 'quasi' qualification being, on a case-by-case basis, more or less significant. The phenomenon is there. It is undoubtedly growing. It is therefore likely to have a sociopolitical impact of some significance, which is likely to be, at least in the short run, mainly beneficial, but which in any case ought to be recognized and understood. It is, admittedly, a minor detail in the global picture of how the world ticks today, but is it not important to identify trends as they are budding?

6

Expanding Human Loyalties

Douglas Roche

Some years ago, the Club of Rome published a time-interest chart which graphically portrayed people's interests. Most people, it was shown, are interested in what is happening in their own lives and their families' and immediate surroundings this week. Only a small fraction of people are concerned about what will happen to the world twenty-five years from now.

The concentration of public attention on the here and now is one of the chief impediments to the implementation of public policies for stable and equitable planetary development. If, twenty-five years ago, governments had adopted a comprehensive nuclear test ban and shut down the nuclear arms race, if private and public investment in developing countries had been greatly increased with full attention paid to education and health services, if treaties had been adopted to stop pollution and clean up the waters and atmosphere, today the worldwide problems of armaments, poverty and environmental deterioration would have been arrested.

Project ahead a quarter-century. Who thinks about the 2020s today? Only a rare person, perhaps the odd media presentation, certainly not the political system. Yet, as Robert D. Kaplan warned in his prescient article, 'The Coming Anarchy',[1] present trends show that in the first decades of the twenty-first century nations may break up under the tidal flow of refugees from environmental and social disasters. Wars will be fought over scarce resources, especially water, and war itself will become continuous with crime as armed bands of stateless marauders clash with the private security forces of the elites. Action now to implement the global UN strategies for demilitarization, sustainable economic and social development, and protection of the environment would head off looming disasters. But the public consciousness and hence the political will are not awakened and energized. We live for the present. We inter-relate with those in our vicinity. We are loyal, in a fashion, to those in the sphere of our daily sentiments and business.

Technology has raced ahead of not only our political systems but the vision of human beings. We may see on television the human tragedies of our time in Bosnia, Somalia, Rwanda, Haiti, Iraq – indeed, in all the squalor and horror that pass for human habitation in both rich and poor countries around the world – but we do not comprehend that such immense suffering is the consequence of public policies that tolerate massive violations of human rights. We have not yet reached a level of civilization that demands the same protection for the rights of the Bosnian child, the Rwandan farmer, the Haitian worker, as we demand for ourselves.

This is not necessarily because we are callous, though aid-weariness has clearly become a characteristic of our age, but because we have not absorbed the integral nature of human rights in a technologically united world. Human beings are slow to adapt themselves – much slower than they can produce new technologies. For instance, we have grown accustomed to instant technological adaptation whether in communications, cars or space exploration. But the human being cannot be adapted like a piece of machinery; our culture, mores and patterns of thinking are slow to change. Our horizons, while technologically expanded, are mentally limited by our conditioning which has, until this explosive time of world change, always been local, not global.

The expansion of loyalties outward will only come, in my

view, from a better understanding of the inherent quality of human rights. Such an understanding will help us to see that in a world that is whole, my human rights are inextricably interconnected with the human rights of the Bosnian child, the Rwandan farmer, the Haitian worker. I must express a loyalty to these people, even if I do not personally know them, if I am to be loyal to myself. The widespread personal discovery of this dimension of human rights would drive the public policy agendas forward.

****

To explore this global extension of loyalty, I want to concentrate on development. What is development?

Although many planners still equate development with efficient economic growth, others repudiate this reductionist view and plead for the multi-dimensional advance of society in all its realms – economic, social, political, cultural, environmental and spiritual. As Denis Goulet, a development specialist, points out:

> Modern men and women must come to recognize that they are the bearers of multiple, partial overlapping identities and loyalty systems, no single one of which can claim their total allegiance.[2]

Only by examining the whole world as a community bonded by our common humanity can we understand what development should entail. Development, in its most comprehensive sense, can best be understood by exploring the meaning of the stirring photo of the earth brought back by the astronauts. There it shines as no earth dweller had ever seen it before: blue, flecked with white cloud patterns, a beautiful small globe set against the black void of space through which it is whirling at incredible speed. Spaceship Earth, Barbara Ward has called it, a unique space vehicle, providing a viable ecosystem for human beings, but with quite limited resources. The fundamental lesson of the photo is the oneness of our humanity on earth – a oneness that must triumph over the artificial divisions of the world.

This brings us directly to the key question of the value of each human being. For if we do not remember what it is that makes a human being human it is all too easy to submerge the dignity and rights of the individual in the name of progress. This approach is equally productive whether we are a Christian putting our faith in the gospel of Jesus; a Jewish believer in *Mitzvah*, the divine commandment to alleviate poverty and restore the image of the divine in every person; or a secularist who perceives that the harmony of creation has been broken. People of diverse religious outlooks can converge on the same practical principles and conclusions, provided that they similarly revere, perhaps for quite different reasons, truth and intelligence, human dignity, freedom, brotherly love, and the absolute value of moral good.

In this view, all things on earth should be related to the human person as their centre and crown. But what do we mean precisely when we speak of the human person? The philosopher Jacques Maritain offers this description:

> We do not mean merely that he is an individual, in the sense that an atom, a blade of grass, a fly or an elephant is an individual. Man is an individual who holds himself in hand by intelligence and will. He does not exist only in a physical manner. He has a spiritual superexistence through knowledge and love; he is, in a way, a universe in himself, a microcosm, in which the great universe in its entirety can be encompassed through knowledge; and through love, he can give himself completely to beings who are to him, as it were, other selves, a relation for which no equivalent can be found in the physical world.[3] [At a later time, I believe Maritain would have used inclusive gender language.]

This description of humanity provides the framework for development. For true development is not about things but about the whole person. Development includes the passage from misery towards the possession of necessities, but it also means victory over social scourges, the growth of knowledge, and the acquisition of culture.

The Dag Hammarskjold Foundation summed up this point:

> Development is a whole; it is an integral, value-loaded, cultural process; it encompasses the natural environment, social relations, education, production, consumption and well-being.

True peace with social justice require the development of a world community characterized by what Maritain has called 'integral humanism'.

Development therefore requires a political, social and economic order that will affirm and develop the dignity proper to every person. This is the proper meaning of human liberation, and this is why the political liberation achieved by most of the developing world since World War II has been followed by demands for economic liberation.[4]

A liberated person is one who has the economic basis and political freedom to develop his or her true potential as a human person in keeping with the common good. Each person must be allowed to discover his or her true self and express a personal authenticity. The liberation of the human being does indeed have a deeper dimension than economic but without access to food, shelter, education, employment, and health care there can be no liberation.

Any process of growth that does not lead to the fulfilment of the basic needs of food, shelter, education, employment, and health care – or, even worse, disrupts them – is a travesty of the idea of development. Just as poverty is destructive of the well-being of the person, superabundance and the satisfaction of endless wants is destructive.

A growth process that benefits only the wealthiest minority and maintains or even increases the disparities between and within countries is not development. It is exploitation. The experience of a quarter of a century shows us that the 'trickle down' theory, in which the poor are better off as the rich get richer is illusory.[5] What of the next quarter-century?

The satisfaction of basic needs opens the way to those other values and goals of development: freedom of expression, the right to give and receive ideas and stimulus, the right to find self-realization in work, the right not to be exploited as another tool in the hands of the employer. There is, finally, a deep social need in people of all colours and cultures to participate in shaping the basis of their own existence, and to make some contribution to reshaping the world's future.

We can now see, in this larger view of development, that the idea that the developing nations should become like the North is ludicrous. For just as it is wrong to debase development by having no floor for economic realization, it is equally wrong to treat the life-support systems of the world as if there were no ceiling. That is what we have done in the industrialized world.[6]

The ideas of progress, creative growth, expansion, surpluses and inexhaustible resources have been synonymous with the development of Western people since the industrial revolution. Science and technology have been the driving forces behind us. This is true no matter whether people live under a capitalist or socialist system of government. Industrial civilization is predicated on expansion. When we are not growing, we are in trouble. Growth has thus become an end in itself. Now, however, we are starting to realize that unlimited industrial production and economic expansion to satisfy an artificially stimulated consumer demand are a voracious trap for the industrialized nations.

****

Loyalty to all humankind has both a philosophical and pragmatic imperative. It can be expressed and taught in a practical manner. The multi-dimensional agenda for world concern has been set out by the United Nations: removal of threats to peace, including the nuclear threat; respect for the principle of non-use of force; resolution of conflicts and peaceful settlement of disputes; confidence-building measures; disarmament; maintenance of outer space for peaceful uses; development; promotion of human rights and fundamental freedoms; decolonization; elimination of racial discrimination; enhancing the quality of life; satisfaction of human needs; protecting the environment.

A wide-ranging programme of action is opened up by this definition. Moreover, this approach enables us to comprehend better that peace is established by the implementation of a system of values. Peace demands the attaining of true human security so that people everywhere can live free of the threat of war, free of violations of their human rights, free to develop their own lives to attain economic and social progress. All this is clearly an advance in global thinking. This advance constitutes a signal of hope to a humanity that has for far too long been fractured and frustrated in the attaining of enduring human security.

Though patience is required, today's turbulence has created an urgent situation. There are too many people suffering, there is too much political frustration, too much fear of global devastation to allow a mood of passivity.

In short, loyalty to all humanity means inculcating in people an *attitude* – not only to the world as it is but as it can be. It means helping them understand the magnitude of the transformation occurring in the world. It means opening up their powers of creativity so that they do not just cope with the world but enlarge the community around them.

As the Club of Rome's latest report, *The First Global Revolution*,[7] points out, the global society we are heading towards cannot emerge unless 'it drinks from' the source of moral and spiritual values.

> Beyond cultures, religions and philosophies, there is in human beings a thirst for freedom, aspirations to overcome one's limits, a quest for a beyond that seems ungraspable and is often unnamed.[8]

The militarism, poverty and assaults on nature that continue to undermine the global agenda for human security underscore, rather than destroy, this resilient human need.   Cultural contradictions, excessive nationalism, loss of identity with its concomitant demoralization must be overcome by the assertion from a thousand avenues of life that there is meaning – a profound meaning – to the life of every individual on the planet.

The trend line of history is favourable to the empowerment of individuals because virtually everywhere society is more open and informed.

The idea of solidarity is changing from a concept limited to the family tribe to a much broader concept, while its strictly tribal connotation may be openly discredited.[9]

Universal norms and values, extending now to the global community, embrace freedom, human rights and responsibilities, family life, equal rights for men and women, compassion for the aged and disabled, respect for others, tolerance, respect for life and peace, and the search for truth.

The first requisite in helping people understand this new reality is to give them a sense of world consciousness in which every individual realizes his or her role as a member of the world community. The historian Paul Kennedy declares that today 'we are all members of a world citizenry', which requires a system of ethics.[10] The educator Edwin Reischauer, in his book, *Toward the 21st Century: Education for a Changing World*, said we will never operate successfully unless the bulk of the people develop a sense of world citizenship:

> This is clearly the biggest educational task of all, for millenniums of history have conditioned men to think in terms of smaller and more exclusive units, while suspicion and hostility toward other groups lie deep in their patterns of thought.[11]

If education is to meet its responsibilities, it must give young people the stimulus to find and develop better ways of organizing global society than by dividing it into hostile, warring factions. Professional educators are the first to know that education can break down feelings of suspicion and hostility and provide an empathy for peoples of diverse histories, cultural and religious backgrounds. This is the work of forming young people's attitudes in the new age of transformation. As Virginia Satir notes in *The New Peoplemaking:* 'Creating peace in the world strongly resembles making peace in the family'.[12]

The late U Thant, Secretary-General of the UN, held that education must produce 'a veritable mental renaissance' to build the conditions for lasting peace. We need a renaissance generation who, although they have inherited a restricted loyalty association, will expand their sense of loyalty to all humanity.

REFERENCES

1.   R.D. Kaplan, 'The Coming Anarchy', *The Atlantic Monthly*, February 1994.

2.   D. Goulet, 'Development: Creator and Destroyer of Values', *Human Rights in the Twenty-First Century: A Global Challenge*, Martinus Nijhoff: Dordrecht, 1993.

3.   J. Maritain, *Principes d'une Politique Humaniste*, Paul Hartmann: Paris, 1945, pp.15-16.

4.   D. Roche, *Justice Not Charity: A New Global Ethic for Canada*, McClelland and Stewart Limited: Toronto, 1976.

5.   *Human Development Report, 1992*, United Nations Development Programme.

6.   *State of the World 1994*, W.W. Norton & Company: New York.

7.   A. King and B. Schneider, *The First Global Revolution*, Pantheon Books: New York, 1991.

8.   *Ibid.* p.237.

9.   *Ibid.* p.240.

10.   P. Kennedy, *Preparing for the Twenty-First Century*, Random House: New York, 1993, p.341.

11.   E. Reischauer, *Toward the Twenty-First Century: Education for a Changing World*, Alfred A. Knopf: New York, 1973.

12.   V. Satir, *The New Peoplemaking*, Science and Behaviour Books: Mountain View, California, 1988, p.368.

Part II

Education for World Citizenship

7

Introduction of Courses on World Citizenship into the Curricula of Schools and Universities

Ana Maria Cetto

THE FIRST LESSONS ON WORLD CITIZENSHIP

The lessons on world citizenship start at home and in the early school years. They start when the child begins to learn that they are not alone in this world, and they gradually becomes aware of belonging to a family, a neighbourhood, a group of children, a gender, an ethnic group, a cultural group, a socio-economic group, a community, a religion, a city, a country . . . a civilization, and to humankind.

Each one of these memberships entails adopting certain attitudes and values and acknowledging a number of rules, which are normally more or less spontaneously followed to ensure one's continued belonging to one's various groups. Sociologists have established the importance that these various memberships bear for the individual; they give them a sense of protection and reliance, of being 'somebody', of having a place in society. In fact, the disappearance or disruption of one such social group or community is recognized as a major threat to the personal well-being, stability and sense of security of its members. Those who are suddenly deprived of their social entourage move erratically, like blind men who use their walking sticks to sense the contours of the new, foreign environment to which they must adapt to survive.

On an individual scale, people can respond to the loss of their sense of security, and of security itself, with aggressive attitudes and antisocial acts. On a collective scale, the effect can be a destabilization with unpredictable consequences. Security, which has become such a crucial issue in the political arena, and has always been a central element of concern for Pugwash, does not only have to do with the protection of nations from the risks of war and other disasters – security is an extremely dear notion for human beings on all scales, at all ages. The social groups or communities play an important role in this respect, by providing their members with safe conditions, protecting them from risks, and supporting them in adverse circumstances.

In addition to the establishment of codes of conduct, the constitution of any social group implies a definition of its common attributes and its boundaries, of all those individual features that allow identification of its members, and distinguish them from the members of other groups. A value is normally placed on these distinctive features, transforming them into socially defined qualities, which helps to establish a normativity, to give cohesion to the group, to guarantee its survival, and to set the basis for its further development. It is natural, then, that the members of the group defend these values, which have become part of their idiosyncrasy, and that they defend them against the values of the others, if necessary. Or is it natural?

This is a matter where education, both formal and informal, can play a decisive role. We can learn to place more emphasis on the similarities than on the differences. We can be taught to discriminate in the sense of recognizing, understanding and appreciating the differences; but we can also be trained to discriminate in the sense of singling out for special favour or disfavour. As is illustrated by the very use of one and the same vocable, sometimes the distance that separates these two aspects of discrimination becomes imperceptible. The difference between them is, however, essential. It is as important to understand one's own place in society as it is to understand that everyone has a place in society; it is as important to defend one's own rights and values as it is to appreciate – or at least tolerate – the values of others and respect their rights. The structural, cultural and educational patterns of traditional liberal societies, whose individualistic character has been further enhanced by neo-liberalism, work much in the direction of overemphasizing the differences between groups and allowing – sometimes even fostering – discriminatory actions against the weaker ones. The puritanical tradition in some societies does not make the situation better by masking these discriminatory actions with a moralistic disguise. On the other hand, socialist experiences of this century have failed to demonstrate that human beings can transcend their individualism and become consciously collectivist.

So we see that a positive task for education is to provide people with the elements for an understanding of their roles as human and social beings and of their place in history. It is important to develop capabilities of recognizing the rich diversity that actually exists in the world, and of realizing that different cultures, traditions and viewpoints, even conflicts of interests, are not something to be afraid of but are a normal state of affairs in a diverse and changing society. What we need to be afraid of is the nonexistence of mechanisms to bring these different viewpoints and interests together to search for common solutions.

In this context there is a basis for education on global peace and world citizenship. The choice of the contents of the courses is of course important, to ensure that the student learns from the early years about the history of civilizations and their legacies; nature and its evolution; the organization of social and political systems; the rich variety of peoples that cohabit on our planet, their cultures, their traditions and their values; about themselves as a human being; about their future rights and responsibilities as a citizen, and so on. This kind of knowledge is an absolutely necessary element of educating for world citizenship. However, in itself, it can hardly be successful if it is not accompanied by a practice whereby the students learn basic norms of behaviour based on mutual respect, coexistence and cooperation, and face real dilemmas and conflicts of interest and learn to manage them in a peaceful way. Also, it can hardly develop a student's conscience if it is not accompanied by a process of self-inquiry, of self-reflected learning as opposed to indoctrination, as has been clearly pointed out by the Freirian school.[1] In addition, it can hardly induce in the student an attitude of tolerance, understanding and solidarity if it is taught in an atmosphere of prejudice, sectarianism, seclusion, or segregation.

The fact is, unfortunately, that our educational systems more often than not reproduce and reinforce the compartmentalized structure and organization of our societies. In many Western countries, the recent privatization trends and the weakening of the state's role in education have only contributed to widening the gap between the state school system open to all, and the private system accessible only to the elites. Even in the more pluralistic societies this problem exists, as was recently observed by a researcher referring to the British school system: if you are white, middle class, protestant and male, you are well off, but if you fail to satisfy any of these requisites, you are in difficulty. What sense can it have to tell children in school that all are equal and yet treat them differently? How can a person be taught to have respect for other human beings if they are not fully respected? How can a person be expected to work for the collective well-being and benefit of society if they cannot consider themselves to be a full member of this society?

The development of a sense of respect for others and of a collective conscience requires that people acquire also a sense of dignity, self-respect and self-reliance. This is an aspect that can vary widely among different cultures and nations. It is, for instance, typical of people who have lived historically in conditions of oppression to have great difficulty in achieving a state of self-reliance, that is, reliance on their own resources – intellectual and material – as the primary stock to draw on in the pursuit of their own objectives. On a global scale, this feature is typical of cultures in the Third World as opposed to those of the First World. Internally, it is reproduced by the respective education systems, thus contributing to perpetuating a cultural and economic dependence even beyond the formal acquisition of political independence. The lack of self-reliance in some parts of the world or in some groups has of course its counterpart: namely, the excess of reliance in other parts of the world and in other groups within the same parts of the world. Even though we are told that we are citizens of one and the same world, we learn that we belong to different worlds – and to different strata within these worlds. Our education systems have still to invest a great deal of effort into changing these patterns of which they themselves are accomplices and victims.

Here we touch upon a concept that has been the subject of much misuse and much debate, namely that of development. For a long time, and even today, 'development' has been identified with the mechanistic notion of the production and multiplication of physical assets and the increase of flow of economic goods and services. This notion has been much used to classify human beings, social groups and even entire nations in a discriminatory way, and to subordinate some groups to others. However, the deep tragedy of 'underdevelopment' is not that people have remained poor – and are becoming poorer – but that, in their state of subordination, they are inhibited from authentic development as humans. One might even say that the very notion of 'poverty', conventionally conceived in consumerist terms, leaves totally aside some inherently human needs, such as the need to fulfil our creative potential in ever new ways, which is what most clearly distinguishes us from any other species. Development does not mean receiving the basic material needs, but learning to think for ourselves and to do things ourselves, devising and constructing the means to do them, building up our capacity for self-determination. For people to develop a sense of responsibility for the whole of mankind, they must first acquire a sense of humanness, of being full members of this humankind to which they owe their existence. In the words of Anisur Rahman: 'experiencing humanhood thus is a great leap forward, the first necessary step in anybody's development'. A healthy collective, social development rests on this development of the individual as a human being. The education system can contribute significantly to this task by fostering independent reflection and self-reflection; by stimulating creativity in all areas of human activity; and, most importantly, by inducing students to think creatively. The educational system can and should do much in the way of paying attention to those humanistic aspects of development that have been almost completely left aside. This implies, however, a revision of the traditional teaching approaches and methodologies in the majority of our schools, a revalorization of the teachers' role, and a critical attitude towards the paradigms of progress, rather than just a change in the curricula.

THE CURRICULA FOR SCIENTISTS

There is an ever growing intervention of the human being in nature and the course of evolution; the living conditions on our planet are gradually becoming more determined by our acts on nature than by nature itself. The spontaneous pace of phenomena has been dramatically distorted, and the events themselves depend to an ever greater extent on human decisions. This confronts human beings with an unprecedented responsibility: we are not any more simply responsible for the most immediate effects that our deeds may have within a more or less stable and predictable framework; our acts and decisions may contribute to changing the framework itself.

Our increasing knowledge of the natural world and our increasing capacity to interfere with it are to a large extent a result of the impressive efforts and advances in the natural sciences and science-based technologies. Too often, however, these advances seem to be aimed at exploiting nature and taking control of it rather than at understanding it and assessing the consequences of this exploitation. Science and technology have been more successful in creating new means for an intense and efficient interaction and communication with other human beings – and sometimes also for a more efficient control over their lives – than in understanding the human beings themselves. Science and technology have been more successfully applied to the development of weapons, than to dealing with the secular problems of war and oppression. An unprecedented responsibility thus falls on us as scientists at a stage where the applications of scientific progress can have increasingly global effects on a system which is not even properly understood. What consequences should this situation have on scientific curricula? What conclusions can be drawn regarding the training of future scientists? What can be done to induce in scientists a sense of responsibility appropriate to this new situation, in which the future of the whole of mankind is at stake?

To find an answer to these questions is a task that requires much analysis and can lead to intense discussions. Certainly, the questions of how to revise the orientations of science and how to induce in scientists an appropriate sense of responsibility had not been properly answered when they constituted a simpler problem – in fact, they had not even received adequate attention. Now the problem is compounded by the increasingly global nature of the problematique and by the growing power acquired by science. Moreover, it is clear that this responsibility is not exclusive to the scientific community proper, but pertains to all those who in some form or other have an influence on the development of science or share the benefits of its advances.

One initial, almost immediate answer relates to scientific education at high-school level. This first formal contact with science is at least as crucial for the majority of students, for whom it is probably also the last formal contact, as it is for those very few who will become scientists. It is of course important that everyone learns the basics about the phenomena of nature, the laws that govern its processes, and the methods of scientific endeavour. But the whole of science acquires a different meaning for the student – in fact, one could say that it acquires a meaning - when the student also learns about how and why science has emerged and evolved; the place it has in our knowledge system; its most relevant contributions to civilization; its enormous tasks, its limitations and potentialities.

As to the students of the sciences proper, it is particularly important that in addition to receiving a solid knowledge basis, they become aware of all those aspects which give a social meaning to the scientific enterprise, and that they are made to participate in the inquiry into the social role of the sciences. However, it has been characteristic of scientific institutions not to provide a space for such inquiry, which is normally disqualified simply as non-scientific, or even anti-scientific. For the scientific community at large, the only valid criticism of science is the self-criticism conducted within the boundaries of its own normativity, and only its members with credentials are qualified to undertake whatever renovations the scientific project is considered to require. Science has thus acquired a dogmatic character – sometimes as dogmatic and coercive as religions can be – which it uses to protect itself from critics and from intruders. The government bureaucracies, private enterprises and funding agencies that support scientific research could not be more satisfied: they want scientists to do their job, as efficiently as possible, without extraneous interferences. Indeed, paradoxically, many colleagues still claim that science must be held immune from the influences of social and historical situations, while at the same time they are eager to prove the enormous influence that science has had on all aspects of our lives and of society, and the utmost importance it has for the future of humanity.

Science has also acquired a sort of exclusivity by disqualifying anything that cannot be stated in precise terms, that cannot be quantified and systematized, that comes from our intuition, our feelings, our traditions. This scientific discourse of purely rational thinking, objective knowledge, quantifiable relations, and so on, has spilled over to other disciplines, and one finds it in the history and philosophy of science, the sociology of science, even science policy. All analyses of science must be undertaken under the scientific rationale so as to arrive at 'valid' conclusions. Anything else is speculation, ideology or superstition.

The doctrinaire character of science makes it extremely difficult to perform a serious critique from within (those few who dare run the risk of being ostracized); its elitist character makes it almost impossible to propose a critical revision from outside. There is at present a widening gap between the practitioners and defenders of established science and its paradigms, and the vast number of people who are distant from science, basically ignore it, mistrust it, or simply do not believe in it. It seems to be easier for scientists to see the negative effects of this process of separation on the people who are outside science than to appreciate its consequences for science itself. It seems to be easier for us to assess the extraordinary achievements of science and its impressive successes than to acknowledge that fundamental questions related to the human being and his basic individual and collective needs are yet to be addressed.

This state of affairs is manifest in the schools and universities where the young scientists are trained. An important part of the training consists in learning the rules of the game of doing science; elaborate rules that are a result of scientific evolution and that can be learnt only by close contact with the practitioners of science. An effort is made in the universities to incorporate the future scientists into research projects as early as possible, thus ensuring a more efficient transmission of this elaborate know-how, along with the transmission of scientific knowledge. This merging of the educational process with the research functions of the institution, which is very convenient for training purposes, does, however, at the same time undermine the critical function of the academy, by inducing the student to 'perform well' as a prospective scientist. The distance needed for the acquisition and self-appropriation of knowledge is thus shortened; the space for a critical apprehension of this knowledge does not exist.

If we expect future scientists to be conscious people, aware of the possible consequences of their work and of the potential of scientific endeavour, these are certainly not the optimal conditions. The scientific system should be more open to criticism and to self-criticism; it should leave space for a revision of its objectives, methodologies, approaches, sets of values, and structure; for an analysis of its achievements and its failures; for an extension of its scope. The sciences themselves would be the first ones to benefit from such revision. With this purpose in mind, it is desirable that the curricula for scientists contain specifically designed courses and seminars where different aspects of science are analysed: its history and evolution, its philosophical implications, its contact with other disciplines, its relations to society. In these activities, natural scientists should closely interact with sociologists and philosophers of science, both in the organization of the courses and the preparation of the reading materials. The positivist approach to teaching purely scientific disciplines as bodies of established knowledge pertains to other times, when scientific progress of itself was a priority. Now that the great edifice of science has been erected, it is time to revise what we want to do with it. We cannot expect future scientists to act responsibly if we do not invite them to participate in this self-reflection on science. Such a broadening of the scientific education provides a concrete foundation for the development of the notion of world citizenship among our future scientists.

REFERENCE

1.   The Freirian school is the school of Paulo Freire, a Brazilian pedagogician. His classic texts include: *La educación como práctica de la libertad,* Siglo XXI: Mexico, 1969; and *Pedagogía del oprimido,* Siglo XXI: Mexico, 1982.

8

Promotion of Exchanges Between Young People

Jeffrey Porten

There are two primary types of international youth organizations. There are those that do not explicitly include an international agenda but which bring students together through conferences and exchange programmes. An example of this type of organization is Student Pugwash USA, which focuses on scientific issues; while international issues may be addressed in the process of its deliberations, they are not the main focus of this group. Other groups have an explicit agenda for international political action or social change but are focused on the youth of a single country, such as student programmes organized by the World Federalist Association (USA). The primary focus for youth organizations tends to be firmly in one category or the other, although there are occasional exceptions to this rule as some organizations arrange conferences and agendas with international scope and membership, such as the recent Youth '95 conference held during the United Nations 50th anniversary celebrations.

There is no 'right' way of going about youth networking; both types have their own particular strengths and failings. International youth organizations that do not address international issues lose a potentially valuable opportunity to harness youth energies towards global processes; national youth organizations with a global outlook may not realize how insular they have become and how little their solutions may apply in different cultures, economies and social systems.

Endemic to both types of movement is the danger of losing sight of primary purpose and reaching out organizationally to an initiative that belongs in the other issue area. While some groups have the resources and tenacity to create a synergistic combination of the two, the likelihood is far greater that this sort of impact will be broad but not deep.

Youth organizations adopt a wide range of organizational styles. Many youth organizations give the impression of having been thrown together on a shoestring budget after an all-night brainstorming session by college or secondary students. This is entirely appropriate because many groups, including many successful ones, are founded in exactly this fashion. At the other end of the spectrum are well-funded organizations run with the formality of old banking firms, often a characteristic in the United States of politically conservative youth groups.

Of course, this dichotomy exists in all organizations, but it creates unique reverberations in a youth-run or youth-oriented group. Many students gravitate to youth organizations immediately after the end of, or as a sabbatical from, their schooling; an organization with a dress code of denim jeans and T-shirts, and less-than-strict attention paid to a timeclock, holds great attraction. This informal atmosphere does not detract from the work of a smaller organization but it causes massive and sometimes catastrophic growing pains when a group decides to increase its staff or enlarge its mandate.

On the other hand, a formal atmosphere is no solution. Hierarchical structures have a tendency to shake out the older members (even older youth) at the top and the younger at the bottom, a phenomenon which excludes newcomers and can lock an organization in stasis, dooming it to disintegration when members move on. Hierarchies are also limited in that they only have a place within them for certain types of activity, aimed in specific directions. The same energy that can create a movement overnight can be stifled in a bureaucratic structure, and there is no surer method of disillusioning a nascent activist.

The trappings of formality require (and attract) funding, which in turn makes continued funding at that level a major ongoing organizational goal. Less funded and unfunded groups often see these groups as having 'sold out' their goals for money, whether this is objectively the case or not. For many youth activists the open credo of the 1960s, 'Never trust anyone over 30', has unconsciously become in the 1990s, 'Never trust an NGO with budgets over $30,000'.

Due to their agendas, volunteers and constituencies, youth organizations are subject to considerable difficulties in several areas. The problems enumerated here are by no means unique to student and youth organizations, but these are those areas in which youth organizations have particular difficulty overcoming internal division or external pressure.

Inability to create a representative cross-section of youth or youth movements

Every culture, class and socio-economic group on the planet has its share of young people. When trying to put together a representative group for input, there is always one more constituency not present, one more point of view that is not being expressed, one more group of youth whose needs are not being met by the decisions being made. At some point, it becomes necessary to simply say that perfect representation is impossible, and that whomever is present will have to be close enough to get to work. Unfortunately, for many this is not seen as a mere concession but as a debilitating strike against the principles guiding the organization. Youth are by and large less than willing to compromise principles for pragmatic goals, and much energy is expended uselessly over this inevitable outcome.

This plays just as strongly between organizations. There is no central clearing-house of information on youth organizations, nor can there ever be, simply because the organizations resist the centralization of data and control that such an effort would require. As a result, the youth movement is riddled with countless instances of duplication of effort and wasted energy, because it is rare that any organization is fully cognizant of what others in its topic area are doing. A good amount of this effort is in the area of simply trying to keep track of who else is out there; nearly every major youth organization has extensive files of printed information generated by other youth groups and distributed at conferences, which invariably are out-of-date, incomplete and rarely referenced. A youth organization will create dynamic links with perhaps a dozen or so other groups, and will be well informed of their activities, but there is always a ceiling on the number of groups that can coordinate in this manner.

Efforts have been made in the past by individual organizations to act as central banks of information for a wide variety of youth movements. This is most effective under the rubric of organizing a conference, as the primary organizers have the institutional advantage of a shared goal. Such centralization invariably breaks down when any attempt is made to move the coalition in any single ideological direction. It is simply impossible to catalogue and disseminate information without stamping one's own agenda on that information. This agenda is frequently resented, preventing the creation of a permanent centralized organizing body.

This situation may change in the near future due to new communication technologies such as the Internet, which facilitate the centralization of information from a decentralized organization of individuals or groups, even on an *ad hoc* basis (see Chapter 11).

Following a youth conference in New York in October 1993, several participants were struck by the enormity of wasted effort in the system and tried to come up with a way around it that did not cause the problems I have mentioned. That conversation was the genesis of the 'Noodle Club', a bi-weekly informal dinner meeting of youth activists working in the Washington, D.C. area. The Noodle Club has no agenda, no goals other than informal discussion, no dinner speakers, and no rules save that the rotating location of dinner must be in a restaurant with cheap entrées (since most youth activists work for little or nothing). In

Washington, cheap usually means pasta, which was the source of the name of the group. One member keeps the Club's records, which is nothing more than a list of everyone who has ever shown up, and a fax and electronic mail announcement each month of the next location. Since the Noodle Club never set out to accomplish specific objectives, it has been a resounding success, bringing organizations together and helping spread information about initiatives and employment opportunities.

Youth organizations, like youth themselves, tend to be poorly funded.

It is rare to find a youth organization – other than one with an official government sinecure – that has enough funding to begin to cover its agenda. Even in those groups with funding, it is common to find that financial power is in the hands of an adult steward who has final say over where the funding will go. Since organizational power follows money, this has the end result of fomenting the sort of disillusionment discussed earlier.

Youth tend to be passionately committed to their agendas, leaving little room for compromise.

During the same conference that spawned the Noodle Club, a meeting was scheduled to create a youth coalition for activities leading up to the 50th anniversary of the Bretton Woods institutions in 1995. A previous coalition, titled Youth '92, had been instrumental in getting youth positions to the negotiating tables in the preparatory committees to and at the Rio environmental conference, and it was envisaged that the new coalition, called Youth '95, would have much the same impact. Three hours were set aside to draw up a preliminary agenda.

The meeting was approximately ten minutes old when someone raised the question: 'Exactly what is meant by the word "youth"?' This was greeted by a few unkind chuckles around the room – myself included – because it seemed like an overly bureaucratic thing to say. The chair of the meeting said: 'Let's call it between the ages of 15 and 25', a range no doubt dictated by a pragmatic appraisal of the span of ages in the room.

That was effectively the end of the meeting, as the following three hours were taken up by interminable debate on the meaning of 'youth'. A Latin American student said that in his country, someone was considered young until the age of 30, and that a cut-off of 25 excluded many organizations. Another representative said that his group worked with many 12-year-olds, whose thought processes were different from those of teenagers, and that barring the younger range of the spectrum would hurt the coalition. And so on. When a compromise of 'under 30' was suggested, a new argument was raised on the grounds that such a wide constituency could never be adequately served, and that if anyone proposed bringing a six-year-old to a United Nations conference, we would all lose our credibility.

The meeting adjourned a half-hour late, forming a committee to debate the issue. The committee met for an additional ten to twelve hours, then presented a muddled statement to the collected group three days later; only about half of the original group attended. The statement did not begin to cover a preliminary agenda, so the conveners of the meeting wrote one themselves over the following six months, and presented it at a later conference. Since this agenda had been written through a closed process, it was not well received and caused a new round of debate.

On the face of it, the argument at the conference seemed ludicrous, but it was not. The issues involving the definition of 'youth' are cross-cultural and strike at the heart of many of the organizations that were in attendance at the meeting. However, I am rather certain that if that same group of people were reconvened in ten years, with the same goal in mind, the debate would have been more quickly tabled even if the emotions and faith in principles still ran as strong.

Youth organizations are made up of a very unseasoned bunch of people which is at once one of their greatest strengths and failings. The best and the brightest of our generation naturally gravitate to these groups, as do our most ambitious and egotistical. Often these are the same people. It is here that young leaders learn the techniques of diplomacy, ethical and unethical uses of power and manipulation, the intricacies of organizational management. Their instructor in this course is the time-honoured method of trial-and-error, and the cumulative impact of these errors is an ongoing barrier for the efficacy of youth movements. This can only be solved by keeping the young out of positions of influence, a solution which is worse than the problem. In many ways, this training of future leaders is the best service that a youth organization provides to the greater society.

Since youth feel themselves not to have the resources to effect change, there is the danger of their energies seemingly going towards nothing. This is especially the case on the 'conference circuit', which is the primary *modus vivendi* of many youth organizations. At nearly every youth conference I have attended, the end of the conference was filled with pronouncements about the plans that had been laid for the next conference in the series, or the spin-off meetings that had been spontaneously planned during the conference.

This is perfectly understandable as a youth conference is one of the most dynamic experiences open to a student, and is one of the more glamorous perks of involvement in a student organization. But one still wonders at the end of the conference: 'What was the point, other than to plan and get invited to yet another conference?'

Many organizations are side-tracked into the belief that activism is committee meetings, that generating paper and electronic mail is the same as solving a problem. A large fraction of scarce financial and human resources is wasted in this manner.

Even when youth overcome these problems, they are frequently sabotaged by their elders. A number of my colleagues have spent months planning and organizing conferences only to have a senior speaker make an offhand comment at a keynote plenary about youth being ineffectual that coloured the entire conference. Students will prepare to be heard as an equal in a session, only to have their position immediately degraded when they are sent to fetch coffee or be the errand runner for the seniors. A Board of Directors of an umbrella organization, including a youth group, may disregard the needs and opinions of the youth as tangential to their true organizational priorities.

There is a general perception among many 'less youthful' people that the young should wait their turn, that they say nothing worth listening to. This is a universal perception, as many graduate students will disregard undergraduates, who ignore high school students, and so on.

It is important for all of us to remember that every time we dismiss someone on account of age we close one more door in our minds, and risk turning a proactive, questioning individual into a passive reactor to world events. This is especially true of the young, who will look to their elders – often unconsciously – for approval of their activities until their own sense of self is sufficiently developed to know that what they are doing is right.

So much for the failings of youth organizations. I have been explicit in the specifics of our problems because I do not know how clearly delineated they are to outside observers. The problems that I have outlined are not at all unique to youth movements; in many cases, these sins are more easily forgiven in youth precisely because they stem most often from extreme dedication to a cause.

I do not mean to convey the impression that youth organizations are irreversibly crippled – if anything, the youth movement grows stronger and more vibrant each day, because of our following strengths, which I feel to be such obvious truisms that little elaboration will be necessary.

Youth have a near-infinite supply of energy, which when properly focused can work miracles. I do not wish to restate a cliché or the obvious, but it cannot be emphasized enough that when a group of young people are energized towards a common goal, the amount of effort and activity that can result is tremendous. Youth are physiologically able to go on little sleep, food and recreation for weeks at a time, and psychologically willing to subject themselves to that sort of abuse if the cause is right.

This flows naturally into its corollary: since the young do not understand why a project is impossible, they may be the only ones able to accomplish the impossible. I need not reproduce here a litany of events precipitated by young people when their elders thought such action was impossible. This can be seen in innumerable small and large ways by watching the changes that youth organizations are causing today, especially in environmental activism. Youth will go further on fewer resources. Like every generalization, there will be frequent exceptions to this rule. But youth on the whole have fewer financial obligations, fewer commitments and fewer ingrained expectations on what they absolutely need in terms of material possessions. The young also tend to be much faster to adopt newer technologies that make new things possible at much lower cost; examples include International Student/Young Pugwash members holding a meeting via the Internet, and Chinese-American activist groups staying in contact with Tiananmen Square protesters via fax machines.

Youth movements must be nurtured and supported, because the alternatives are far worse. The greatest enemies of world harmony are apathy and disillusionment, insular thinking and devotion to personal self-interest. The young learn these attitudes from their elders, many of whom have already been beaten down until their cynicism is the only way of maintaining their dignity.

But youth are naturally optimistic and will always see not what is but what can be. The vast majority of us slide into adulthood having lost these traits, waiting to beat negative ideas into the heads of our own children. Youth movements are a natural rebellion against that path of least resistance, and will always spontaneously form no matter the greater social context. These movements will either turn out committed individuals ready to continue changing the world throughout their adult life, or dispirited husks who, having dared and failed, are far more bleak about the world's prospects than those who originally remained within their safe enclosures of cynicism. It is vitally necessary that youth movements be supported in order to prevent this kind of human decay.

The young will become the elders of the next generation and, being human, will inevitably make no fewer mistakes than our own elders and mentors are making with us. What will hopefully be different is that if enough of us are brought through powerful mechanisms for growth, such as International Student/Young Pugwash, or the thousands of organizations like it that dot the globe, we in turn will help nurture our own young through this process, in a continually self-affirming process. There is never a lack of things to be done and there can never be too many youth activists – or activists of any age.

Youth movements nurture activism. They reach people at an early age, reversing trends of cynicism and replacing them with real tools for effecting change. Many youth organizations are conscious of their role of turning youth into leaders and incorporate leadership development training into their programmes – hands-on training in political and social mobilization that can be found nowhere else. Specific goals of the organizations are similar to the following, taken from the Youth '95 mission statement:

> The Youth '95 Initiative strives to empower youth to participate in, strengthen, and reform the United Nations system and its goals on local, national, and international levels through grassroots mobilization, global education, and a sustainable working partnership among youth organizations and UN agencies.

Youth organizations replace the seeds of hatred and bigotry in the newest generation by reaching individuals before these opinions can calcify. Every student that works on a global issue or meets a young person from another nation is far less capable of ever seeing members of another nation as the 'other', or too foreign to understand or care about. This type of bridge-building may be the cheapest form of peacemaking available to humanity as a species. Indeed, it is the only way of ensuring that ethnic hatreds are truly reduced over time, from generation to generation.

The problem is not so much the promotion of exchanges between young people. Like any group with something in common, we naturally mingle with each other, and given resources, we set up our own mechanisms for promoting this on a global scale. Of course, it is vitally important that these resources be made available, as many youth organizations do not have the means of raising sufficient funds on their own. Left to themselves in a vacuum, the odds against a youth movement rise exponentially.

As important, however, is the 'promotion of exchanges between young people and the less young', because so long as we impose an artificial chasm of 'we' and 'they' on a group that should simply be seen as 'us', we will always run the risk of losing vital knowledge, losing important battles, and worst of all, losing people, our spirits, and our humanity.

Seeing the global issues that must be addressed in the coming century, we no longer have the luxury of keeping that particular old way of thinking.

****

A comprehensive overview of youth movements and organizations that work towards global interdependence would be an extremely useful tool for members of such organizations and others who wish to track their work; such was the original scope of the work from which this chapter is derived. Unfortunately, that was quickly discovered to be an impossible task, due to the great number of such organizations and their impermanence.

Youth organizations are amorphous, turbulent, quick to form and often quick to disband or dissolve from lack of resources. Many times an organization is itself a coalition of other groups, making it even more difficult to determine the range of its scope and its overall impact. Even those student organizations which have demonstrated longevity and commitment to a single set of issues may change their organizational priorities from year to year, so any exhaustive description of 'the youth movement' would lose most of its accuracy in a very short time.

Further complicating the situation, my experience with various youth organizations leads me to believe that the only viewpoint that accurately describes these organizations is an internal one; one that stays to watch the development of initiatives over several years. I can confidently speak of a number of organizations over the past several years but my assurance is much lower when I speak of other youth groups that I have worked with, but, crucially, not in.

So, given the infeasibility of its first premise - which shines some light on the nature of the topic – this chapter was switched from an encyclopaedic format to an essay of observations on youth organizations in general and the specific ones with which I have been involved. I have no way of knowing whether my personal experience is with a representative cross-section of youth organizations. Further, it has become more clear to me that the assumptions and structures of these movements are indelibly rooted in Western beliefs and, all too often, American culture. That will undoubtedly also colour my appraisal here, and I apologize for any Western bias that readers of different backgrounds may recognize, when my comments here do not translate to their own cultures.

I would like to thank Timothy Larson, formerly of Student Pugwash USA, and Aaron Knight, Director of Development and Special Programs at the World Federalist Association (USA), whose comments were invaluable during the preparation of this paper.

9

Making Information Widely Available: The Media and World Affairs

Nigel Calder

Reading foreign newspapers when you travel, or watching the television of other countries, tells you that news is a geographically variable concept. You may look in vain for updates on stories that were making banner headlines in your own country when you left home. Instead, you will find local and regional matters reported, involving people and places of which you know very little. A few big stories from around the world, typically wars and disasters, will find their way into the media everywhere, but otherwise what a well-informed person is supposed to know depends on where he or she lives.

The human perspective, in which near events seem more important and interesting than remote ones, is reinforced by linguistic differences and by the organization of the world into nation states. Indeed, the media and the nation states evolved together, so that leading newspapers and broadcasting organizations stand alongside the flag and the football team as durable emblems of nationhood in an otherwise melding world. Parliamentary democracy relies on the national focus of the media to keep voters informed about the personalities and issues.

The idea that anyone can be well informed about the world as a whole is far-fetched. No individual brain could cope with the events and concerns among billions of busy people in dozens of regions. Instead, the media highlight certain events. Although often arbitrary (why this war, or this famine, rather than another?) their selections influence what national leaders and the UN Security Council deem to be worthy of attention.

One could feel better informed during the Cold War. When two superpowers threatened the world with nuclear war at short notice, it was obvious what was most newsworthy. The top concerns of the media matched the geopolitical perspectives of the US President and the Soviet Chairman. Readers of newspapers and viewers of television news broadcasts wanted to know how this event or that was playing in Washington or Moscow, and on the whole they were told.

Alarm bells rang whenever anything perturbed the interface between the rival alliances, or brought the interests of the superpowers into conflict, actual or potential. Ugly things could happen outside their main spheres of influence, in Africa or China for example, with much less attention. Events deep inside the main power blocs were of lesser interest too, except as local news. But if you read the newspapers and watched the television news bulletins you could believe you knew how the world wagged. With hindsight it was the blinkered view of someone subconsciously checking that it was not yet time to head for the fall-out shelter.

In the end, everyone from President and Chairman downwards turned out to be ill-informed, by their intelligence services as well as by the media. All were surprised by the chain reaction of events in the late 1980s that led to the dissolution of the Soviet bloc and eventually of the Soviet Union itself. The media played their part in the process, not least in the broadcast television signals that conformed to the laws of physics rather than of nations. They freely crossed the frontiers, and disclosed to people in the Warsaw Pact countries the upheavals going on among their neighbours.

Now what? Those who wish conscientiously to follow world events find similar news services continuing to serve them with their soothingly rhythmic and prepackaged bites of information. Technically they are better than before. But the news has lost its primary focus and the shedding of Cold War blinkers reveals a wider world with a quasi-infinite amount of information that might be retailed. It exposes more clearly the arbitrary nature of editorial judgments about what is newsworthy.

The media are so habit-forming that one can hardly imagine a world without newspapers, radio and television. But in most places and at most times people did without them. The classical Chinese and Roman empires had no media in the modern sense. Nor did Venice, half a millennium ago, when it was the leading city of commerce, analogous to New York or Tokyo today. Individuals paid 'foreign correspondents' to send them handwritten newsletters, but on the whole news travelled by word of mouth.

Those needing information of particular kinds would share their knowledge in gossip with colleagues. When, in *The Merchant of Venice*, Shylock asks: 'What news on the Rialto?' he refers to the place where traders from all over the known world gathered to do business and pass the time of day. There you could hear from your fellow merchants about war and peace, piracy, the economy of nations, commodity prices, and the outcome of mercantile ventures. In exchange, you imparted news you might have heard from a returning sea captain. The course of events in Shakespeare's play hinges on a lack of news and vague reports of shipwrecks.

I suspect that our children will return to personalized newsgathering habits like those of the Venetian merchants. While technology is, for the time being, giving a boost to global news services for the conventional media, other trends are making them less important in the practicalities of everyday life. But I shall also argue that news should be evaluated in respect of its emotional impact, as well as for its analytical content. Then the media, flawed though they may be, are seen to be very valuable in promoting a sense of world citizenship.

GLOBAL MEDIA OF THE 1990s

Old-time journalists had umbrellas or parasols; their successors carry folding satellite dishes. Telecommunications satellites make the gathering and distribution of news much easier. But coverage costs money – whether to send a television crew to an obvious trouble-spot, or to retain stringers in residence in sleepy places where nothing noteworthy happens from one year to the next.

Radio is the cheapest mass medium, and the BBC World Service, based in London, was able with a modest budget to build up a reputation for reliable reporting and informed commentary. It is still unrivalled in the number of languages on offer in its direct transmissions (about forty) and the number of countries where its material is rebroadcast by local companies (about 100). But in the size of its regular audience, BBC World Service radio is being overtaken by worldwide television news, in the first instance by CNN.

A television news service with pretensions to global coverage has to be big and financially powerful. Ted Turner of Atlanta, Georgia, instituted CNN International in the mid-1980s, and it leapt into the limelight during the Gulf War. By 1994, according to *The Guardian's* latest Media Guide, CNN's 24-hour worldwide television news service was reaching 145 million households in 143 countries, via eleven satellites and associated cable distribution. The BBC is challenging CNN with World Service TV in many parts of the world, and it aims, as with radio, to provide the news in the regional languages. In cooperation with the BBC, Rupert Murdoch's Star TV has established a dominant role in satellite television in India and China.

The news agencies shadow the broadcasters, providing them with material. In 1992 Reuters Television of London took over Visnews, a pioneering television news agency, and now it dominates the field. In 1994 Reuters employed 1350 journalists, cameramen and photographers in 123 bureaux in 80 countries, to serve 900 broadcasters in 81 countries (*The Guardian* data for 1994).

The mind boggles at the scale of the operations. This is the visual analogue of the news agencies for text, among which

Reuters itself dates back to the early days of the electric telegraph, circa 1850. Text too multiplies, and a flourishing news agency will make available to newspapers, every day, as many words as in Tolstoy's *War and Peace*. Add to the global operations the zeal of individual newspapers and broadcasters in sending out their own teams in pursuit of stories, and no-one can doubt that there is a lot of news flowing around the world, some of it acquired at great personal risk by the journalists concerned.

The sheer abundance of data can nevertheless induce a false sense of security, as Goethe observed more than 160 years ago. The resources even of the largest networks and agencies are strictly limited. So are the number of pages in a newspaper and the number of minutes in a TV news bulletin. Editors have to assign their teams to stories most likely to sell and eventually to reach the public. In the case of agencies, there are two filters at work: the selections of the agency editor and the selections of the newspaper or television station acquiring the material. Objectivity in reporting is something that individual journalists can strive for, on the spot, but objectivity in the choice of stories is a much more difficult goal. Could sincere, well-informed editors in, say, Paris, Bombay and Caracas ever be expected to agree on the top ten news items of the day?

An illusion of consensus comes with the 'media circus' in which large numbers of reporters and cameras turn up at the same event. The media are incestuous. For fear of missing a big story, they watch what their competitors are doing and do likewise. They are also very reliant on their own memories and their files of past stories, which tend to define who is famous and what parts of the world are most interesting. An example of that sort of historic bias is apparent in science, where news of discoveries and inventions from the USA is favoured over equivalent or stronger stories from Europe and Japan. Editors have been conditioned over the years to think of North America as the source of great science, just as South America is a source of great footballers.

Even global news networks have headquarters located in particular places, and a bias that goes with that provenance. Typically, they favour the North over the South, the West over the East, the interests of the wealthy over the concerns of the poor, and English in preference to other languages. In the case of television, spectacular pictures and easy access for live reports will encourage the selection of particular news items and guarantee them more air time.

The news media are not educational enterprises dedicated to enlightening the public comprehensively and objectively about world affairs. They are selling information as other people sell fruit, and the tastes of the customers shape the news. Editors match their selections of news to what they believe their audiences, highbrow or lowbrow, want to hear about.

More deliberate distortions occur, as a result either of partisan orientations or of government censorship and mendacity. A public relations industry is dedicated to influencing what appears in the media, in promoting or stifling particular stories on behalf of the clients. The media affect the events they report. Pressure groups of various kinds, including those campaigning in support of the most laudable of causes, find themselves playing the same sort of game in pursuit of column inches or seconds of air time.

Battles are staged or halted for the benefit of the cameras. A grotesque example occurred in Somalia when American marines assaulting a beach at night were unexpectedly dazzled by TV lights. It was by a miracle of forbearance that young men fearing for their lives did not open fire on the assembled newsmen. Thoughtful journalists are perturbed by the way atrocities stop when the foreign press turn up in a trouble-spot and resume when they move on. At the time of writing, I see a Chechen woman pleading with a Western news team to remain in Grozny because otherwise the Russians would step up their air attacks.

Entrepreneurial pressures concentrate media power in the hands of a few global operators, serving or controlling many outlets. Media moguls can make or break individual ministers, if not entire governments, by their slants on the news. Conversely, Silvio Berlusconi, Prime Minister of Italy during 1994, wielded television power that a dictator could envy. He simultaneously controlled his own privately owned channels and made appointments to key positions in the state television service. He could address the nation whenever he liked and used this power shamelessly in trying to cling to office amid corruption scandals.

LIFE IN ZAPPERVILLE

Maybe none of this will matter very much in the future. The effectiveness and, therefore, the importance of television is probably declining. We live in the age of the zapper. The hand-held remote control device makes it so easy to change the television channel that viewers wander from one to another, among the dozens of channels on offer, as if they were strolling through a fairground. News channels and documentary programme-makers compete from moment to moment with all other offerings, from game shows to drama. Television is being trivialized more surely by the consumer than by the media bosses.

A recent personal example illustrates life in Zapperville today. A production company in the UK invited me to script several hours of documentary material on meteorology, for a US educational television channel. With apologies, the producer briefed me to write it in the form of self-sufficient sequences of two to three minutes. On no account should I attempt to develop ideas coherently through a 25-minute programme, because few viewers would stay with it for more than a small fraction of the time. Then the invitation was withdrawn. The US broadcasters thought I was too well informed. They wanted a writer ignorant of the subject, apparently to avoid any risk of straining the viewers' brains with non-superficial information.

More means worse. Roughly constant money, from advertising revenues and direct expenditures by consumers, has to sustain the multiplying television and radio channels, thicker newspapers, and a ridiculous number of book and magazine titles. The hours per week that people spend attending to the media do not change much, except to the extent that home computers, videos, optical compact discs and electronic games eat into the time available for the more traditional media.

Programme-makers, editors and writers find that the affordable effort per minute of air time or per page of print goes down, and quality suffers.

Good work still appears. On-the-spot reporting by individual journalists and teams may have improved over the years. The media are more investigative, on the whole. Certainly they are less deferential to authority and more reluctant to believe official hand-outs. Yet in the end the picture of the world disseminated by the media is a caricature of reality.

Perhaps it was always so. But never was it so clear that journalism is just a branch of the entertainment industry, with news services competing with all the other media that clamour for attention on a shrill planet.

TOWARDS A TOTAL INFORMATION SYSTEM

During the Cold War, the sense of a never-ending crisis was intensified by the presumed availability to commanders-in-chief of total information concerning military matters all around the world. Chance brushes between troops or distant ships, which in the eighteenth century would not have been heard of for several months, were supposed to be calculated and controlled from the superpower bunkers. Conversely, the military satellites and communications systems were high on the target lists, with 'decapitation' of the opponent on offer as a way of winning a nuclear war.

Of course the systems were never perfect, but military and civilian needs have between them wired up the world to an astonishing degree. If you are a serious player in the markets for stocks, commodities or money, you plug into a network uniting the main centres and follow the action from minute to minute, as vast sums flow around the northern hemisphere in a financial jet stream. In the process, electronic money has become a force in its own right, as psychologically detached as gambling chips from the goods and services, or wealth and poverty, that it represents.

The World Meteorological Organization has for many years coordinated the daily harvesting of information from weather stations in every country, and from ships and aircraft. The data feed the supercomputers that generate the weather forecasts by global calculations. It is an equable system, because those contributing data receive the forecasts in return, together with relevant weather satellite imagery and data. Perhaps this reciprocity should be extended to other data-gathering systems, so that everyone has the right to knowledge assembled with their active or even passive participation.

Democratization of the wired world comes with the Internet, at least for many millions of people with computers, modems and the wherewithal to use the system. The Internet is expanding and changing so rapidly that anything written about it is likely to be out of date by the time it appears in print. Scientists, as professional users of computers, had a head start in their access to data-exchanging systems and e-mail, and CERN established the World Wide Web as part of the Internet.

Whether seen as a global tool for the serious-minded or as a hobby for computer buffs, the Internet is anarchistic, both in the benign, anti-authoritarian sense of the word and in its potential for chaos. It illustrates strengths and weaknesses of the idea of total information. Material available on the Internet ranges from cooking recipes and pop music to DNA sequences and abstracts of scientific papers. Much of the information is free, but there is also access to commercial sources and services for which payment is required.

People chat and set up *ad hoc* discussion groups on the Internet. They follow up enthusiasms of the moment. The combined attention of astronomers and eavesdroppers overloaded the system when it was pooling information about the impacts of Comet Shoemaker-Levy 9 on Jupiter, in July 1994. Traditionally-minded researchers are made uneasy by scientific papers circulating freely on the Internet, without the normal refereeing of formal publication. Traditionally-minded journalists are bemused by the lack of editorial quality control on other information.

THE ELECTRONIC RIALTO

Low data-rates on telephone lines limit the present effectiveness of the Internet. High-rate optical fibre systems, capable for example of carrying video material, will make anything that is convertible into digital form accessible to anyone, at least in theory. Every satellite image of the Earth's surface, every movie and newspaper article, the speeches of every politician, results of opinion polls in Bolivia and Botswanaland, the outcome of every football game or scientific experiment . . . the list is endless.

Of course, total information is totally indigestible. The process of selection, whether done by the individual user or by a newspaper-like service on his or her behalf, is unavoidable. It may be technically trivial to program one's own selection of information to be downloaded routinely on to one's computer/ receiver, as a kind of home-made newspaper, but it is not clear that this will be a good way to stay informed. The conventional media are better able to respond to the unexpected, and to tell you things you didn't know you would be interested in.

The human species seems likely to revert to gossip, in the electronic Rialto, as the way to keep informed. People with shared interests will pool what they know, while perhaps subscribing to specialized news services closely matched to their needs. A model exists in the network of scientists active in a particular field of research, who exchange preprints and read much the same selection of journals.

Pugwash itself is another model. Indeed, misgivings about the media fall into a less perplexing perspective if you focus on the needs of a particular group. In Pugwash this means scientists interested in world affairs. The information that they as a group require is precisely that which they wish to discuss with one another.

The general media were only one contributor to the information available after Hiroshima to concerned individuals and local groups among the 'atomic scientists'. Others were: (1) their professional scientific knowledge; (2) the erudite conversations in which scientists indulge over their coffee or beer; (3) their privileged access to the suburbs of policymaking;

and (4) their scholarly ability to seek out information by consulting other experts or delving in libraries.

Individuals and local groups pooled their knowledge. This happened among Western scientists with the *Bulletin of the Atomic Scientists*, which made their knowledge and opinions influential. In a less public way, Pugwash extended the process across the Iron Curtain and into the Third World. The tradition in Pugwash that its discussions should be closed to the press emphasizes its independence from the media. Had the invention of nuclear weapons occurred forty years later, concerned scientists would now be exchanging their knowledge and opinions by e-mail and issuing their bulletins and manifestos on the Internet. This is certainly a practical method for building up a body of knowledge on current issues, such as nuclear proliferation and the trade in fissile materials. But people will still want to meet in private to consider politically sensitive ways of dealing with problems.

LONG-TERM ISSUES

Fundamental questions arise about the social system. Information is power, and there will be strong tensions between those who want privileged access for financial or political reasons, and those who invoke the technological possibilities to make everything accessible. It is worth recalling that, at the height of the Cold War, the USA and USSR joined forces to squelch a French proposal for an international system of photo-reconnaissance satellites, which would have ended the superpowers' advantage in espionage from space.

A total information system can be abused by a dictatorial regime. When George Orwell wrote *Nineteen Eighty-Four* the technology available to Big Brother was rudimentary by comparison with what even credit card companies have today, never mind the potential combination of modern surveillance techniques and computerized monitoring of troublemakers. The dictatorship could be global, as in Freeman J Dyson's grim scenario of a world police state dedicated to the prevention of nuclear proliferation.

The best defence against dictatorship is supposed to be democracy, but one must ask whether the rise of information-sharing among special-interest groups, not tied to particular geographical areas, is compatible with conventional systems of government. The continuing love-hate relationship of politicians and the media is a reminder of the symbiosis between the press and parliamentary democracy. If the media dissolve into specialized and geographically diffuse information services, on the electronic Rialto, this may undermine parliamentary democracy at the national level.

The door might then open to national tyrannies. But equally it could show the way to the demise of the nation state, and its replacement by other systems of human organization on a local, continental and/or global scale. The anarchism of the Internet may foreshadow political anarchism in its literal sense of doing away with governments. But here the crystal ball grows very cloudy. Perhaps no-one alive today has the imagination to foresee the full consequences of current developments in information technology.

Would-be world citizens have to confront the problem of language. Differences in language remain the chief impediment to mutual understanding around the world. Although English has become *de facto* the global language of politics, commerce and science, its use disadvantages the individuals and cultures that are not natively English-speaking, and excludes the less well-educated from the global discourse. Some newsgroups actively challenge the hegemony of English on the Internet. A recent listing shows offerings in Arabic, Chinese, French, German, Persian, Polish, Portuguese, Russian and Turkish.

These are not among the thousands of 'small' languages now disappearing worldwide, and taking with them an incalculable treasury of culture. There is a grim contradiction between the wish to remove the barrier of language differences, and the wish to preserve cultural diversity and the right of people to speak the same language as their parents. Perhaps technology can help (see Chapter 11).

Computer scientists and linguists have pursued machine translation for forty years. They wrestle with technical and philosophical problems that make even the plasma physics of fusion reactors seem tame by comparison. Deeper insight into language, combined with the brute-force power of twenty-first century computing, may carry the technology forward from the present faulty literal translations by machine, which have to be edited, to something really useful in everyday discourse. For example, it may be possible some day to phone a friend in Tokyo and hear him speaking your language, while he listens to you in Japanese.

AWARENESS OF OTHERS

While the media may never supply the world with a fair, comprehensive and wholly objective body of information about the state of the planet, they already do a superb job in fostering the ideal of world citizenship. In this respect, the judiciousness of the news menu is less important than the sight, every day, of the faces of faraway people moved by grief or joy, anger or reason, conviction or doubt. The resulting empathy cuts across ethnic, religious and political divisions more effectively than any abstract pronouncements about the unity and interdependence of the human species.

Here the media parallel and support other benign influences such as tourism, sport and international action programmes. Experts in nutrition may question the priorities in famine relief, but if ordinary individuals around the world are moved to give money to help hungry people seen on their television screens, they are paying a voluntary welfare tax as world citizens. Similarly, while Earth-system scientists can and should debate whether the information circulating about threats to the global environment is technically sound, it has implanted the idea that we all share a lonely and vulnerable planet in the desert of space. At this same emotional level, political critiques of UN success and failure in peacekeeping matter less than the images of men in blue berets, far from home, facing hardship and danger on behalf of people whose languages they cannot speak.

In their piecemeal way, the media also monitor political

behaviour worldwide, exposing examples of repression and corruption to the international gaze. Even authoritarian regimes pay lip-service to worldwide norms of decent behaviour, legality and human rights, and adverse publicity embarrasses them. Exposés also alert the citizens of the world to the ever-present danger of tyranny.

The danger of weapons of mass destruction, on the other hand, is less clearly expressed nowadays. The media pay some attention to concerns about nuclear proliferation and the smuggling of nuclear materials. But with the diminished threat of an all-out war between Russia and the Western allies, the horror of nuclear war may become attenuated in the public mind. During the Cold War, a fairly steady trickle of factual and fictional descriptions reminded people of the effects of nuclear weapons. Now we may be rearing a generation of youngsters with little idea of the orders of magnitude of destructiveness that separate nuclear from conventional weapons.

Those concerned with world citizenship should try to use all available media – starting perhaps with the Internet – to educate young people about weaponry in the post-Cold War world. Clear explanations of nuclear weapons, and of trends in chemical and biological weapons too, should be made available as widely as possible and should leave no doubt about the horrors their use would bring. But the idea that it is quite all right for some countries to possess nuclear weapons, while utterly wicked for others to try to acquire them, will not be self-evident to budding world citizens. When they realize that the permanent members of the UN Security Council are themselves armed to the teeth, they may come to mistrust the present arrangements for policing the world.

The human species has to find a long-term solution to the control of weapons of mass destruction. Public information, public opinion and the vigilance of scientists and journalists will have crucial parts to play, along with the awareness of other peoples and their legitimate concerns which global reporting can cultivate. I recommend a worldwide debate in the media about military power in the twenty-first century as a practical exercise in world citizenship that should begin now.

10

Exposing and Eradicating Misleading Information

Shalheveth Freier and
Carin Atterling Wedar

INTRODUCTION

It is desirable that information should be 'objective', that it gives a balanced picture of the world – that what we see and hear about the world is true. With an increasingly interdependent world the importance of understanding all of that world is growing. This interdependence cannot be built on misunderstanding – it is often no more than misunderstanding that brings conflict. Often, all that is necessary to find tolerance for one's neighbour is to be able to understand what they are and how they live.

In order for our discussion of 'objective information' to be meaningful we have to consider information in the context in which it is given. This is simply illustrated by looking at the statement 'he drove at 150 km/hr'. This is an objective statement, in that it is demonstrably true. The person we are speaking of either did or did not drive at 150 km/hr. However, information is rarely given in such a bald way, but is presented in context. Firstly, context is provided by the preconceptions we bring to the information; how we view the world colours how we understand the information that comes to us about it. It cannot be helped that some information will tend to support our sincerely held beliefs, and some we will reject because it runs counter to those beliefs. This can be taken advantage of, when information is manipulated to appeal to these beliefs, and we shall look at how this has been done in the case of Bosnia, below. We are talking here of those cases where the media have attempted to produce information that is true, not where the aim has been to spread lies or outright propaganda, although the means to prevent these are much the same. There are two main ways to avoid information becoming biased by our cultural preconceptions. The information should be balanced, covering all sides of an issue and not just those that immediately appeal to the prejudices of those who provide or those who consume the information, and the recipients of the information should have a broad education, so that they can understand and empathize with the context for the information.   Secondly, context is given by surrounding information. The statement 'he drove at 150 km/hr' takes on new meaning when we are informed that the driver sped recklessly to impress a lady sat beside him, or that he was speeding to the aid of a friend in distress. The news we receive of the world does not reach us as a succession of bald facts. Each objectively true fact comes in its own little package. To prevent misleading information we need to ensure both that the facts themselves are discernible and are disseminated, and that the packages they come in are themselves objective. If we can do the former, we can eradicate lies and propaganda, since they will be thrown into high relief by the objective facts that are uncovered.

We must remember, of course, in what follows, that we, ourselves, are part of the Western democratic consensus, and that our views on this subject have their own context and are coloured by it. We are taking as given that each person is entitled to uncensored information, that they should be empowered to ponder issues pertinent to them and take action to support their enlightened convictions. These are not necessarily objective goods in themselves. Some countries have arguably only achieved progress through manipulating information: it is doubtful, for example, whether China could have been guided towards prosperity through congenial liberal means. But it is with this Western democratic bias that we must, perforce, approach the subject in hand.

INFORMATION IN CONTEXT

When we use the word 'objectivity' in connection with the media, we are not doing so in absolute terms. We refer more to the notion that the media should always present all sides of a story. This is because information is always presented in a context, and for information to be understood by all it is important that all should understand the context in which it is presented.

The natural sciences approximate most closely the ideal of objective 'information in context'. The attributes of natural phenomena, the methods of observation, and the rules of inference are agreed. Paradigms – the ways of looking at natural phenomena – are the context. These change occasionally, but after a change a new paradigm is agreed, inasmuch as it succeeds in explaining diverse phenomena. The constraints of nature, which are demonstrable, and the rules of logic form the objective basis for these paradigms, and tell us what is permissible and what is not.

To a lesser degree, such conceptual constraints exist in other areas of human life but they have much smaller scope than the paradigms of the natural sciences. Different cultures, different values, different senses of pride and identity are the differing conceptual backgrounds – the different contexts – in which information, and its pertinence, are embedded. We all tend to cling to conceptual clichés. These confer a measure of certainty, of which we stand in apparent need, as we wish to negotiate the inconsistencies within us and without. We need this certainty as a point of departure for our opinions and decisions. There is almost a compulsion to select information and present it in support of these clichés, which offer ready comfort.

Information given in context is in this way inherently biased. The simplest way to alleviate this bias is to broaden the context, by allowing ourselves a broader base of knowledge and values. The main reason for unwillingness to accept new ideas is often lack of knowledge – life experience, broad education, and insight into what could be called basic international knowledge. This should include a certain amount of history, politics, ethics, religion, literature, ethnography and economics. Without a basic knowledge of other parts of the world we cannot talk to each other, or at least cannot understand what one another is saying.

The phrase 'my freedom fighter is your terrorist, your terrorist is my freedom fighter' is well-known, but if I knew more about your terrorist I might be tempted to call him a freedom fighter too. Nelson Mandela provides an example. Many inside and outside South Africa thought him a dangerous terrorist, imprisoned as he was for terrorist offences. But for those people, when they saw the impressively clothed, well-spoken gentle man who appeared from jail, he ceased to be a terrorist and became a spokesman. This may appear a banal example but a serious insight underlies it. If more people had known about the real Mandela earlier, about his history, his roots, his social background, his reasons for fighting, attitudes might have changed two decades earlier.

MEANS OF PROVIDING A BROADER CONTEXT FOR INFORMATION

One of the means of providing a broader context for information is already to some extent in place. The means of access to information have greatly expanded in recent times. Time and place, if not immaterial, are nonetheless under our control. We and our colleagues no longer have to even be in the same hemisphere even to carry out our daily routines together. We can all connect to the same computer and the same information. The vast mine of information available through the Internet illustrates the potential for cross-global communications.

These resources are available to those in the North more

readily than in the South, it is true. There is enormous potential to use the available resources, if they can be coordinated. The SatelLife project has shown what can be done, by linking African health professionals through modem and satellite to data resources in the North and worldwide.

There is no substitute, though, for mutual exposure of citizens of countries in opposition, and indeed of countries from very different parts of the world. Such exchange visits, embracing all types of people – from lecturers to students, schoolchildren to ordinary people – should be encouraged. It would be useful for UNESCO to have a fund dedicated to this purpose, especially where money is needed to support such exchanges. Clearly, people from the West are in a better position to visit the rest of the world than those from the South, say. The UN could help support North-South, East-West, or any type of exchange. One can imagine the effect in the Cold War if these exchanges had been more common. Xenophobia is based on lack of knowledge of outsiders. It is difficult to hate someone when you know them well, know their culture and the reasons for it. Fear of the new can keep us from making progress; but if the new is familiar to us we can embrace it without fear.

Nationalism looks like the greatest obstacle on the path to a united world. The wish to cling to 'our nation', 'our values', and defend them against all-comers, is strongly imbued in many in the world today. But if we can understand other values, other cultures, we can begin to accept them, incorporating them into our own system of beliefs, and perhaps begin to see the world as our nation, its values in all their diversity as our values.

Much space and time should be dedicated by the mass media to increasing our awareness of issues concerning global and regional interdependence, showing up the damages of petty or shortsighted policies. As permanent features – advertised as such – we suggest such subjects as global and regional interdependence and common hazards. So many problems in the world need global effort, and in their solving there will inevitably be conflicts with national interests and policies; these features could show that the need for joint action is ineluctable.

Just as there is a State of the Union address in the USA and other nations, the Secretary-General of the UN could present a State of the World message yearly. This should be a balanced, factual report, reflecting contending views where necessary, and containing a survey of areas of unhappiness and despair throughout the globe. It should become statutory for all nations to discuss this statement in their legislatures (where they have them) and one would hope it would be extensively discussed in the media. This message should illustrate and insist on common interdependence and hazards.

Above all else, though, for information not to mislead, both its providers and recipients must be knowledgable, well educated. This will require a new approach to education. This must start at school, in the early years. What we now think of as adult education must become a part of elementary schooling for young children. Many countries are currently re-evaluating their schoolbooks and curricula to reflect the need for global education; this is encouraging.

There is a need for better teacher-training. Teachers at the lowest levels must have better qualifications in order to include more advanced education during the first years at school. If global attitudes can be inculcated at a very young age, they will become a firm part of each child's conceptual background.

One of the authors (CAW) is involved in an educational experiment to introduce a new subject onto the syllabus: international human relations in literature and history. It is a small project thus far, without systematic evaluation, but it has shown the possibility of producing fairly objective information, and also that young people are prepared to see things from different perspectives. The students are aged 12-15. In one term they worked in groups, reading extracts from Russell, Nietzsche, *The Koran*, *The Bible*, modern poetry, *The Brothers Karamazov*. The aim was to sort out certain views of humanity. The project included seeing *Schindler's List* after a thorough consideration of *Letters from Stalingrad*. Many very balanced comments were made afterwards by the students, who could see that evil exists all around, but so do good, humanity, loneliness, the yearning for peace, friendship, lasting values and consideration.

A new area will be cross-global education. One of the

authors' (CAW) investigations led her to CNN and Turner Educational Services Inc. CNN's former head in Scandinavia became actively involved. They had already worked on plans to broaden teaching by computer in different countries. This included a project aimed at using computers as tools, not just as a subject for study. Computers are a means of quickly gaining new knowledge and through them students can discuss different subjects with students in other countries in a 'live' situation. The idea of a TV series with the same content directed at schoolchildren throughout the world is a good step towards being educated as world citizen. Objective information can be guaranteed in such a programme by a mix of editors with special knowledge of the subject in question.

There is an experimental class of nine-year-olds in Stockholm using computers and videos in its daily lessons. The class is linked to seven other classes throughout the world. So far, maths, geography and history lessons have been shared globally. Objectivity in the information children receive can become possible through direct discussions in the media of video and computer. Questions are free and so are answers. There is no need for the teacher to interpret anything. The speakers are their own jury and can come up with their own judgments. Doubts and differences freely expressed can help cover a great distance on the journey to objective information.

OBJECTIVITY IN NEWS PRESENTATION

There are many examples of media reporting that breaks with fundamental reporting principles. These principles are: describing as far as possible both sides in a conflict and not disturbing the balance of a report, so that what could be a positive report comes out as negative.

Ideally, we should wish to see a balance in the types of news presented. Unfortunately, the requirement that the media present objective reports is obscured by an unwritten law that the destructive, horrible, violent and spectacular in life is the most newsworthy. Why is this so? One answer, of course, is that people want to hear about the spectacular. Bad news sells. The media do not have to choose illness before health, brutality ahead of sympathy, and indeed are not responsible for this choice. The choice is already made by the public that receives the media's output, it is their values and interests that form the context for the information.

It is true that small, 'good news' stories, such as the famous picture of the policeman in Tokyo stopping the traffic to allow a mother duck and her offspring to cross the road, are sometimes given the headlines. But the real top sellers are about murder, disaster or presidential love affairs. The latter is of some importance, of course – a politician's actions have effects outside their private life. However, there is no paradigm of values wherein the president and the ducks can be ranked. In the final analysis it is a question of which values we wish to focus on.

The media can contribute to our view of human beings by the most banal and innocent means. One of us (CAW) remembers an argument with a headline writer many years ago when working in the media. She was especially irritated by the following: 'An earl drove too fast and killed chickens.' She thought that anyone who drove too fast and ran over poultry should be pilloried – whether or not they were an earl. Whatever one's views on aristocrats, they ought to be attacked only when their earlness is relevant. It is seldom interesting to write stories about metal workers or the unemployed. The worry is that this type of reporting maintains and reinforces class divisions. Class divisions are dangerous when they become permanent groupings. They become useful for dictators and racists to exploit in times of crisis.

This somewhat light-hearted example serves to show that the media can cause harm even with the smallest story. There is a great deal of value in the old, sacred rule for all journalism: whether you are dealing with a fire in a small shop in a small town, a report from the local council, or a civil war, all these stories have the same dignity and should demand the same approach, the same ethics, and the same standards.

CULTURAL CONTEXT AS A BARRIER TO OBJECTIVE
INFORMATION – BOSNIA: A CASE STUDY

Political conflicts and war reporting are, of course, the ultimate
test of serious journalism. The effects of war reporting can be
severe and long-lasting. They can lead to a permanent picture of
good and bad. The war in Vietnam is an extremely important chapter in
media history. It produced many examples of objective
information mixed with nationalist loyalty. 'Our boys are doing
their best and are on the receiving end of grim, bestial
behaviour.' Nobody could say this was untrue, but the lack of
balance, and of reports from the other side, had considerable
political effects. Vietnam was fought in the full glare of the
media's attention and has set the tone for those that have
followed, including the object of our case study, the struggle over
Bosnia.

The war in the former Yugoslavia provided journalists with
a unique role in terms of their direct, subjective involvement in
politics. The difficulty of freeing oneself from national, political
and ethnic loyalties, and remaining objective, has nowhere been
more clearly illustrated.

The war has put to the test the journalistic principle of
reporting the truth as far as possible. One example of a journalist
so tested is Milos Vasic, who works for the independent Belgrade
newspaper *Vreme*. The paper has become one of the most quoted
sources of news in the former Yugoslavia precisely because of its
political independence and commitment to objectivity. *Vreme* is
owned by a US-based liberal lawyer, Srdja Popovic. In an
interview in 1993, Vasic said: 'We are journalists – that is our
nationality.'[1] This is an important concept – that one can have
a greater loyalty, a higher 'nationality'. We are a stage nearer to
a global loyalty when professional knowledge and common aims
are given greater priority than traditional nationality where
freedom of expression can be denied. 'We stole the international
stage from Milosevic', says Vasic. 'Our recipe is simple. We
have professional standards and we don't fall for cheap tricks.'

Vreme was founded in October 1990. In December 1993 it

had achieved a circulation of 30,000. 'Our aim is to be the only real winners in this war.' *Vreme*'s journalists have a very strict rule that all facts are checked thoroughly; its journalists strive to be well-informed and reliable. 'All information is checked carefully. In the past six months we have not needed to correct any false facts.' The newspaper is neutral. Winning the war for them means simply winning their freedom of expression – 'telling it how it is.'

The paper's neutrality is strict, it has no national or political sympathies. Journalistic values are the only ones that are recognized. This has been *Vreme*'s route to providing objective information. On the domestic level, this has not been appreciated by the media who are loyal to the existing regime. 'They pretend we do not exist. Unfortunately, they do not attack us. If they did, it would be good advertising. Our editor says that he would give up one year of his life for a 30-second attack by the state TV network.' The editor's prayers have since been answered; he has been branded a warmonger in Bosnia by the state TV.

During its early days many of *Vreme*'s journalists found it hard to shake off the practice of self-censorship that was so common in formerly communist Yugoslavia. Other journalists simply did not want to break with the past, rupture their conceptual make-up. Milos Vasic lays a heavy burden on the shoulders of some of his colleagues: 'If the large, government-controlled media centres in Serbia and Croatia had had the moral strength to stick to the truth, the war would never have occurred. Events since then are the result of two or three years of propaganda from both sides.' But this propaganda is in some cases obviously intended to mislead:

> Lying is an art-form . . . and a propaganda war requires experts! But here they are quite scandalously bad. News is invented. Massacres and gruesome monstrosities are thought up at breathtakingly frequent intervals. They are quite unbelievable, statistically unbelievable too. The whole business has turned into the worst sort of violent pornography and in some journalistic quarters there seems to be a competition to invent stories with the most sordid details. Not so long ago it

was claimed that some Croatian Ustasha soldiers wore armbands made from children's fingers and necklaces made from the eyes of Serbian corpses. It was a war crime to print this sort of thing.

On another occasion a story was spread about a group of brutal murders of children in Vukovar. Some of this reached Swedish newspapers, for example. Not one word was true. The formerly well-respected newspaper *Politika* was the source. *Politika*, the Yugoslav equivalent of *The Times*, was under the strict control of Milosevic's Serbian government for a decisive period. Propaganda is used to legitimate attacks on the opposition. As more and more incredible stories are printed people cease to believe what the media report. 'One day a newspaper reported the astonishing news that Croatia had access to nuclear weapons . . . in a small paragraph on page 6 or 7. How are people expected to believe this.'

It is increasingly becoming accepted that a part of winning wars is to win the media war, to control the media. The need for objective reporting is never more evident than in wartime. Facts are all too easily coloured by which side you happen to be on, by interference from government or external sponsors. There may be a case for an UN-sponsored news agency, in the form of a global contact programme, its staff drawn from across the globe, with no agenda other than to report the truth. How this agency would gain access to the people in whose country the war is being fought is another question, though radio may be the answer. Nearly every home in the world has a radio, and radio transmissions, unlike newsprint, cannot be confiscated. The UN could attempt to get signed agreements that their agency would not be impeded in its work, but imposing these would be difficult. The UN needs most definitely to take a part in this area. UNESCO in particular needs to present a clear media programme, proposals on providing and disseminating objective information. The main difficulties will be those regimes that suppress free expression.

SUGGESTIONS FOR CORRECTING MISLEADING INFORMATION

All the mass media should be invited to adhere to a convention obliging them to set aside space and time for the airing of views running counter to editorial policies. This should be a proper, formalized right to reply, wherein all sides of an issue may be aired. Where a newspaper, for example, has taken one political stance, other viewpoints ought to be allowed equal space. Adherence to the convention would be well publicized. This is important especially for those countries where the government controls editorial policies.

As far as information that is intended to mislead we suggest examining the possibility of learning from the laws of libel that are common in many countries. There could, possibly, be a new crime of international libel, where a panel of judges drawn from a broad spectrum of countries could decide cases of misleading information. The decisions of the court could be publicized and repetition or dissemination of the offending information could become an offence punishable under international and national laws.

It will be very difficult to prevent the spread of lies. People will always lie, one cannot rely on their integrity. But through making access to objective information easier, and educating people so that they have more knowledge and thus more ability to perceive what is true and untrue, and by doing what is possible to punish those who seek to mislead, some progress can be made.

Shalheveth Freier did not review the final text due to his untimely death.

REFERENCE

1. S. Sommelius, 'Mediernas krig i forna Jugoslavien', Stockholm, 1993.

11

A Global Community Through Electronic Communications

Mark Esdale

Much unhappiness has come into the world because
of bewilderment and things left unsaid.

Feodor Dostoevsky

Communication is arguably the most important tool for the
construction of a peaceful world. Throughout history, as technology improved, so did
communication. Indeed, in many cases, the need for improved
communication between groups – normally armies – created
technological advances in themselves.

Today's powerful communication services allow telephone
and facsimile calls to be made virtually anywhere in the world.

The use of computers for communication is almost as old as
computer technology itself. The early electronic computers were
large and very expensive, so a single central unit was connected
to several terminals. The use of the central processor for storing
messages was part of the main operating system of the computer.
Thus, the seeds for electronic mail were sown very early on.

Devices for allowing terminals to be connected remotely

from the central computer, via normal telephone lines, also appeared early in the computer's history. These devices would encode the data by modulating a carrier signal and then demodulating it at the other end. The term *mo*dulator-*dem*odulator became contracted to modem.

A modem, a terminal and a connection to a mainframe computer could allow a user to send messages to any other user of that system. This tended to be restricted, however, to those, normally computer programmers, who used the central computer. To allow more people to have access, a dedicated piece of software is used, called a bulletin board. These have telephone numbers which are published in various magazines – normally computer orientated – and allow anyone with a terminal and a modem to connect to them. They are limited to leaving mail for someone else, reading one's own mail, or transferring computer files to or from the bulletin board.

Computer technology has moved on from the days of a central mainframe computer with dumb terminals attached, to today's system consisting of powerful personal computers often connected to each other via a network. The principles of electronic mail, however, have remained the same.

Computer 'conferencing' systems allow messages to be placed in a location where they may be read by other users who may add a comment to the original message. Both the originals and any comments are then visible to all users, thus making it possible to follow an entire thread of a discussion.

An experiment in the United States led to the formation of the 'Internet'. The Internet is a collection of individual networks connected together, allowing electronic mail to be sent virtually anywhere in the world.

CYBERSPACE

Electronic mail is discussed in Chapter 5 as a means through which international communities of scientists are formed. It is growing clear, however, that electronic mail systems do more than help build camaraderie among academic colleagues; in many cases, the technology fosters a sense of community between all users of electronic communication, crossing differences in background, profession, or nationality.

This concept is summed up in the term 'cyberspace'. It is not a location, although it is thought of as one: an ethereal realm that co-exists with the physical world. It is, in a technical sense, the sum total of all computer-based communications and data storage that is accessible via computer network. Its largest manifestation is the Internet, a global computer network that now extends in one manner or another to 170 countries around the world.

In the early days of the telephone in the United States, lines installed to the home were 'party lines', shared by a community and operated by switchboard operators who connected, when necessary, to outside lines. Since one could pick up a phone at any time and reach other people from the neighbourhood (usually unavoidably), the telephone strengthened local community ties and was to a great extent marketed as an emergency aid rather than a method of reaching people at a distance. Since the national implementation of the telephone was sporadic, it was extremely uncommon for the new device to be used for anything other than local communication.

The technological underpinnings of electronic communication, however, opened up new vistas to the users of that technology. Using local telephone lines (and usually incurring no greater costs than a local call), an individual reached the same sort of party line community found on the telephone in the early part of the century – but thanks to the Internet, the other people on the line could be around the corner or around the world.

Early on, users of electronic communication developed unique metaphors to describe their activities and the virtual locations in which they interacted. These metaphors have taken on the weight of a divergent culture, a separate world view which dictates the means by which people communicate electronically. In many cases, individuals develop entirely different personae which exist only in the virtual realms of cyberspace.

By cyberspace, we mean the location in which people meet

each other, discuss issues of importance and insignificance, store libraries of information for public dissemination, create fictional aliases, play games, and occasionally fall in love. The concept is taken from the book *Neuromancer* by William Gibson, in which he wrote of a future in which people cabled their nervous systems directly to a computer network and 'jacked in' to a virtual realm. Present day use of computers proves that such high-tech interaction between man and machine is not necessary to create a virtual space.

The strength of this metaphor cannot be underestimated. For users of the Internet and other large scale computer-based communications systems, cyberspace is an actual place, as real a location as the home, office or local playground. More importantly, it is a place where people live – a place to speak with colleagues, trade information on computers or automobiles, chat about a television show, or simply to wander about.

Every metaphor about using the Internet extends this sense of place. When speaking of the libraries of data it contains, it becomes an ocean, something to be surfed or navigated. When using its tools to get files or information from a remote location, the common shorthand is to speak of 'going there'. Again, this information may be in Japan, Australia, or on the IBM of a college student in the American Midwest – in cyberspace, distance has little meaning, so one thinks little of the physical location of any data that might be found, or of the people one might meet.

Just as in any other human interaction, when people meet and converse in a common setting, a sense of community begins to form. On the Internet, that sense is often strong. The same culture that spawned the metaphor of the Internet as place has also created its own dialect, rules of etiquette and interaction, and in some areas a form of democratic government.

The USENET computer bulletin board system allows over ten million people to read and post information in any of approximately 4000 different ongoing discussions. Approximately 40,000,000 bytes of information are typed onto it daily – the equivalent of volumes A to G of the *Encyclopaedia Britannica*. It has developed a two-tiered system for creating new discussions. Anyone can create an 'alternative' discussion, merely by announcing its creation in a particular public forum. In order to create a discussion in 'news', 'society', 'computer', or one of the other formal hierarchies, a three-month period of debate over the new discussion's merits and goals must be held, followed by a vote open to the USENET readership. The new discussion must receive at least a two-thirds positive vote, and one hundred more yeas than nays, in order to be created. Many computer system administrators, faced with limited storage for USENET discussions, do not carry 'alternative' discussions, but only those that have been elected into the USENET hierarchies; it is recognized that each owner has total rights over what will and will not be carried on their own systems.

In this manner, the USENET community – and it is self-aware of its nature as an international community of ten million people – has devised a form of self-government in an inherently anarchic system, balanced a strong cultural belief in freedom of speech with limitations on the power to tax system resources with unneeded conferences, and apportioned finite computer capabilities in a way that has weathered the phenomenal growth of the community from a half million to its current size, in much the same manner as a well-written national constitution.

USENET may be the largest and most obvious form of self-government on the Internet, but it is by no means the only one. Internet users – sometimes called 'Internauts' – self-consciously refer to themselves and each other as members of a virtual community. Physically, they may be sitting in front of their computers, doing nothing differently than if they were using their word processors. Conceptually, they have entered and become inhabitants of cyberspace.

As they travel from one interest group or discussion to another, they are visiting each of their own 'quasi-nations' in turn. Internet culture is robust enough to sustain subcultures of its own, and many of the discussions and forums, from *Star Trek* fanatics to communications scholars, have developed their own jargonistic terms that would be incomprehensible to other Internet denizens.

It is worthwhile to note the nature of Internauts. An

Internaut has no inherently observable race, ethnicity, nationality, gender, age or physical handicap. The textual nature of Internet, and its substitution of arcane (or user-defined) names for ones that may be gender or ethnicity-specific, allows anyone to cloak their identity with a certain degree of anonymity.

In short, many of the defining characteristics that give rise to difference, conflict and hatred are shed in cyberspace. Any Internaut may choose to display publicly their various identifications to others, but only through the means of their ideas and writing. That which is normally learned through visual cues can only be picked up through the subtext of communication – which means that one Internaut cannot practice racial hatred or ethnic discrimination against another until he has listened closely to him at least once. Even then, all attacks other than verbal are impossible recourses over the Internet, and verbal attacks are commonplace enough for other reasons that the sting of hatred is almost entirely removed.

Given an international community that in many ways transcends ethnic and national boundaries, it may be legitimate to include the Internet community as a possible progenitor of international peacekeeping.

Do Internauts share a common set of interests? On a universal scale, they are all using the same basic component of communication – a computer – and usually a shared language. (All languages that can be expressed with variations of the Latin alphabet included in the ASCII character set have their own place on the Internet, and a large section of USENET takes place in German, but the majority of communication is in English.) On a smaller level, every Internaut can take part in any of 4000 USENET discussions, 5000 public electronic mail discussions, or countless other private associations.

Just as academics form relationships through personal contact and correspondence, so too do many Internauts make friends through private electronic mail spurred by public discussion. Internauts also congregate physically at various conferences and local gatherings, furthering the sense of community with a little face-to-face interaction (or f2f, as an Internaut would put it).

Do Internauts share a common set of values? This may be

harder to discern, but again seems to hold true. Freedom of speech is widely held as a transcendent value on the Internet, which is often extended to include free (that is, no economic cost) access to information. Countless millions of man-hours go into maintaining libraries of information, or creating 'shareware' software which is then circulated freely. As befits a community where skin colour, religion and gender are invisible, discrimination on any level is frequently discouraged (and 'flamed' into non-existence when found).

Therefore, Internauts may rightly claim 'quasi-national' status (see Chapter 5). As for considerations of territory, this is a culture that is quite proud of the fact that is has transcended territorial and national considerations. (In fact, a large amount of discussion is currently taking place as to how to handle problems of conflicts between international transmission of information and national laws against certain data, as in the case of a Toronto student who was questioned by police about his involvement with an Internet document concerning a trial that was off-limits to Canadian publishers.)

This is a community that is also divided along certain lines, and faces occasionally internal conflicts. The nature of the system makes physical violence an absurdity – in fact, any form of punishment more severe than public censure is impossible. Internet borders are so vast and anonymity so assured that even in those few cases when an Internaut was 'deported' – that is, when a forum decided that someone's actions were unethical enough by Internet standards to merit banishment, and a system administrator who had the power to do so agreed – the individual often 'repatriated' himself through another provider of Internet service in a short period of time.

The Internet has an estimated citizenship of forty million – larger than many members of the United Nations. More importantly, it is undergoing a huge wave of immigration, sometimes estimated as high as a twenty per cent increase a month. Initiatives such as the United States' National Information Infrastructure, and similar efforts in Canada and Europe, promise that within the next decade or so all citizens of those nations will have the opportunity to become Internauts if they choose – and this sort of 'dual citizenship' may be part of their educational upbringing.

Of course, there are caveats to the ways in which this virtual near-utopia will interact with global systems. A cursory examination of most of the Internet will show that the majority of Internauts are from the world's wealthier nations – it takes a rich country to be able to spare the sort of capital required to lay high-speed data cabling. Access to the Internet is available for a much smaller investment through systems, which use individual personal computers wired serially to relay messages to an Internet 'gateway'. But even this solution requires personal computers, modems and spare telephone lines – luxuries too dear for many countries. Without care and serious investment from the West, the Internet will become yet another division between the rich and the poor, both internationally and intranationally.

Even so, the promise of electronic communication for promoting international understanding is great. Ignoring all of the positive benefits that the Internet culture could convey to other global systems, the opportunities for simply increasing communication between nations and peoples are enticing enough that a major effort should be undertaken to bring the Internet to as many people as possible as quickly as possible. The Vice President of the USA, Al Gore, speaks of the rural schoolchild in Tennessee going home and having access to the Library of Congress; greater still are the possibilities of every child gaining access to the world's information resources.

Yet, when one considers the vast benefits of Internet culture, transcending racial, political and ethnic boundaries, one begins to see a true, pragmatic method for creating a parliament of mankind. Not a world court of national representatives, or an annual conference of peoples, but an ongoing, open forum where the world's population can continuously interact, teach and learn from one another. The world could do far worse.

This 'Brave New World' will not be achieved, however, without overcoming some difficulties. The remainder of this chapter will attempt to address some of the practical issues which arise from the desire to use modern computer and communication technology to enable or increase communication between 'world citizens'.

PRACTICAL ISSUES IN COMPUTER
COMMUNICATION

There are two distinct areas which are encompassed by the concept of this form of electronic communication: (1) Intimate person-to-person communication; (2) one-to-many communication.

At a technical level, there is little to distinguish between these two areas. At a user's level, however, there may be quite different 'cultural' requirements.

Intimate person-to-person communication may be likened to communicating via a fax machine or by letter. It is not the same as a telephone call, as the recipient is unlikely to be connected to the sender at the same time, unless this has been previously arranged. The sender composes a letter and sends it to the recipient at their Internet address. At some later time, the recipient connects to the Internet and collects their mail. Communication at this level is private, unless the sender chooses to send copies to other parties, but even in this case, the communication is restricted to a chosen group. This method of person-to-person communication is known as electronic mail, or e-mail.

One-to-many communication is more like a discussion group, open to the public. A user will send a message to a newsgroup. Any subscriber to that newsgroup will see the message next time they connect to the system. Any subscriber may reply to that message, with the reply also becoming part of the newsgroup. It is possible, of course, to send a private reply via normal e-mail. It is also possible to have newsgroups which can only be read – with the moderators being the only people with the power to post messages.

One of the more popular facilities currently available on the Internet is called the World Wide Web. This allows individual users and companies to set up pages of information which are then available to all Internet users. These pages (or computer screens) normally contain text and pictures but are increasingly including other multi-media elements, such as sound and video pictures. Each page can also contain links to other pages which may be located on the same host computer, or on the other side of the world. Although accessing these pages (known as 'browsing' or 'cyber-surfing') is enjoyable and educational, it tends to be a one-way link and so does not have the same intimacy as the two-way communication of the USENET and other conferencing systems.

Demystification

One of the first tasks is the demystification of the technology. This is not a call for increased education in the fields of computer science and digital communications, rather a need for the user's interface to be made simple and intuitive.

The Internet is still very much a like private club, despite having millions of users. This is because the vast majority of its members are computer users first and Internet users second.

E-mail must be made as easy to use as, for example, the telephone. In general, producers of software have realized that to sell their products, the computer must adapt to the user, not the other way round. On the Internet, however, much of the software used for communication is not produced on a commercial basis, thus it often tends to be somewhat esoteric in its use.

Language

Some of the problems of language have been addressed by the commercial aviation industry. Indeed, aviation can almost be considered a 'world community'. A German pilot coming in to land at a Chinese Airport must be able to communicate quickly and effectively with air traffic control. To enable this, the international aviation governing body (IATA) has standardized on English as the language of aviation and so almost all air traffic control is now done in English. There are still ethnic anomalies, however – French air traffic control, for example, tend to issue their initial call in French, resorting to English only if necessary. The use of English works: most airline pilots tend to be well educated and highly motivated, so learning English is not a problem. Most aircraft operation and maintenance manuals also tend to be written in English. In this case, the users may not be so well educated and their command of English not so great. To help with this situation, airlines use a language called 'Simplified English.' This language contains only 3000 words and the meaning of those words is very precise.

The main language of the Internet today is also English. The main reasons for this are both historical and technical. As most of the initial work in setting up the Internet was carried out in the United States, it followed that English would be its first language. The operating system, the interface and the system-generated messages were also all in English.

In order to allow the maximum number of people access to the Internet, a basic standard character set has to be used. The initial choice for this was ASCII (American Standard Code for Information Interchange). This defines a set of characters using a 7-bit word allowing 128 different characters. The character set is enough to define the numerals, the letters A to Z (both upper and lower cases), a number of punctuation marks and 16 control codes used by the communication systems. The lack of accented characters in ASCII virtually rules out any language other than English. There are, however, several 8-bit character sets which include accented characters. An 8-bit character set allows 256 different characters which, in theory, permits the construction of a single set which would allow the use of any language based on Latin characters. However, when given an extra 128 characters, the computer designers chose to use most of them for special characters, such as line drawing, currency symbols, and so on. The result is that there is still no single character set available for use, although any single language has a set which represents its entire character set.

The situation is further confused by Semitic languages, which apart from running right to left, are also self modifying (in Latin languages, the form of a character does not change; in Semitic languages, a character's form may depend on its position and surrounding characters). Iconic languages, such as the various Chinese languages, also pose problems. Apart from the vast number of characters in such languages, the actual graphical representation requires additional complexity within the computer.

The ultimate goal must be to allow the use of any language within the communication network. One of the recurrent points in the discussion on world citizenship is the need to preserve ethnic ties, including language.

There are two steps needed to achieve this goal. Firstly, the technology must be adapted to cope with any language the user wishes to employ. Most of the actual software needed for this exists today – for example, Microsoft have word processors available in 39 different languages.

Secondly, computerized translation facilities need to be introduced. Merely supporting many languages is fine, provided that the sender and all the recipients speak a common tongue. On the Internet today this happens, and there are many newsgroups which operate in languages other than English. To achieve the ultimate goal, the system must allow a single message to be reproduced in multiple languages. Computer translation is getting better, but it is still a long way from being near perfect. All information on the system, apart from personal mail, would be stored in one single 'meta-language'. This would then be translated into whatever language the user desired. One of the main obstacles in computer translation is idiom; a method of helping the process of communication, until better translation is achieved, is for users to use 'simplified' versions of their native languages. The choice of meta-language, whether a real language such as English, or an artificial language such as Esperanto, or even a binary language understandable only to computers, will depend on the level of simplicity required and the ability of the meta-language to convey the sense – some concepts may be too complex to be automatically translated.

Misuse

An open system, such as the Internet, is always open to misuse. As its use grows, so too, will the misuse. There are five main areas of concern.

Commercialism

In general, the Internet is not intended to be used for commercial purposes. The ideal was to set up a system to allow free access to as much information to as many people as possible. There are two threats from commercialism which need to be addressed. Firstly, the distribution of advertising through e-mail. This is already happening on fax machines and, given the open nature of the Internet, will be difficult to control. Secondly, the charges made by service providers for access to the Internet are arbitrary, there being no governing body. Currently, most service providers charge only enough to cover costs with a small profit. This will almost certainly change when the large commercial institutions recognize a potential profit-making concern.

The area of commercialism also includes the problem of who pays for the main backbone of the Internet. The bulk of the data is carried on fibre optic links running at very high speeds. These links are normally paid for by the government of the country. In most of Europe, this funding is indirect – through the universities. As the use of the Internet grows and it becomes more commercial, governments will come under more pressure to start charging realistic commercial prices. This is already being suggested in the United States and is something which should be deplored. We do not want this new form of communication to become a plaything only for the rich.

Control

There is always a danger that any information system can be used to gain political or other control over its users. Most service providers can, and many do, control which newsgroups they will carry. It is feasible for a service provider even to manipulate the data being transmitted through its network.

Abuse/Flaming

Although, as stated above, Internet users tend to regulate themselves, it is still possible to offend a very large number of people at very little cost. When an offensive/abusive comment is made, the damage is done long before the responses come back. It may be necessary to examine the limits to free speech.

Pornography

This is one of the most frightening aspects of today's communication technology. While most people are gradually becoming aware of the Internet's potential, and are slowly putting their toes into the water, a group of people have already found a way of sullying the Internet's good intentions. Perhaps computer pornography is the apple in the Internet Garden of Eden?

Even though most of the world is appalled and disgusted by child pornography, there are individuals and groups and even nations where it is considered acceptable. Who draws the line defining acceptability on a worldwide, non-governed network?

As it is technically feasible to keep such material away from anyone except those with the correct access rights, should such material be policed at all? Most service providers do maintain a control over which newsgroups they will carry – but, as mentioned earlier, this can also be used to manipulate the spread of legitimate information.

Viruses

There is always the danger of a computer virus being spread through the Internet. It is important to remember that data themselves cannot do damage. Accessing the billions of pieces of information on the Internet is as safe a reading a book.

Viruses are spread by modifying code contained in executable computer programs. When an infected program is run, it spreads the infection to the new computer. This computer will then infect a disk inserted into it, which in turn infects the next computer, and so on. Luckily, the incidence of computer viruses is decreasing, partly because the 'thrill' of building them has died away, and partly through the increase of anti-virus software which detects and kills viruses before they can do damage. The most common source of viruses is from illegal copies of computer games – a source which is not connected to the Internet at all.

Minimum requirements

The absolute minimum requirements for a connection to the Internet are: a computer; a phone line; and a modem.

Communications software

The computer does not have to be at all sophisticated. The very early IBM PCs, or Acorns, or the BBC computers are sufficient as are the current PCs, including Macintosh and Amiga – even hand-held Psions can connect to the Internet. Any computer running UNIX, or DOS, or Windows is suitable. Virtually all mini- and main-frame computers (IBM, ICL, DEC, and so on). All they need is a communication port and a VDU terminal.

The phone line is an ordinary phone line. It can be the same line as used for voice communication. The only caveat is that if the line quality is very bad this can severely slow down the computer communications – making connection much more expensive.

The modem is a unit which connects between the computer and the phone line. The normal minimum standard is 2400 baud, which is roughly 2400 bits-a-second or 240 characters-a-second.

As with the computer, the communications software does not need to be sophisticated. A very simple terminal emulator program, which sends out the keys which the user presses and displays the incoming characters on a screen, is sufficient.

Having established the minimum, one can then build on this – faster computers and modems, better software, dedicated phone lines, and so on. In general, the faster the system, the lower the on-line connection costs – up to a point!

The Way Forward

Pugwash has set up a newsgroup on USENET. This is another mechanism through which members of Pugwash could communicate, and a springboard from which to spread the word about the Internet. Although the existing newsgroup was set up by Student Pugwash, it is available to all members. There is also a listserver which can be set up to automatically mail members with the latest information. Pugwash has an information page on the World Wide Web. Important Pugwash documents can be read at this site.

Most universities have connections to the Internet, so members with University connections can get themselves an Internet address, and start sending and receiving e-mail almost immediately.

For the rest, the connection can be made either through a service provider locally or, if there is not one available, through one of the dial-in networks such as CIX or CompuServe. Both these networks support a piece of software called an 'Off-Line Reader' or OLR. This allows the user to connect to the network for a very short time (often less than a minute) and load all the new information onto their local computer. The user can then browse through this information at leisure, formulate responses and connect again to the network to send the replies. Using this mechanism it is financially feasible to connect over international phone lines, where no local service is available. The use of OLRs also enables 'old technology' computers to be used for this form of communication as the speed of the connection – thus the time on-line; and hence the cost – is governed by the modem and the capabilities of the phone lines.

Even in the remotest spots, the proliferation of lap-top computers, and cellular or even satellite telephone systems, means that users can keep in touch from literally anywhere in the world – and even out of it.

This chapter incorporates ideas presented by Jeffrey Porten in a paper 'Cyberspace and the Virtual Community as a Component of the New World Order' discussed at the Pugwash Workshop, **Social Tensions and Armed Conflict***, held in Pugwash, Nova Scotia in July 1994.*

12

Communication and Community: Promoting World Citizenship Through Electronic Communications

David V.J. Bell and Robert Logan

The term citizenship is usually defined in relation to membership in a state with its attendant rights and responsibilities. It would be an appropriate term for membership in a world state had we achieved a form of world government more powerful than the existing United Nations. Lacking this development, and focusing on consciousness and civic responsibility (in particular, the importance of educating the public about the need to develop a sense of responsibility for the whole of mankind), rather than on formal legal rights and privileges, world citizenship can be seen as an aspect of a sense of community which can coalesce around any number of possible identities. The multiplication of such identities is indeed a hallmark of the postmodern age. Identities based on gender, sexual orientation, privilege or its absence, disability, have taken their place alongside more primordial identifications based on ethnicity, language, religion or race. All of these identities vie for recognition and formal attention.

Like any sense of community, identity entails the capacity for communication with others who share the identity and are part of

the community. Accordingly, transformations in the technology
of communication have a profound impact on identities and on
the definition of community. In many respects, the development
of the modern state is closely associated with the development of
the printing press. By the same token the new technologies of
the late twentieth century, which have supplanted print as the
dominant medium, have brought with them the capacity to
transform identities and destabilize the attachment to the nation
state. Ironically, they have enhanced the attractiveness of both
sub and supranational identification. When subnational identities
are enhanced, the nation state's continued existence is threatened.
It is not surprising that a number of large multi-ethnic states have
broken apart under the combined pressures of economic change
and the communications revolution. When ethnic identities are
enhanced, the result can be painful, bitter and violent. The
examples of Yugoslavia, Rwanda and Chechnya are chilling cases
in point.

Can we avoid the tension and violence associated with ethnic
conflict by enhancing supranational identities and awareness? As
a corollary to this question, what impact will person-to-person
information sharing networks (such as e-mail) have on this
process. In undertaking this analysis, we are well aware of some
of the ground breaking work done by previous theorists of
communication and media. Most significant in this regard is the
work of Harold Innis and Marshall McLuhan. These Canadian
theorists appreciated the impact upon political cultures of new
media and new modes of transportation. Marshall McLuhan was
best known for his famous aphorism 'the medium is the
message'. The media through which people communicate
profoundly affect the content of communication and also the way
in which content is interpreted. Media are not transparent vessels
that carry meanings between people. Indeed, communications
scholars use the term mediation (or mediatization) to refer to the
'impact of the logic and form of any medium involved in the
communication process'.[1]

McLuhan's ideas about communications were largely derived
from the work of Harold Adams Innis, who saw communications
as the material base of culture. His remarkable studies of the

historical development of civilization led him to the conclusion that the mode of communication available to a society conditions its approach to both space and time, thereby giving rise to unique cultural epochs and political formations. Thus, Innis distinguished oral from written cultures, and identified the invention of the printing press as the necessary and sufficient precondition for the emergence of modernity.[2]

Innis also saw political institutions as shaped and limited by the available means of communication. He distinguished types of polities on the basis of their relationship to both space and time, and this crucial relationship depended in turn on how the available modes of communication permitted society to adapt to and manipulate these two dimensions. Media that were heavy and permanent (such as clay tablets) favoured time over space, and generated small, compact polities that cherished history and tradition. Lighter media that could be transported easily (for example, parchment) permitted polities to expand their boundaries over large areas, thus making possible the emergence of vast empires. Developments in technology of communication (for example, the invention of the printing press) in his view had enormous effects on culture and political forms. Indeed, the printing press ushered in the modern age of politics, permitting the expansion of political participation to the masses, challenging the narrow hierarchies of both church and state, and underpinning the emergence of political ideologies.[3]

Of course, neither Innis nor McLuhan had the opportunity to study the role of computers in detail. Nor did they witness the astounding technological advances of the past quarter century, such as the micro computer or the Internet. One of the main components of the new global electronic network is the Internet. The Internet grew from having 30,000 computers connected to it in 1987 to nearly 40 million in 170 countries by the end of 1995. Given the current growth rate of 12 per cent a month, it is estimated that there will be over 100 million users by the year 2000.[4] The exponential growth in the use of electronic networking has allowed for the creation of what are called 'virtual communities' in 'cyberspace' (see Chapter 11). What began as a US Department of Defense initiative in 1969 has become a worldwide tool of interpersonal communication. The bases of this development are technological changes that have made it possible for tiny portable and personal computers to have a capacity several orders of magnitude greater than the earliest mainframe machines (which were so huge they required large air-conditioned warehouses for siting). Developments in computer technology, when coupled with the capacity for global telephone links involving satellite and other technologies, have produced a breakthrough technology that will undoubtedly transform social relations in the twenty-first century. As with many other technologies, the Internet and electronic networking have helped foster a culture among its users. For the most part, it is a culture of cooperation. The many virtual communities that have formed around various interests and activities have looked to one another for support, assistance and information.

The Internet has obvious political implications. As Howard Rheingold points out in his book entitled *The Virtual Community*,[5] 'the effectiveness of . . . government is heavily influenced by how much the governed know about the issues that affect them'. Whereas modern mass media are largely controlled by elites, electronic networking has the potential to be democratically based and widely accessible. If access is maintained as a right open to nearly everyone, as contrasted with a privilege extended to the favoured few, we can foresee enormous democratizing potential in this technology.

Against this optimistic view, critics argue that this technology is at best double-edged. They contend that the technology will always be at its highest level in elite closed organizations, such as defence and security bureaucracies. Moreover, 'the same channels of communication that enable citizens around the world to communicate with one another also allow government and private interests to gather information about them'.[6] Along with the democratizing potential of this form of communication is the potential to use it as a form of surveillance and control. Indeed, in some organizations, the measure of workers' productivity and responsiveness is the time taken by them to respond to random messages from their supervisors. In this case, e-mail becomes a twenty-first century form of big brother.

This book's concern with world citizenship is juxtaposed with a focus on globalization. It is instructive to note the factors that are an aspect of globalization. The term globalization implies transformations that have taken place with respect to markets, production, finance, ownership structures and information itself (see also Chapter 3). While this chapter is placing special emphasis on information, we should not ignore its links with these other global factors. It is heavily and interactively related to each of them. Future developments in information will be related to the impact (direct and indirect) of major world class economic actors. Indeed, the globalization of finance is itself a product of the technologies of electronic networking. As Paul Kennedy reminds us:

> Without the vast increase in the power of computers, computer software, satellites, fibre-optic cables, and high-speed electronic transfers, global markets could not act as one, and economic and other information – politics, ideas, culture, revolutions, consumer trends – could not be delivered instantaneously to the more than 200,000 monitors connected into this global communications system.[7]

COMMUNICATION AND COMMUNITY

Before pursuing our analysis of person-to-person information sharing networks, and their possible impact on world citizenship, let us turn to the general study of the relationship between communication and community. We are particularly interested in how a change in communication patterns or the creation of new means of communication leads to changes in a community. The intimacy of the connection is betrayed by their shared root: 'commun'.

Speech distinguishes humans from other animals and allowed the creation of human society based on the cooperation that communication permitted. The first social units must have been families – clans and tribes in which a common language bound together its members into coherent social units. These early social units grew and spread out geographically. As they lost contact their languages evolved in isolation from each other. New dialects, languages and cultures emerged.

It was during this pre-literate tribal form of existence that ethnic identities formed. An individual was not a citizen of a tribe or ethnic group but rather one's participation in the cultural life of one's tribe created a bond that required no definition. A simple rite of passage often marked the transition from childhood to adulthood, but no other concept of belonging was required.

The advent of literacy had a powerful effect on many aspects of social, cultural, political and economic life. Writing arose initially as an administrative tool and was used for the promulgation of legal codes as a way of formalizing the relationship of an individual to the collective, that is, the citizen to the state. The state operated most efficiently by imposing uniformity on the transactions of its citizens through administrative regulations. Small differences in the dialects of the different tribal groups making up a state began to disappear because of the uniformity that a working system imposed. Furthermore, the state took on an identity of its own and developed an imperial imperative, sometimes to increase its efficiency by realizing economies of scale and other times because of greed and the desire for power.

The next communication technology to change the nature of community was the printing press.

> The spirit of nationalism that engulfed Europe and led to the formation of today's modern nation-states was the product of the printing press and the many fallouts of this new technology, including the translation of the classical works into vernaculars, the establishment of vernacular literature and culture, the Reformation and the public education system. The printing press played the central role in the rise of nationalism first by releasing the forces that generated the movement and then by providing the medium whereby the movement took hold. This parallels the role it played in the Reformation.[8]

Print, through the promotion of the use of vernaculars, gave rise to national languages and cultures through which the aspirations of nationalism could be expressed and a national consciousness could emerge.

> By the end of the sixteenth century the flexibility of the alphabet and printing had contributed to the growth of diverse vernacular literatures and had provided a basis for divisive nationalism in Europe.'[9]

With printing, similar dialects merged into national languages in which small to medium variations were smoothed out. National languages led to literate national cultures. The nation states that arose increased their sphere of influence (usually) by military conquest which led to the imposition of their national language and culture upon the vanquished. The vanquished operated publicly in the language of the conqueror, particularly in written publications and in public oral utterances. The private spoken language used in the home allowed for the preservation of their ethnic identity or culture.

In some cases, the ethnic identity and their national identity overlapped as in the case of a Parisienne or a Londoner (if he was not a Cochnaigne). In most cases, individuals would carry identities reflecting their local culture, which in the case of the people of Bretagne or the Basque region involved a totally different language, or in the case of Burgundy or Normandy a different dialect. (The French Revolution involved among other things a sustained, often brutal, attempt to impose a uniform language throughout the territory of France.)

With the advent of electrification of information through the mass media, including the telegraph, telephone, radio and television, the possibility of a new identity emerged, namely, that of the world citizen. It was McLuhan who first recognized the global village and gave it its name. He observed 'that everybody in the world has to live in the utmost proximity created by our electric involvement in one another's lives'.[10]

Electricity brings information instantaneously from all parts of the planet and invests distant events with an immediacy and a personal dimension as though they occurred in one's own community. Local communities across the globe become intertwined in each other's affairs giving rise to a sense of global belongingness or world citizenship.

We are now in a position to identify four levels of belongingness that pertain to any individual. First, there are the basic family connections which existed even before humans possessed speech. Second, there are the bonds of a people with a common language and culture. Third, there are the bonds and responsibility of a people who are citizens of a nation state and share a common system of government, economics, and written or public language. Fourth, there is the bond of world citizenship among those who share a sense of a global community and understand that we all share a common ecological system, and that pollution and the degradation of the environment know no boundaries.

In using this framework we must be careful to understand the subtle distinctions between these different forms of belongingness. Family ties, while institutionalized by religion, are actually totally informal and are regulated almost totally by tradition and custom. Ethnic ties are also largely traditional but they are reinforced by informal community sanctions. National citizenship, on the other hand, is extremely formal, entailing very rigid responsibilities prescribed by written law and enforced with authority. World citizenship, as we are using the concept, is once again an informal tie entered into voluntarily.

The concept of world citizenship that we are describing is the one that arises naturally out of the electronic forms of mass media and not the kind associated with a world government in which member nation states have surrendered their sovereignty. The concept of world government might make sense theoretically, but given the rather poor performance of the United Nations it is perhaps wiser to try for the more modest goal of inculcating through education a sense of responsibility for humankind throughout the globe.

In this nuclear age, when the continued existence of our civilization, perhaps even of all mankind, is threatened by advances in science and technology, advances which are making the world ever more interdependent, it is becoming essential to extend loyalties beyond national frontiers.[11]

At the same time that people across the world feel a great affinity for each other and a common cause as citizens of the same global village, their national or nationalistic identities are weakening while their attachment to their ethnic identities are becoming stronger. The explanation to this paradoxical result lies in understanding the way in which television robs individuals of their personal identity. As McLuhan put it: 'Television sucks the brain right out of your skulls.' The individual, therefore, feels a much greater affinity for their ethnic identity over their national identity because it is more personal and more closely tied to the language they speak in the home, their own personal dialect. This phenomenon explains the many movements that have arisen across the globe since World War ll.

In Canada the Quebec sovereigntists have aspired to create a new pluralistic, territorial, multi-ethnic nation state; but they find themselves dragged back by atavistic references to ethnic purity (*'pur laine'* Quebecois) exemplified in Premiere Parizeau's bitter reference in his referendum night speech to the defeat of the sovereignty referendum by 'money and the ethnics'.

The new electronic communication technologies (which include fax, satellites, fibre optics, VCR, cellular phones, modems, CD Rom, as well as the computer and the Internet) have been introjected into a rapidly changing social and geopolitical environment. With the end of the Cold War, the major threat to peace and security in today's world (beyond environmental degradation) is no longer the conflict between nation states or blocs of nation states but rather the struggles between ethnic groups which more often than not find themselves within the same nation state. The aspirations of aboriginal peoples is one source of these conflicts. Examples include the Maori, the Amerindians, the Inuit and the Sami people. The aspirations of ethnic groups which were incorporated before the twentieth century into modern nation states is another source and includes, for example, the aspirations of the Scot, Welsh, Bretagne, Basque and Catalonian nationalists. The break up of

Western Colonial empires after World War II has resulted in the creation of a number of artificial nation states in Africa, Asia and the Middle East, whose borders more often reflected the former needs of the colonial administrators than the desires of ethnic groups for a homeland. The break up of the Soviet Union and Yugoslavia, as well as the collapse of the other communist regimes in Eastern Europe, have given rise to another class of ethnic conflicts. This latter group of conflicts is perhaps the most volatile because of the region's political and economic instability, and the most dangerous because of the potential involvement of nuclear weapons. A fourth class of ethnic conflicts with the potential for global consequences are the conflicts which cross civilizational lines, such as the one between the Armenians and the Azeris. The danger here, or in Bosnia, is that these local wars could escalate into a global conflict between the West and the Islamic states. Samuel Huntington predicts that: 'the clash of civilizations will dominate global politics. The fault lines between civilizations will be the battlelines of the future.'[12]

The force that drives many of these conflicts is complex. We must not forget the significant impact of environmental factors, analysed so impressively by Thomas Homer-Dixon.[13] But an additional (related) factor is the aspirations of ethnic groups for a homeland of their own. Each group would like to form a nation state and control a territory with well-defined borders. This presents a number of problems. In some cases, these aspirations helped cause the break up of existing nation states, while in others the ethnic group is only seeking a greater degree of autonomous rule. The most volatile situations are found where ethnic groups live side by side, particularly where an enclave of one ethnic group finds itself surrounded by another group. A partition of territory to create ethnic homelands is impossible in many of these cases except by armed conflict or the still more odious practice of 'ethnic cleansing'. Even where peaceful break up is possible, economic hardship is sure to follow because of the break up of the economic infrastructure.

While some of the worst cases of ethnic conflict are a result of the current political instability during this period of political transition, history has taught us that ethnic conflicts are very stubborn and persist over many generations, even over many centuries.

The central problem in ethnic conflict, the one that leads to the greatest violence and social unrest, is the coupling of ethnic identity with the concerns of territory, in particular the establishment of a national state with a contiguous land mass and well-defined borders. This aspiration of ethnic communities and the needs of modern nation states are often in conflict (see also Chapter 4).

CONFLICT BETWEEN ETHNIC COMMUNITIES AND THE NATION STATE

In order to understand how this difficult and complex conflict could be resolved in a peaceful and productive manner, we shall show how the roots of the conflict between ethnic aspiration and nationhood can be traced historically to the economic and communication systems that led to the formation of nation states. The concepts of ethnicity and nationality are not universal and give rise to a number of misunderstandings and mutually conflicting aspirations among people with diverse cultural backgrounds who share a common territory or border.

'Ethnic' and 'national' identities are often confused. We use the adjective 'ethnic' to identify a people who share a common culture, language, religion and social institutions, and are not necessarily tied to a particular territory or land mass. The term 'national' or 'nationality' will be used to identify a multi-ethnic people who occupy a modern nation state with a common land mass with well-defined borders and a national government. This form of identity is territorial.

There is always the possibility that a nation state will correspond to a common single ethnic community. The actual cases of this are extremely rare and possibly non-existent. At any rate, our focus will be on the overwhelming majority of cases in which nation states contain more than one ethnic community, and where often the aspirations of ethnic communities and the needs of the nation state come into conflict.

Ethnic identity, as we indicated earlier, actually began with the tribal associations of nomadic people who subsisted through hunting and gathering, and hence were not tied to territory. With the advent of agriculture, peoples began to settle permanently on the land, but this did not immediately result in the formation of nation states. With the formation of city states in which agricultural produce was traded at the wholesale level and irrigation systems were organized and administered, nation states began to emerge. One of the results of these activities was the advent of literacy which in turn pushed the development of the nation state even further. At the same time, we saw the beginning of the territorial imperative, military conquest, the acquisition of lands, and the creation of empires as nation states.

These new nation states became multi-ethnic. The first examples include Mesopotamia, ancient Egypt, Greece and Rome. The creation of the first forms of codified law, such as the Hammurabic code, were attempts by 'national authorities' to create uniformity within their states so as to regulate and facilitate commerce. These codes not only had a moral base to them, which insured 'peace, order and good government', but they also regulated the price of bread, beer, transportation and labour and insured standard weights and measures. With a written code, a national language emerged from the many dialects and languages spoken within the nation state by different ethnic groups.

These new states which incorporated literacy into their central administration also organized schools to teach the new skills of reading and writing. A bourgeoisie arose in this manner because, in fact, the middle class was actually the literate class. The new educated bourgeoisie became the prototype of the new national citizens.

In some cases, ethnic identity and national citizenship were identical, in other cases, they differed. Joseph, the Hebrew of Biblical fame, who became an advisor to Pharaoh of Egypt, is an example of a person with a mixed identity. Babylon is another example of a multicultural state consisting of the original non-Semitic speaking Sumerians and their conquerors, the Semitic speaking Akkadians. Babylon recognized this duality through the creation of bilingual dictionaries. From this, we may deduce that a certain degree of ethnic diversity was at least tolerated and possibly encouraged by the authorities. As conquest enlarged the size of empires, ethnic diversity increased. One can find similar models in the history of ancient Egypt, Greece and Rome.

Although ethnic diversity was tolerated within ancient empires whenever it did not interfere with state policy, authorities were quite ruthless when it came to suppressing those groups who opposed central authority. The history of Athens during the Peloponnesian wars, as described by Thucydides, is one example; the Roman suppression and dispersal of the Judeans is another.

The conflict between the 'nation state', with its need for uniformity, and that of 'ethnic communities', with their need for cultural preservation and diversity, is the inherent conflict between the literate or bureaucratic forms of organization and the oral or tribal ones. The different modes of organization of ethnic communities and nation states are summarized in Table 1.

Table 1

Type of Community	Ethnic Community	Nation State	Global Village
Communications	Oral	Written	Electronic
Organizational Mode	Diversity	Uniformity	Universal
Government	Tribal	National	UN or world
Land Base	Settlement	Territory with borders	Whole Earth
Commonality	Culture	Economics	Environment
Commerce	Hunting/ gathering	Agriculture/ Industry	Post-Industrial

With the breakdown of the Roman empire, Europe entered the Dark Ages during which central authority collapsed. In addition, widespread literacy fell into eclipse and was only preserved in monasteries isolated from the mainstream of everyday life. During this period, European culture was more characterized by ethnic collectivities and local associations than by nation states. As Europe emerged from the Dark Ages into the high Middle Ages, national forms of organization began to reassert themselves together with a resurgence of literacy and public education, as exemplified by the Italian city states and Charlemagne's empire.

With the advent of the printing press, there was a concomitant rise of literacy, education, national languages, nationalism and, eventually, industrialization. The printing press was the first example of mass production. The type fonts used in the printing press had to be uniformly mass produced using hot lead moulds. The products of the printing press were the first mass produced uniform manufactured goods. With industrialization nation states increased central authority and imposed greater uniformity. In order to make mass manufacturing more efficient, the schools served as an instrument of national policy by training youngsters to use the same national language. They were also taught the principles of obedience, punctuality and the ability to do rote work so as to transform them into efficient factory workers and citizens of a national state.

In such a climate, short shrift was given to the concerns of ethnic communities that did not conform to the national model. Ethnic minorities within powerful nation states had to comply with the will of the central authorities as they had no means by which to make their case. In fact, ethnic cultures were suppressed, and many languages and cultures were lost during this period, particularly those languages for which a vernacular press was never created.

The conflict between nation states and ethnic cultures is not so much the conflict of one group of people with another as it is the conflict of two different systems of organization, one based on orality and the other on literacy.

PEACEFUL COEXISTENCE OF ETHNIC COMMUNITIES AND NATION STATES

Having identified the potential source of conflict between ethnic communities and nation states, how do we resolve the inherent conflicts? We would like to offer the following proposal as a possible long-term solution.

(1) We should try to create a world in which two kinds of 'nations' exist. One would be a 'nation state', based on territory, which is multicultural, pluralistic, democratic and concerned with the economic, political and social well-being of its citizens. The second kind of 'nation' would be an association of peoples of a common ethnic background who would be linked by different forms of communication – oral, written and electronic – which would transcend the borders of nation states and would allow them to share a common cultural heritage.

(2) At the same time that we try and reinforce ethnic identities and protect them from the 'imperialism' of nation states, we should also promote the notion of world citizenship in which we all share a mutual concern for world peace, security, prosperity, health and the environment. Ethnic difference should become something that enriches us not an excuse for selfishness and violence.

The idea of world citizenship is integrated into the concept of 'environmental citizenship' which is the focus of a 'Primer' published in 1993 by Environment Canada (the Federal Ministry of the Environment).[14] The approach links awareness with responsibility and relates both to the existence of community at various levels from the local to the global:

> Our responsibilities are rooted in the communities to which we belong. The most immediate of these is the family. On a larger scale, we are also part of local and national communities. In fact, on a global scale, we are members of the community of all human beings – the human species. Each of these communities can generate responsibilities. Environmental citizenship is about recognizing that we are part of these communities, and acknowledging the environmental

responsibilities that membership in these communities brings. Specifically, we have an obligation to care for the Earth, our common home.

The notion of levels of community (from the local to the global) can be modelled nicely by simply conjugating the number 10 through the powers of 0 to 10.

10^0 – individual
10^1 – family, executive committee or cabinet
10^2 – neighbourhood, advisory council
10^3 – village, large assembly
10^4 – small town
10^5 – small city
10^6 – medium size city
10^7 – large city, small state or province
10^8 – medium size state
10^9 – large state, continent, regional bloc or 'civilization' in Huntington's term
10^{10} – entire globe

What electronic networking permits is instantaneous communication across space at nearly any level – and the result is sometimes a sense of personal intimacy, usually found only at the level of the family.

Calling for a stronger sense of world citizenship is extremely idealistic. The new information technologies, however, are opening up new possibilities for change. The interactivity of the new technologies and the enormous powers of networking are creating new forms of community.

The Internet and e-mail will soon be as common as the telephone. Unlike the telephone, with its costly long distance charges, the rates for the Internet use are so modest that users can afford to use it as much as they want. But herein lies the biggest challenge. Will the current open accessibility arrangements be allowed to persist, or will 'the political and economic big boys slice it, sensor it, meter it, and sell it back to us'?[15] How ownership and access are decided will have a crucial impact on the way this new technology gets used and the purposes to which it is put.

Electronic communication is not without its problems. Even if the rates for using the Internet were zero, other problems of access remain. One must have access to a computer and to telephone or other forms of connection to the 'information superhighway'. Beyond these hardware problems are subtler problems of computer literacy and basic knowledge, education and linguistic ability. To make the Internet a tool of democratic discussion and exchange will require widespread electronic 'communicative competence' (to adapt Jurgen Habermas' term). At present the users of the Internet are *de facto* members of an 'information elite'.

> In the future, that's where the net culture in the rest of society will come from worldwide – those who connected with it in college. Will the future see an increasing gap between the information-rich and the information-poor? Access to the Net and access to college education are going to be the gateways, everywhere, to a world of communications and information access far beyond what is accessible for traditional media.[16]

Among administrators electronic communication can have dysfunctional effects. The President of York University, who was introduced to e-mail after assuming the presidency in 1992, offered this comment:

> E-mail encourages haste, flippancy, off-the-cuff remarks. Its conversational tone is seductive but because the other person isn't there, the dangers of misunderstanding are great (no tone is heard, no gesture observed, no reaction registered). It is easily forwarded to others . . . [Perhaps] there should be a corresponding message to the one that pops up when you cancel a note (do you really want to cancel?); it should say 'do you really want to send this note?' That being said, there's no doubt the transmission of messages in this form speeds things up, eliminates paper and phone calls and is kind of fun![17]

Nor is everyone supportive of the democratizing potential of the new technology. In Ontario, a recently passed Environmental

Bill of Rights mandates the use of a computer network, called the Environmental Registry, to link members of the public into regulatory measures involving environmental legislation across a broad range of issues. A noted environmental lawyer expressed grave concern that combining computer communication technology with a new legislated 'right to participate in decision making' will establish a new direct link between the public and the bureaucracy, bypassing elected representatives, transforming lobbying patterns, and creating 'a long term adverse impact on the role and effectiveness of local municipal government'.[18] Environmental activists take a rather different view, and see the new developments as potentially progressive and empowering. The actual effects will become clear as use of the new system is phased in. The use of the Internet promotes participatory democracy.[19] Rather than having one's views represented by an elected official, each individual can express and communicate their own ideas directly. The Internet retrieves the tribal council fulfilling McLuhan's prediction that the electronic flow of information reverses the social forms of literacy society and returns those of the oral tradition.[20]

Clearly undesirable uses of e-mail are already evident. Among the thousands of networks and bulletin boards that have sprung up around the globe are some that specialize in child pornography, and that permit users to exchange 'graphic image files' depicting children and paedophiles. Another abuse that is the topic of a recent Internet survey concerns sexual and other forms of harassment by e-mail.

Notwithstanding dangers and abuses, electronic networking has many supporters and enthusiasts who have found through their computers an opportunity to construct 'virtual communities' that combine emotion with reason, information with empathy, and knowledge with passion. The positive potential for building world citizenship holds out great hope for the future.

EPILOGUE

While this paper may be criticized for its lack of practicality and the fact that it offers very little in terms of short term solutions to the horrible problems of ethnic conflict that now face our world, we believe that it provides a viable model for long-term future development. It will involve nation states surrendering sovereignty to world bodies and providing ethnic communities with greater autonomy and respect for their human rights. In this respect our prognosis parallels that of Nicholas Colchester, who commented that as the role of the nation state continues to evolve: '[g]overnment will become a more stratified affair, with power, and a little identity, shifting up above national capitals and identity, and a little power, shifting down below them'.[21]

  The new communication technologies, including electronic networking, will play a significant role in the cultural, economic and political transformations occurring all over the world as we prepare to enter the twenty-first century.

REFERENCES

1.   D. Altheide, 'The Elusive Mass Media', *Politics, Culture and Society* 2:3, Spring 1989, p.416.

2.   C. Couch, 'Mass Communications and State Structures', *Social Sciences Journal* 27:2, 1990; K. Lang, 'Mass Communications and Our Relation to the Present and the Past', *Politics, Culture and Society*, Spring 1989.

3.   M. Walzer, *The Revolution of the Saints*, Harvard University Press: Cambridge, 1965; D.V.J. Bell, 'Global Communications, Culture, and Values: Implications for Global Security', in D. Dewitt, D. Haglund, and J. Kirton eds, *Building a New Global Order*, Oxford University Press: Toronto, 1993.

4.   J. Carroll and R. Broadhead, *Canadian Internet Handbook*, Wiley: Toronto, 1994.

5.   H. Rheingold, *The Virtual Community: Homesteading on the Electronic Frontier*, Addison Wesley: Reading, Mass, 1994.

6.   *Ibid.*, p.280.

7.   P. Kennedy, *Preparing for the Twenty-first Century*, Harper Collins: Toronto, 1993, pp.50–1.

8.   R. Logan, *Alphabet Effect*, Morrow: New York, 1986, p.223.

9.   H.A. Innis, *Empire and Communications* – Introduction by Marshall McLuhan, University of Toronto Press: Toronto, 1972, p.55.

10.   M. McLuhan, *Understanding Media*, McGraw Hill: New York, 1964.

11.   J. Rotblat, letter announcing the meeting of the Pugwash study group on Social Tensions and Armed Conflict held in Pugwash, Nova Scotia in July 1994.

12.   S. Huntington, 'The Clash of Civilizations', *Foreign Affairs*, Summer 1993, p.22.

13.   T.F. Homer-Dixon, 'Global Environmental Change and International Security', in D. Dewitt, D. Haglund and J. Kirton eds, *Building a New Global Order*, Oxford University Press: Toronto, 1993.

14.   A Primer On Environmental Citizenship, Ministry of Supply and Services Canada: Ottawa, 1993.

15.   Rheingold 1994, *op.cit.*, p.5.

16.   *Ibid.*, p.68.

17.   S. Mann, personal (e-mail) communication to David Bell, 1994.

18.   H. Turkstra, faxed Newsletter to clients of Turkstra Garrod Hodgson, 1994.

19. L.K. Grossman, *The Electronic Republic: Reshaping Democracy in the Information Age*, Viking: New York, 1995.

20. R. Logan, *The Fifth Language: Learning A Living in the Computer Age*, Stoddart: Toronto, 1995.

21. N. Colchester, *Globe and Mail*, July 21, 1994, A–23; see also, Kennedy 1993, *op.cit.*, pp.131–3.

Index